ᵀᴴᴱ HUTCHINSON

DICTIONARY OF
COMPUTING, MULTIMEDIA, AND THE INTERNET

^{THE} HUTCHINSON

DICTIONARY OF
COMPUTING, MULTIMEDIA, AND THE INTERNET

Helicon

First published 1997
Reprinted 1997

Helicon Publishing Ltd
42 Hythe Bridge Street
Oxford OX1 2EP

ISBN 1-85986-159-8

British Cataloguing in Publication Data

A catalogue record for this book is available from the British Library

Terms which are known to be trademarks or service marks have been
appropriately capitalized.

The use of a term in this book should not be regarded as affecting the validity or
legal status of any proprietary rights which may be claimed in that trademark or
service mark.

Printed and bound in Great Britain by
The Bath Press, Bath

Acknowledgements

We would like to thank the following for screen shots of proprietory
software: Adobe (Illustrator), MegaTech Software GmbH (MegaCAD),
Microsoft Corp. (Excel, Internet Explorer, PowerPoint, Word),
Netscape (Navigator); and the following WWW pages:
AltaVista (http://www.altavista.digitial.com/),
Infoseek (http://guide-p.infoseek.com/),
Lycos (http://www.lycos.com/),
Pepsi (http://www.pepsi.com/),
Yahoo (http://www.yahoo.com/).

Contents

Illustrations

Features

Tables

Contributors

Wendy Grossman is a journalist and regular specialist contributor to magazines such as *Internet Today* and the computer and technology supplements of the *Daily Telegraph*, the *Guardian* and *The Times*.

David Gould is a freelance writer and was formerly editorial manager of the highly successful Chronicle publications and Reader's Digest's *How it was Done* series.

Jack Schofield is a journalist and is technology correspondent for the *Guardian*.

Other contributors

Paul Bray writes regularly about technology for the *Daily Telegraph* and the *Sunday Times*.
Ian Kingston is a freelance editor, writer, and typesetter.
Peter Lafferty is a freelance writer and editor.
David Penfold is a freelance writer, editor, and publishing consultant.

Introduction

It may be possible to avoid computers altogether, but for an increasing number of people they are a fact of life. Whether your starting point is an interest in computers and what they can do, bewilderment at how they work, or a desire to know a bit more, *The Hutchinson Dictionary of Computing, Multimedia, and the Internet* contains information you will find useful, whatever your level of understanding.

The entries are arranged alphabetically so that if you know what term you are looking for it can be found immediately. If, however, your interest is in a particular area of computing, help is at hand. By using the thematically arranged appendix you can quickly locate all entries relating to specific topics under headings such as 'Computer Types', 'Electronic Mail', 'Internet and On-line Services', etc.

As well as articles and the appendix, the dictionary provides signed feature essays by journalists whose business it is to spot developments. Subjects include 'Digital Future', 'Censorship of the Internet', 'Industry Standards', and others. There are over sixty illustrations, twenty-two useful tables such as 'Acronyms in common use on line', 'Programming languages' and 'Search engines' which help you compare like with like. Finally, the dictionary has a special 'Tips' feature. These handy hints are displayed alongside the relevant entries.

Editorial director

Anne-Lucie Norton

Project editor

Christopher Brown

Editors

Catherine Thompson
Edith Summerhayes
Tracey Auden

Proofreader

Barbara Newson

Art and design manager

Terence Caven

Page make-up

TechType

Design

2 H

Illustrations

Mike Ing

Production

Tony Ballsdon

absolute (of a value) in computing, real and unchanging. For example, an *absolute address* is a location in memory and an *absolute cell reference* is a single fixed cell in a spreadsheet display. The opposite of absolute is ⌒relative.

accelerator board type of ⌒expansion board that makes a computer run faster. It usually contains an additional ⌒central processing unit.

acceptable use set of rules enforced by a service provider or backbone network restricting the use to which their facilities may be put. Every organization on the Internet has its own *acceptable use policy* (AUP); schools, for example, may ban the use of their facilities to find or download pornography from the Internet. Originally, when the Internet was publicly funded, acceptable use banned advertising, and although funding is moving to private enterprise and advertising is now becoming commonplace, some service providers still do not allow commercial exploitation. The US National Science Foundation's NSFnet, for example, imposes a strict AUP to prohibit commercial organizations from using the network.

access the way in which ⌒file access is provided so that the data can be stored, retrieved, or updated by the computer.

access privilege authorized access to files. The ability to authorize or restrict access selectively to files or directories, including separate privileges such as reading, writing, or changing data, is a key element in computer security systems. This kind of system ensures that, for example, a company's employees cannot read its personnel files or alter payroll data unless they work for the appropriate departments, or that freelance or temporary staff can be given access to some areas of the computer system but not others.

   Certain types of restrictions may be applied by users themselves to files on their own desktop machines, such as private e-mail; others may be granted only by the system administrator.

   On all client-server systems, all data, even private e-mail and personal letters, can be accessed by the system administrator, who needs system-wide privileges in order to manage the network properly. Data which is encrypted, however, will not be readable unless the system administrator knows the user's individual password. The privacy of employee e-mail is a contentious issue, as many employees assume their e-mail is private, while many companies presume ownership of all data stored on company systems.

access provider another term for ⌒Internet Service Provider.

access time or *reaction time* the time taken by a computer, after an instruction has been given, to read from or write to ⌒memory.

account on a computer network, a ⌒user-ID issued to a specific individual to enable access to the system for purposes of billing, administration, or private messaging. The existence of accounts allows system administrators to assign ⌒access privileges to specific individuals (which in turn enables those individuals to receive private messages such as e-mail) and also to track the use of the computer system and its resources.

On commercial systems such as CompuServe or America Online, users are given an account when they dial up the system and give the number of a credit card to which usage may be billed. On other types of systems, accounts are typically issued by the system administrator. In all cases, accounts are protected by a password, which should be carefully chosen.

accumulator a special register, or memory location, in the ⌐arithmetic and logic unit of the computer processor. It is used to hold the result of a calculation temporarily or to store data that is being transferred.

ack radio-derived term for 'acknowledge'. It is used on the Internet as a brief way of indicating agreement with or receipt of a message or instruction.

ACM abbreviation for the US ⌐Association for Computing Machinery.

Acorn UK computer manufacturer. In the early 1980s, Acorn produced a series of home microcomputers, including the Electron and the Atom. Its most successful computer, ⌐BBC Microcomputer, was produced in conjunction with the BBC. Subsequent computers (the Master and the ⌐Archimedes) were less successful. Acorn was taken over by the Italian company Olivetti 1985.

acoustic coupler device that enables computer data to be transmitted and received through a normal telephone handset; the handset rests on the coupler to make the connection. A small speaker within the device is used to convert the computer's digital output data into sound signals, which are then picked up by the handset and transmitted through the telephone system. At the receiving telephone, a second acoustic coupler or modem converts the sound signals back into digital data for input into a computer.

Unlike a ⌐modem, an acoustic coupler does not require direct connection to the telephone system. However, interference from background noise means that the quality of transmission is poorer than with a modem, and more errors are likely to arise.

Acrobat program developed by Adobe to allow users of different types of computers to view the same documents complete with graphics and layout. Launched 1993, Acrobat was designed to get around the limitations of existing systems when transferring data between types of computers, which typically required all formatting to be stripped from the documents. The program to generate the code that makes the documents transferable with formatting intact must be bought, but the program for reading the documents is available free of charge.

By 1996 Acrobat was in common use on the World Wide Web for distributing certain types of company documents, and the program had been enhanced to integrate with Web ⌐browsers.

Acrobat coding was designed to turn computers into information distributors that would allow Mac users to view a document in its original form, and can be generated directly from ⌐PostScript files.

acronym abbreviation that can be pronounced as a word, for example *ASCII* (American standard code for information interchange) and *MUD* (multi-user dungeon). People in the computer industry often incorrectly refer to all abbreviations as acronyms. Both are frequently used as industry jargon and as shorthand to save typing on the Net. See also ☞TLA (three letter acronym).

Abbreviation	Meaning	Abbreviation	Meaning
AFAICR	As Far As I Can Recall	OIC	Oh I See
AFAICT	As Far As I Can Tell	OLR	Off Line Reader
AIUI	As I Understand It	OTOH	On The Other Hand
ATM	At The Moment	OTT	Over The Top
BTDT	Been There Done That	OTTH	On The Third Hand
BTW	By The Way	OVSN	Out Very Soon Now
DQM	Don't Quote Me	PIM	Personal Information Manager
DWIM	Do What I Mean		
FAQ	Frequently Asked Question	PMFJI	Pardon Me For Jumping In
FOAF	Friend Of A Friend	PMJI	Pardon Me Jumping In
FOC	Free Of Charge	POV	Point Of View
FOCL	Falls Off Chair Laughing	ROTFL	Rolling On The Floor Laughing
FUD	Fear, Uncertainty, and Doubt	RSN	Real Soon Now
FWIW	For What It's Worth	SO	Significant Other
FYI	For Your Information	SOTA	State Of The Art
IIRC	If I Recall/Remember Correctly	TIA	Thanks In Anticipation
		TIC	Tongue In Cheek
IKWYM	I Know What You Mean	TLA	Three Letter Abbreviation/ Acronym
IMO	In My Opinion		
IOW	In Other Words	TPTB	The Powers That Be
ISTM	It Seems To Me	TTBOMK	To The Best of My Knowledge
ISTR	I Seem To Recall/Remember	TTFN	Ta Ta For Now
IYKWIM	If You Know What I Mean	TTYL	Talk To You Later
IYSWIM	If You See What I Mean	TYVM	Thank You Very Much
LCW	Loud, Confident, and Wrong	UKP	United Kingdom Pounds (sterling)
LOL	Lots Of Luck/Laughing Out Loud	WRT	With Respect To
		WYSIWYG	What You See Is What You Get
NAFAIK	Not As Far As I Know		
NALOPKT	Not A Lot Of People Know That	YHM	You Have Mail
		YKWIM	You Know What I Mean
NIMBY	Not In My Back Yard		

Acronyms and abbreviations in common use on line

active matrix LCD (or *TFT (thin film transistor) display*) type of colour ⤶liquid crystal display (LCD) commonly used in laptop computers. Active matrix displays are made by sandwiching a film containing tiny transistors between two plates of glass. They achieve high contrast and brightness by applying voltage across the horizontal and vertical wires between the two glass plates, balanced by using a small transistor inside each ⤶pixel to amplify the voltage when so instructed.

To create ⤶VGA colour, each pixel must also integrate colour filters; essentially, each logical pixel is made up of three physical pixels, one for each of red, blue, and green, the primary colours of light. The consequence of this – and the reason active matrix screens are such expensive options – is that a VGA display requires approximately a billion transistors, and even minute imperfections render the screens useless for computing purposes. A high refresh rate means that the screens are extremely responsive, so the cursor does not disappear as a mouse is moved quickly across the screen.

Active matrix displays began to appear on laptops 1992, and are expected by many to eventually replace the older cathode-ray technology for television sets as well as display monitors.

active window on graphical operating systems, the ⤶window containing the program actually in use at any given time. Usually active windows are easily identified by the use of colour schemes which assign a different colour to the window's title bar (a thin strip along the top of each window bearing the name of the window's specific program or function) from that of the title bars of inactive windows.

On a true ⤶multitasking system, each window may represent an active program, but the active window is the one into which the user may enter data. A user might, for example, be typing a document into a word processor in the active window while in the background other programs back up files or sort data in a database.

ActiveX set of technologies developed by Microsoft 1996 to enable interactive content on the World Wide Web. It is a trademark.

Ada high-level computer-programming language, developed and owned by the US Department of Defense, designed for use in situations in which a computer directly controls a process or machine, such as a military aircraft. The language took more than five years to specify, and became commercially available only in the late 1980s. It is named after English mathematician Ada Augusta ⤶Byron.

ADC in electronics, abbreviation for ⤶analogue-to-digital converter.

adder electronic circuit in a computer or calculator that carries out the process of adding two binary numbers. A separate adder is needed for each pair of binary ⤶bits to be added. Such circuits are essential components of a computer's ⤶arithmetic and logic unit (ALU).

addiction obsession for working with computers; the inability to stop interferes with and is damaging to the rest of the addict's life. Many computer users describe themselves as being 'addicted' to computers or on-line systems, but the percentage of users who have serious problems as a result seems to be small, although research continues.

Addiction has been used as a defence in ⌖hacking cases, including one of the early arrests of US hacker Kevin Mitnick and the 1993 trial of British hacker Paul Bedworth, who was the first to be prosecuted under the ⌖Computer Misuse Act.

add-on small program written to extend the features of a larger one. The earliest successful add-on for personal computer users in the UK was a small routine which allowed the original version of the spreadsheet Lotus 1-2-3 to print out a pound sign (£), something the program's US developers had thought unnecessary. In 1996 popular add-ons customized Word 6 to produce accurately formatted film scripts or gave personal finance packages like Intuit's Quicken the ability to generate invoices.

address in a computer memory, a number indicating a specific location. At each address, a single piece of data can be stored. For microcomputers, this normally amounts to one ⌖byte (enough to represent a single character, such as a letter or digit).

The maximum capacity of a computer memory depends on how many memory addresses it can have. This is normally measured in units of 1,024 bytes (known as kilobytes, or K).

address means of specifying either a computer or a person for the purpose of directing messages or other data across a network. Addressing e-mail to a person across the Internet involves typing in a string of characters such as 'userID@machine.system.type.country'. To send mail to Jane Doe, for example, whose user ID is 'janed' and who works at a company called Anyco in the UK, a user would type in 'janed@anyco.co.uk'.

Computers do not, however, use these named addresses in routing data. The portion after the address is known as a domain, and the domain name is an easy-to-remember alias for a numbered address that is understandable by a computer. This numbered address, which takes a form similar to 127.000.000.001, is known as an IP (Internet protocol) address. Both the numbered IP addresses and domain names are assigned by the ⌖InterNIC.

ADDRESS BOOK

TIP: Always keep a backup of your address book in case of mishaps.

address book facility in most e-mail software that allows the storage and retrieval of e-mail addresses. Address books remove the problem of trying to remember a particular user's exact e-mail address – and it must be exact, as computers are unable to correct human errors. The best address-book software allows a user to type in just the correspondent's name and fills in the rest automatically.

address bus the electrical pathway or ⌖bus used to select the route for any particular data item as it is moved from one part of a computer to another.

Adobe US company specializing in graphics and desktop publishing software. Founded 1982 by former Xerox PARC researchers John Warnock and Chuck

Geschke, Adobe was the inventor of ⌐PostScript and is the publisher of ⌐Acrobat and Pagemaker. Adobe's enduring contribution to the computer industry is that it facilitated the use of computers to produce the fancy fonts without which desktop publishing would not have been possible.

Adobe Type Manager program from Adobe that manages fonts under Windows 3.1 and allows the printing and display of ⌐PostScript fonts.

ADSL (abbreviation for *asymmetric digital subscriber loop*) standard for transmitting video data through existing copper telephone wires. ADSL was developed by US telephone companies as a way of competing with cable television companies in delivering both TV and phone services. By 1996 it was developing into a possible alternative means for high-speed Internet access. ADSL is one of several types of digital subscriber loops (DSLs) in progress.

Advanced Technology Attachment Packet Interface enhancement to integrated drive electronics (IDE), usually abbreviated to ⌐ATAPI.

advertising the practice of paying to place information about a company's services or products in front of consumers. The earliest advertisers on the Net used to distribute their information as widely as possible in a practice quickly dubbed 'spamming'. By 1996 the practice of advertising on the World Wide Web was becoming commonplace.

Much Web advertising is sold in the same way as advertising in traditional media such as the print and broadcasting industries. Advertisers pay to place a small graphic known as an 'advertising banner' on a particular Web page in a spot (usually the top) where users are expected to see it clearly and click on it to follow the link to the advertiser's own site for more information. More sophisticated systems are under development which allow an advertising agency to track users' interests by watching which Web sites they visit and using that information to choose banners to insert which match those users' interests.

The New York-based company WebTrack Information Services estimated advertising spending on the Web for the final quarter of 1995 to be $12.5 million.

agent software that mimics intelligence by automating tasks according to user-defined rules. The most visible agent on the Internet in 1995 was Firefly, which recommends music that users might like based on information they have already given about their favourite artists. Agents might also select news stories of interest, arrange scheduling with other agents, and filter out unwanted junk e-mail.

Much research on agents is proceeding at the ⌐MIT Media Lab, where Professor Pattie Maes directs the group studying the capability and potential of autonomous agents. See also ⌐crawler and ⌐bot.

AI abbreviation for ⌐artificial intelligence.

Aiken Howard Hathaway 1900–1973. US mathematician and computer pioneer. In 1939, in conjunction with engineers from ⌐IBM, he started work on the design of

AGENT

TIP: An overview of the agent-related resources is available on the Web: http://agents.www.media.mit.edu/groups/agents/.

an automatic calculator using standard business-machine components. In 1944 the team completed one of the first computers, the Automatic Sequence Controlled Calculator (known as the Harvard Mark I), a programmable computer controlled by punched paper tape and using punched cards.

Aiken was born in Hoboken, New Jersey, and studied engineering at the University of Wisconsin. His early research at Harvard in the 1930s was sponsored by the Navy Board of Ordnance and in 1939 he and three IBM engineers were placed under contract to develop a machine to produce mathematical tables and to assist the ballistics and gunnery divisions of the military.

The Harvard Mark I was principally a mechanical device, although it had a few electronic features; it was 15 m/49 ft long and 2.5 m/8 ft high, and weighed more than 30 tonnes. Addition took 0.3 sec, multiplication 4 sec. It was able to manipulate numbers of up to 23 decimal places and to store 72 of them. The Mark II, completed 1947, was a fully electronic machine, requiring only 0.2 sec for addition and 0.7 sec for multiplication. It could store 100 ten-digit figures and their signs.

ALGOL (acronym for *algo*rithmic *l*anguage) an early high-level programming language, developed in the 1950s and 1960s for scientific applications. A general-purpose language, ALGOL is best suited to mathematical work and has an algebraic style. Although no longer in common use, it has greatly influenced more recent languages, such as ↝Ada and ↝PASCAL.

algorithm procedure or series of steps that can be used to solve a problem. In computer science, it describes the logical sequence of operations to be performed by a program. A ↝flow chart is a visual representation of an algorithm.

alias name representing a particular user or group of users in e-mail systems. This feature, which is not available on all systems, is a matter of convenience as it allows a user to substitute shorter or easier-to-remember real names for e-mail addresses. In 1995 CompuServe announced a system of named aliases for its long, numbered addresses.

aliasing or *jaggies* effect seen on computer screen or printer output, when smooth curves appear to made up of steps because the resolution is not high enough. The steps are caused by clumps of pixels that become visible when the monitor's definition is lower than that of the image that it is trying to show. ↝Anti-aliasing is a software technique that reduces this effect by using intermediate shades of colour to create an apparently smoother curve.

ALife contraction of ↝artificial life.

alligator clip small metal clip wired to other similar clips to allow temporary connections. Today's modular phone jacks generally make it easy to hook up modems and telephones. However, in some situations, such as a hotel room where a telephone is hard-wired to the wall or in a foreign country where a visitor's modem plug is incompatible with the local telephone network, the only answer is to take the phone apart and hook the modem directly to the phone line using these small clips.

alpha the first version of a new software program. Developing modern software requires much testing and many versions before the definitive product is achieved. The first versions of any new product are typically full of ⌐bugs, and are tested by the developers and their assistants. Later versions, known as ⌐betaversions, are given to outside users to test.

alpha channel in ⌐24-bit colour, a channel for controlling colour information. Describing colour for a computer display requires three channels of information per ⌐pixel, one for each of the primary colours of light: red, blue, and green. A 24-bit graphics adapter with a 32-bit ⌐bus can use the remaining 8 bits to send control information for the remaining 24 bits.

alphanumeric data data made up of any of the letters of the alphabet and any digit from 0 to 9. The classification of data according to the type or types of character contained enables computer ⌐validation systems to check the accuracy of data: a computer can be programmed to reject entries that contain the wrong type of character. For example, a person's name would be rejected if it contained any numeric data, and a bank-account number would be rejected if it contained any alphabetic data. A car's registration number, by comparison, would be expected to contain alphanumeric data but no punctuation marks.

AltaVista search engine on the World Wide Web run by DEC. AltaVista runs an automated program to index all the pages it can find on the Web, enabling visitors to enter search terms such as a name or subject and quickly retrieve a list of pages to visit to look for specific information. It has a similar indexing program for UseNet.

In mid-1996 DEC claimed the service indexed 30 million pages on 275,600 servers, as well as 3 million articles from 14,000 USENET newsgroups, and was accessed over 16 million times per weekday.

ALT HIERARCHY

TIP: More information about starting an alt group is available on the Net in the Start Your Own Newsgroup FAQ.

alt hierarchy on USENET, the 'alternative' set of ⌐newsgroups, set up so that anyone can start a newsgroup on any topic. Most areas of USENET, such as the ⌐Big Seven hierarchies, allow the creation of newsgroups only after structured discussion and a vote to demonstrate that demand for the newsgroup exists. The alt hierarchy was created to allow users to bypass this process.

Many of the most active newsgroups are alt groups, such as alt.flame and alt.sex.

ALU abbreviation for ⌐arithmetic and logic unit.

American National Standards Institute (ANSI) US national standards body. It sets official procedures in (among other areas) computing and electronics. The ANSI ⌐character set is the standard set of characters used by Windows-based computers.

America Online (AOL) US market-leading commercial information service. America Online was launched 1986 with a bright, colourful graphical interface and a marketing campaign that issued free discs on almost every US magazine cover. In 1995 it overtook the then market leader, CompuServe, and by 1996 had more than 5 million users worldwide. America Online combined with the German publishing conglomerate Bertelsmann to launch a UK version of the service, known as AOL, in early 1996.

Because a number of America Online users, many of them using temporary accounts set up from the many free discs, acted in breach of ⁓netiquette when America Online opened its Internet ⁓gateway 1994, America Online users are held in contempt by many parts of the Net.

Amiga microcomputer produced by US company Commodore 1985 to succeed the Commodore C64 home computer. The original Amiga was based on the Motorola 68000 microprocessor and achieved significant success in the domestic market.

analogue (of a quantity or device) changing continuously; by contrast a ⁓digital quantity or device varies in series of distinct steps. For example, an analogue clock measures time by means of a continuous movement of hands around a dial, whereas a digital clock measures time with a numerical display that changes in a series of discrete steps.

Most computers are digital devices. Therefore, any signals and data from an analogue device must be passed through a suitable ⁓analogue-to-digital converter before they can be received and processed by computer. Similarly, output signals from digital computers must be passed through a digital-to-analogue converter before they can be received by an analogue device.

analogue computer computing device that performs calculations through the interaction of continuously varying physical quantities, such as voltages (as distinct from the more common ⁓digital computer, which works with discrete quantities). An analogue computer is said to operate in real time (corresponding to time in the real world), and can therefore be used to monitor and control other events as they happen.

Although common in engineering since the 1920s, analogue computers are not general-purpose computers, but specialize in solving differential calculus and similar mathematical problems. The earliest analogue computing device is thought to be the flat, or planispheric, astrolabe, which originated in about the 8th century.

analogue-to-digital converter (ADC) electronic circuit that converts an analogue signal into a digital one. Such a circuit is needed to convert the signal from an analogue device into a digital signal for input into a computer. For example, many ⁓sensors designed to measure physical quantities, such as temperature and pressure, produce an analogue signal in the form of voltage and this must be passed through an ADC before computer input and processing. A ⁓digital-to-analogue converter performs the opposite process.

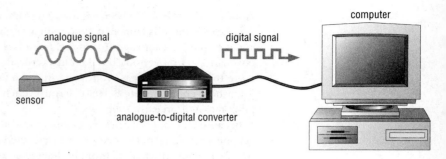

computer

analogue signal   digital signal

sensor

analogue-to-digital converter

analogue-to-digital converter
An ADC takes a continuous signal and converts it into the digital ('off and on') form used by computers.

analyst job classification for ⌐computer personnel. An analyst prepares a report on an existing data processing system and makes proposals for changes and improvements.

analytical engine programmable computing device designed by English mathematician Charles ⌐Babbage 1833.

It was based on the ⌐difference engine but was intended to automate the whole process of calculation. It introduced many of the concepts of the digital computer but, because of limitations in manufacturing processes, was never built. Among the concepts introduced were input and output, an arithmetic unit, memory, sequential operation, and the ability to make decisions based on data. It would have required at least 50,000 moving parts. The design was largely forgotten until some of Babbage's writings were rediscovered 1937.

anamorphic projection technique used in film and in ⌐virtual reality to squeeze wide-frame images so that they fit into the dimensions of a 35-mm frame of film. In film projection, the projector has a complementary lens which reverses the process. In virtual reality, the computer must calculate the amount of deformation and reverse it.

anchor an ⌐HTML (hypertext markup language) tag that turns ordinary text into a ⌐hyperlink. Anchors are used to enable easy navigation within a single large document or to link to remote documents on distant computers. On the World Wide Web, anchor text is underlined, coloured differently, or surrounded by a dotted line in order to mark it out from normal text.

Andreessen Marc born 1972. US systems developer and author of the first widely available graphical ⌐browser for the World Wide Web, ⌐Mosaic. He wrote Mosaic with fellow researcher Eric Bina while working at the National Center for Supercomputing Applications (NCSA), based at the University of Illinois. In 1994 both moved to the start-up company ⌐Netscape Communications Corporation to work on the next generation of browser software. This included the Netscape Navigator, which was made freely available on the Internet and contributed to the explosive growth of the World Wide Web in the mid-1990s.

<> in documentation, brackets that indicate places where the user should input information of the type described between the brackets. Angled brackets are also used in on-line services and on the Internet to indicate that the name used is a user-ID rather than a real name, and on CompuServe as part of certain ⌐emoticons.

<g> on CompuServe, an indicator that the message writer is smiling. The 'g', which stands for 'grin', is similar to an ⌐emoticon in that it helps to identify an on-line writer's state of mind in the absence of facial expressions, tone of voice, and other real-world clues. Variants include <vbg> for 'very big grin'.

animation, computer computer-generated graphics that appear to move across the screen. Traditional animation involves a great deal of drudgery in creating the 24 frames per second needed to deceive the human eye into seeing a moving picture on film. In computer-generated animation, while humans still create the key frames that specify the starting and ending points of a particular sequence – a character running through a landscape, for example – computers are faster and more accurate at calculating the in-between positions and generating the frames.

Computer animation

increasing popularity Traditional animation involves a great deal of drudgery in creating the 24 frames per second needed to fool the human eye into seeing a moving picture on film. In computer-generated animation, while humans still create the key frames which specify the starting and ending points of a particular sequence – a character running through a landscape, for example – computers are faster and more accurate at calculating the in between positions and generating the frames. The first completely computer-generated character to appear in a major motion picture was the sea-water creature in James Cameron's 1990 film *The Abyss*, developed at the leading special effects shop Industrial Light & Magic. It was quickly followed by the liquid-metal man in Cameron's 1991 film *Terminator 2*. The first entirely computer-animated full-length feature film was Pixar's *Toy Story* (1996), which was the first film ever to achieve independent motion of characters and backgrounds in the same sequence.

techniques The basis of computer animation is algorithms developed by academic researchers. These are used to develop software routines which handle the complex calculations needed to work out the precise colour of each pixel in each of the finished frames; the process demands exceptionally powerful hardware with massive storage capacity. For the animator, an image begins as an on-screen collection of lines that look much like a wire frame. There are a variety of techniques to let the animator develop 3-D objects – they can be extruded from a cross section, or 'swept', which is the on-screen equivalent of turning a cross section on a lathe to produce an evenly curved surface. Less symmetrical objects may be defined by a series of Bezier curves.

adding solidity and colour The object then has to be rendered, which essentially means making it into an image of a solid object. To do this, the computer needs four types of information. First, the object has to be located in space. Second, it has to be assigned a colour, specified either by levels of red, blue, and green or by levels of hue, saturation, and brightness. Third, the location and focal point of the camera photographing the object have to be specified. These determine how the object appears on screen, in perspective. Fourth, the location and type of light sources must be specified: colour, brightness and, in the case of spotlighting, the size of the cone-shaped pool of illumination. Ray tracing, meanwhile, calculates how the light directed at the object reaches it, with what intensity and in what areas. From all this information, the computer can calculate the colour intensity of each pixel that makes up the object.

light reflection There is another element, too: how the object itself reflects light. Two techniques model this, each named for its creator. If the object's surface could be described as a mosaic of polygons, Gouraud shading works by measuring the colour and brightness at the vertices of the polygons and mixing these to get values for the areas inside the polygons. Phong shading extends this by taking into account the angle of reflection, so it is more accurate for creating spectacular highlights. Gouraud, because it is simpler, is faster, and there is specialized hardware available for it. Phong has to be implemented in software. Either method produces an object that looks as though it is made of soft, smooth plastic – the smoothness comes from anti-aliasing, a process which removes the jagged edges or stepped effect that mars the edges of diagonal lines on a computer display screen.

mapping for realism Mappings are what make the objects look as though they are made of real-world materials. There are four main types of mapping: texture, environment, bump, and transparency. Texture is the actual texture of the material the object is made of: brick, water, wood, and so on. The system essentially wraps the object in the texture the animator chooses. Environment mapping adds the reflections on the object's surface of its surroundings; a shiny, round, metal object rolling down a hill, for example, must show accurate reflections of the trees and other objects it rolls past. Bump mapping takes into account the shape of the object itself and the way that affects reflections and shadings in its surface colour. Transparency mapping defines what can be seen through the object, with the distortion caused by the substance of the object; this was a key element in animating the monster in *The Abyss,* which was made of sea-water.

fog and haze Finally, fog and haze are important elements of computer animation, particularly for backgrounds, as computerized images tend to look too flat and sharp. The introduction of a little fog hides the sharp edges and makes the scene look more realistic. This is vital for one of the biggest growth areas in computer animation for film and video: simulated flyovers, which are impossible in live action and expensive and difficult in model work.

Wendy Grossman

annotate to add one's own comments to Web pages or graphical computerized documents such as stored faxes.

anonymous FTP (file transfer protocol) method of retrieving a file from a remote computer without having an account on that computer. Many organizations, such as universities and software companies, maintain publicly accessible archives of files that may be retrieved across the Internet via ⇔FTP. An ordinary user who is not affiliated to the organization may retrieve files by entering the FTP address and then typing in either 'anonymous' or 'ftp' when asked for a user-ID or log-in name, followed by the user's e-mail address in place of a password. These users are typically offered ⇔access privileges to only a small part of the company's stored files, and the rest may be cordoned off from access by a ⇔firewall.

anonymous remailer service that allows Internet users to post to USENET and send e-mail without revealing their true identity or e-mail address. To send an anonymous message, a user first sends the message to the remailer, which strips all identifying information from the message before sending it on to its specified destination, identified only as coming from the anonymous server. Because the ability to post anonymously also removes user accountability, these servers are controversial. However, they provide a useful function on the Net in support groups and other areas where the ability to post anonymously allows people to speak freely about confidential matters without the risk of being identified by friends, family, or anyone else.

The best-known anonymous server, the Finnish anon.penet.fi was closed down in Aug 1996 as it could no longer guarantee anonymity following a court case ordering the operator to reveal a user's name. The more elaborate servers use encryption to make the message even more difficult to trace.

anorak term used interchangeably with *geek*, *techie*, or *nerd*. It derives from the stereotype that all technical people resemble the stereotypical anorak-wearing trainspotter; in other words, that they are obsessive, slightly antisocial, and overly knowledgeable about matters that interest very few other people.

ANSI abbreviation for ⌐American National Standards Institute, a US national standards body.

anti-aliasing in computer graphics, a software technique for diminishing ⌐aliasing ('jaggies') – steplike lines that should be smooth. Jaggies occur because the output device, the monitor or printer, does not have a high enough resolution to represent a smooth line. Anti-aliasing reduces the prominence of jaggies by surrounding the steps with intermediate shades of grey (for grey-scaling devices) or colour (for colour devices).

anti-virus software computer program that detects ⌐viruses and/or cleans viruses from an infected computer system. There are many types of anti-virus software. Scanners check a computer system and detect viruses. Other utilities allow a user to edit the data on hard and floppy discs directly or repair system damage. Still other types, which may come with specialized hardware, function by detecting and blocking changes to files or system activities which are typical of how viruses behave.

AOL abbreviation for ⌐America Online; the UK version of the US service.

API abbreviation for ⌐Applications Program Interface, a standard environment in which computer programs are written.

Apple US computer company, manufacturer of the ⌐Macintosh range of computers.

applet mini-software application. Examples of applets include the cut-down word processor WordPad in Windows 95 or the single-purpose applications that in 1996 were beginning to appear on the World Wide Web, written in ⌐Java. These include small animations such as a moving ticker tape of stock prices.

application a program or job designed for the benefit of the end user, such as a payroll system or a ⌐word processor. The term is used to distinguish such programs from those that control the computer (⌐ systems programs) or assist the programmer, such as a ⌐compiler.

applications package the set of programs and related documentation (such as instruction manuals) used in a particular application. For example, a typical payroll applications package would consist of separate programs for the entry of data, updating the master files, and printing the pay slips, plus documentation in the form of program details and instructions for use.

Applications Program Interface (API) standard environment, including tools, protocols, and other routines, in which programs can be written. An API ensures that all applications are consistent with the operating system and have a similar ⌐user interface.

Archie software tool for locating information on the ⌐Internet. It can be difficult to locate a particular file because of the relatively unstructured nature of the Internet. Archie uses indexes of files and their locations on the Internet to find them quickly.

Archimedes microcomputer introduced by ⌐Acorn 1987. It was based on a ⌐RISC microprocessor called the ⌐ARM, and was intended to be the successor to Acorn's BBC Microcomputer.
  Despite its technically advanced design, it did not prove successful.

architecture the overall design of a computer system, encompassing both hardware and software. The architecture of a particular system includes the specifications of individual components and the ways they interact. Because the operating system defines how these elements interact with each other and with application software, it is also included in the term.

archive collection of computer files. The term is commonly used to refer to the files created by ⌐data compression programs, such as the popular PKZIP, which contain one or more files. On the Internet it is also used to refer to a large store of files from which visitors can select the ones they want.

argument the value on which a ⌐function operates. For example, if the argument 16 is operated on by the function 'square root', the answer 4 is produced.

arithmetic and logic unit (ALU) in a computer, the part of the ⌐central processing unit (CPU) that performs the basic arithmetic and logic operations on data.

ARM (abbreviation for *Advanced RISC Machine*) microprocessor developed by Acorn 1985 for use in the ⌐Archimedes microcomputer. In 1990 the company

Advanced RISC Machines was formed to develop the ARM microprocessor. The ARM is the microprocessor in Apple's ⌐Newton.

ARPANET (acronym for *Advanced Research Projects Agency Network*) early US network that forms the basis of the ⌐Internet. It was set up 1969 by ARPA to provide services to US academic institutions and commercial organizations conducting computer science research.

ARPANET pioneered many of today's networking techniques.

It was renamed DARPANET when ARPA changed its name to Defense Advanced Research Projects Agency. In 1975 responsibility for DARPANET was passed on to the Defence Communication Agency.

array in computer programming, a list of values that can all be referred to by a single ⌐variable name. Separate values are distinguished by using a *subscript* with each variable name.

Arrays are useful because they allow programmers to write general routines that can process long lists of data. For example, if every price stored in an accounting program used a different variable name, separate program instructions would be needed to process each price. However, if all the prices were stored in an array, a general routine could be written to process, say, 'price($_J$)., and, by allowing J to take different values, could then process any individual price.

article or *posting* on USENET, an individual public message.

artificial intelligence (AI) branch of science concerned with creating computer programs that can perform actions comparable with those of an intelligent human. Current AI research covers such areas as planning (for robot behaviour), language understanding, pattern recognition, and knowledge representation.

The possibility of artificial intelligence was first proposed by the English mathematician Alan ⌐Turing in 1950. Early AI programs, developed in the 1960s, attempted simulations of human intelligence or were aimed at general problem-solving techniques. By the mid-1990s, scientists were concluding that AI was more difficult to create than they had imagined. It is now thought that intelligent behaviour depends as much on the knowledge a system possesses as on its reasoning power. Present emphasis is on ⌐knowledge-based systems, such as ⌐expert systems, while research projects focus on ⌐neural networks, which attempt to mimic the structure of the human brain.

On the ⌐Internet, small bits of software that automate common routines or attempt to predict human likes or behaviour based on past experience are called intelligent agents or bots. One notably successful AI project is IBM's Deep Blue, which in 1996 was the first chess-playing computer to defeat a human grand master, the Russian Gary Kasparov.

artificial life (contracted to *ALife*) area of scientific research that attempts to simulate biological phenomena via computer programs. The first ALife workshop was held at Los Alamos, USA, in Sept 1987. Research in this area is being conducted all around the world; one of the most significant centres is the ⌐MIT Media Lab.

Character	Binary code
A	1000001
B	1000010
C	1000011
D	1000100
E	1000101
F	1000110
G	1000111
H	1001000
I	1001001
J	1001010
K	1001011
L	1001100
M	1001101
N	1001110
O	1001111
P	1010000
Q	1010001
R	1010010
S	1010011
T	1010100
U	1010101
V	1010110
W	1010111
X	1011000
Y	1011001
Z	1011010

ASCII codes

ASCII (acronym for *American standard code for information interchange*) a coding system in which numbers are assigned to letters, digits, and punctuation symbols. Although computers work in code based on the ↪binary number system, ASCII numbers are usually quoted as decimal or ↪hexadecimal numbers. For example, the decimal number 45 (binary 0101101) represents a hyphen, and 65 (binary 1000001) a capital A. The first 32 codes are used for control functions, such as carriage return and backspace.

Strictly speaking, ASCII is a 7-bit binary code, allowing 128 different characters to be represented, but an eighth bit is often used to provide ↪parity or to allow for extra characters. The system is widely used for the storage of text and for the transmission of data between computers.

ASCII art pictures or fancy graphics created entirely out of ↪ASCII characters such as letters of the alphabet or punctuation marks. ASCII art has existed since the invention of computers. Today it is found in USENET signatures (.sigs), special ↪newsgroups such as alt.art.ascii, and occasionally in messages, both public and private.

ASIC board (abbreviation for *application-specific integrated circuit board*) integrated circuit built for a specific application.

assembler a program that translates a program written in an assembly language into a complete ↪machine code program that can be executed by a computer. Each instruction in the assembly language is translated into only one machine-code instruction.

assembly language low-level computer-programming language closely related to a computer's internal codes. It consists chiefly of a set of short sequences of letters (mnemonics), which are translated, by a program called an assembler, into ↪machine code for the computer's ↪central processing unit (CPU) to follow directly. In assembly language, for example, 'JMP' means 'jump' and 'LDA' means 'load accumulator'. Assembly code is used by programmers who need to write very fast or efficient programs.

Because they are much easier to use, high-level languages are normally used in preference to assembly languages. An assembly language may still be used in some cases, however, particularly when no suitable high-level language exists or where a very efficient machine-code program is required.

Association for Computing Machinery (ACM) US organization made up of computer professionals of all types. Its monthly journal, the *Communications of the Association for Computing Machinery*, is peer-reviewed. Its subsidiary special interest groups, or *SIGs*, focus on areas such as graphics and human-computer interaction. Several of these run major conferences for their areas such as SIGGRAPH (graphics) and SIGCHI (human-computer interaction).

The equivalent UK organization is the ***British Computer Society*** (BCS).

* wild card character standing for multiple characters in most operating systems. It allows a user to specify a group of files for mass handling. Typing 'dir *.bat' in DOS, for example, will return a list of all files with the extension .BAT in the current directory. On USENET, * is used to denote a group of ⌐newsgroups; the phrase 'alt.music.*' means all the newsgroups in the alt.music hierarchy, such as alt.music.pop, alt.music.jazz, and so on. On the Internet, an asterisk before and after a word is a way of indicating emphasis.

asymmetric digital subscriber loop standard for transmitting video data; see ⌐ADSL.

asynchronous irregular or not synchronized. In computer communications, the term is usually applied to data transmitted irregularly rather than as a steady stream. Asynchronous communication uses ⌐start bits and ⌐stop bits to indicate the beginning and end of each piece of data. Most personal computer communications are asynchronous, including connections across the Internet.

asynchronous transfer mode (ATM) high-speed computer ⌐networking standard suitable for all types of data, including voice and video, that can be used on both private and public networks.

Because of its high capacity, flexibility, and scalability, and the need for new networking standards that can handle the large amounts of data required by multimedia applications, ATM is expected to replace ⌐Ethernet as the most popular type of network. The basic technology was developed as part of the Cambridge Ring in the late 1970s, and is now being adopted by companies such as IBM and AT&T.

ATAPI (abbreviation for *Advanced Technology Attachment Packet Interface*) in computing, enhancement to integrated drive electronics (IDE) that allows easier installation and support of CD-ROM drives and other devices. Part of the EIDE standard introduced by hard disc manufacturer Western Digital 1994, ATAPI uses a standard software device driver and does away with the need for older, proprietary interfaces.

AT command set (abbreviation for *attention* command set) set of standard commands allowing a ⌐modem to be controlled via software. These commands are used via special communications software to control a modem's actions from the computer console. The most common are ATZ to reset the modem and ATH to hang the modem up at the end of a call. The set was invented by Hayes Computer Products for its earliest modems.

ATM abbreviation for ⮑asynchronous transfer mode.

attachment way of incorporating a file into an e-mail message for transmission. Within a single system, such as a corporate local area network (LAN) or a commercial on-line service, binary files can be sent intact. Over the Internet, attached files must be encoded into ⮑ASCII characters and then decoded by the receiver. See ⮑MIME.

audio file computer file that encodes sounds which can be played back using the appropriate software and hardware. On the World Wide Web, the latest types of audio files can be played on the user's computer system in real time while they are being downloaded. Apple Macintosh computers have sound capabilities built in, as do multimedia personal computers (MPCs). Older PCs need to have a ⮑soundcard installed in order to achieve good playback quality.

audio-video interleave in computing, ⮑file format for video clips.

audit trail record of computer operations, showing what has been done and, if available, who has done it. The term is taken from accountancy, but audit trails are now widely used to check many aspects of computer security, in addition to use in accounts programs.

augmented reality use of computer systems and data to overlay video or other real-life representations. For example, a video of a car engine with the mechanical drawings overlaid.

AUP abbreviation for *acceptable use policy*; see ⮑acceptable use.

authentication system for certifying the origin of an electronic communication. In the real world, a handwritten signature authenticates a document, for example a contract, as coming from a particular person. In the electronic world, encryption systems provide the same function via ⮑digital signatures and other techniques. In ⮑public-key cryptography, for example, the ability to decrypt a message with a particular user's public key authenticates the message as coming from that user and no one else. Authentication is an essential requirement for electronic commerce.

authoring development of multimedia presentations. Authoring includes pulling together the necessary audio, video, graphics, and text files and formatting them for display.

authoring tool software that allows developers to create multimedia presentations or World Wide Web pages. Typically, these tools automate some of the more difficult parts of generating program source codes so that developers can work on a higher,

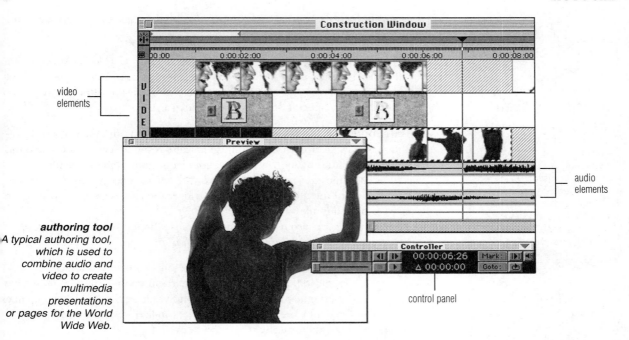

video
elements

audio
elements

control panel

authoring tool
*A typical authoring tool,
which is used to
combine audio and
video to create
multimedia
presentations
or pages for the World
Wide Web.*

ome major authoring programs

Software	Manufacturer	Description
Authorware	Macromedia	icon-driven program for professional authoring
Director	Macromedia	industry standard; with graphics, sound, animation and QuickTime
Netscape Navigator Gold	Netscape	Web authoring software; supports many Netscape extensions
PageMill	Adobe	Web authoring software; ideal for beginners to web-page creation
Premiere	Adobe	effective general-purpose sound and video editor
ToolBook	Asymetrix	popular professional tool, especially for multimedia databases

more abstract level. Popular authoring tools for the World Wide Web include Hot
Metal and HTML Assistant, both available in ⮑shareware versions.

authorization permission to access a particular system. Unauthorized access to
private computer systems was made illegal in many countries during the late
1980s.

AutoCAD the leading computer-aided design (CAD) software package. It is
published by the specialist US company AutoDesk (founded 1982). Users include
engineers, architects, and designers.

autoexec.bat a file in the ↝MS-DOS operating system that is automatically run when the computer is ↝booted.

automatic fallback feature allowing ↝modems to drop to a slower speed if conditions such as line noise make it necessary. Modem speeds are typically rated according to one or another ↝CCITT standard (known as a *V number*). All modems rated for a specific standard are ↝backwards compatible.

auto-responder on the Internet, a ↝server that responds automatically to specific messages or input. A common use for auto-responders is to automate the dispatch of sales information via e-mail. A user requesting such information typically sends a message with specified words such as 'send info' in the subject line or the body of the message. The words trigger the auto-responder to send the prepared information file.

Auto-responders are also used in e-mail systems which can be configured to notify correspondents that the user is on holiday.

avatar computer-generated character that represents a human in on-screen interaction. In the mid-1990s, avatars were primarily used in computer games, but because they take up much less memory or bandwidth than full video, companies such as British Telecom were researching the possibility of building multiparty videoconferencing systems using this technology.

AVI (abbreviation for *Audio-Visual Interleave*) file format capable of storing moving images (such as video) with accompanying sound. AVI files can be replayed by any multimedia PC with ↝Windows 3.1 and a ↝soundcard. AVI files are frequently very large (around 50 Mbyte for a five-minute rock video, for example), so they are usually stored on ↝CD-ROM.

Babbage Charles 1792–1871. English mathematician who devised a precursor of the computer. He designed an ⌐analytical engine, a general-purpose mechanical computing device for performing different calculations according to a program input on punched cards (an idea borrowed from the Jacquard loom). This device was never built, but it embodied many of the principles on which digital computers are based.

Babbage was born in Totnes, Devon. As a student at Cambridge, he assisted John Herschel with his astronomical calculations and thought they could be better done by machines. His mechanical calculator, or ⌐difference engine, begun 1822, which could compute squares to six places of decimals, got him a commission from the British Admiralty for an expanded version. But this project was abandoned in favour of the analytical engine, which he worked on for the rest of his life. The difference engine could perform only one function, once it was set up. The analytical engine was intended to perform many functions; it was to store numbers and be capable of working to a program.

backbone in networking , a high-⌐bandwidth trunk to which smaller networks connect. The original backbone of the Internet was ⌐NSFnet, funded by the US National Science Foundation, which linked together the five regional supercomputing centres.

backing storage memory outside the ⌐central processing unit used to store programs and data that are not in current use. Backing storage must be nonvolatile – that is, its contents must not be lost when the power supply to the computer system is disconnected.

backup a copy file that is transferred to another medium, usually a ⌐floppy disc or tape. The purpose of this is to have available a copy of a file that can be restored in case of a fault in the system or the file itself. Backup files are also created by many applications (with the extension .BAC or .BAK); a version is therefore available of the original file before it was modified by the current application.

backup system a duplicate computer system that can take over the operation of a main computer system in the event of equipment failure. A large interactive system, such as an airline's ticket-booking system, cannot be out of action for even a few hours without causing considerable disruption. In such cases a complete duplicate computer system may be provided to take over and run the system should the main computer develop a fault or need maintenance.

Backup systems include *incremental backup* and *full backup*.

backwards compatible term describing a product that is designed to be compatible with its predecessors. In software, a word processor is backwards compatible if it can read and write the files of earlier versions of the same software, and an operating system is backwards compatible if it can run programs designed for earlier versions of the operating system. Similarly, all modems are compatible with all the standards (V numbers) which precede the fastest one they can handle.

balloon help small cartoon-style bubble which pops up in a graphical computer system to convey ⮠on-line help. In many new products, balloon help is activated by holding the mouse over an icon or other type of control for a few seconds. Such help is context-sensitive.

bandwidth in computing and communications, the rate of data transmission, measured in ⮠bits per second (bps).

bang in ⮠UNIX, an exclamation mark (!). It appears in some older types of Internet addresses and is used in dictating the commands necessary to run UNIX systems.

bang path list of routing that appears in the header of a message sent across the Internet, showing how it travelled from the sender to its destination. It is named after the ⮠bangs separating the sites in the list.

bar code pattern of bars and spaces that can be read by a computer. Bar codes are widely used in retailing, industrial distribution, and public libraries. The code is read by a scanning device; the computer determines the code from the widths of the bars and spaces.

Barlow John Perry born 1948. US writer and cofounder of the ⮠Electronic Frontier Foundation 1991. His writings about cyberspace issues, such as *Crime and Puzzlement* 1991 and *A Declaration of the Independence of Cyberspace* 1996, have circulated widely and influentially on the Net.

He was formerly a lyricist for the US psychedelic rock group, the Grateful Dead.

Barnsley Michael. British computer graphics researcher who in the mid-1980s developed fractal image compression. In *Fractals Everywhere* 1988 he sets out the use of fractal geometry as a language that allows the precise description of any object, thereby making it possible to program computers to produce even the most complex images.

baseband type of ⮠network that transmits a computer signal without modulation (conversion of ⮠digital signals to ⮠analogue). To be able to send a computer's signal over the analogue telephone network, a ⮠modem is required to convert – or modulate – the signal. On baseband networks, which include the most popular standards such as ⮠Ethernet, the signal can be sent directly, without such processing.

BASIC (acronym for *beginner's all-purpose symbolic instruction code*) high-level computer-programming language, developed 1964, originally designed to take advantage of ⮠multiuser systems (which can be used by many people at the same time). The language is relatively easy to learn and is popular among microcomputer users.

Most versions make use of an ⮠interpreter, which translates BASIC into ⮠machine code and allows programs to be entered and run with no intermediate translation. Some more recent versions of BASIC allow a ⮠compiler to be used for this process.

batch file file that runs a group (batch) of commands. The most commonly used batch file is the ⮎DOS start-up file ⮎AUTOEXEC.BAT.

batch processing a system for processing data with little or no operator intervention. Batches of data are prepared in advance to be processed during regular 'runs' (for example, each night). This allows efficient use of the computer and is well suited to applications of a repetitive nature, such as a company payroll.

In ⮎ *interactive computing*, by contrast, data and instructions are entered while the processing program is running.

baud in engineering, a unit of electrical signalling speed equal to one pulse per second, measuring the rate at which signals are sent between electronic devices such as telegraphs and computers; 300 baud is about 300 words a minute.

Bauds were used as a measure to identify the speed of ⮎modems until the early 1990s because at the lower modem speeds available then the baud rate generally equalled the rate of transmission measured in ⮎bps (bits per second). At higher speeds, this is not the case, and modem speeds now are generally quoted in bps.

Baudot code five-bit code developed in France by engineer Emil Baudot (1845–1903) in the 1870s. It is still in use for telex.

BBC Microcomputer microcomputer developed 1982 in the UK by ⮎Acorn for the BBC. The first versions were developed from Acorn's earlier microcomputers, the Electron and the Atom, and based on Rockwell's 6502 microprocessor.

benchmark a measure of the performance of a piece of equipment or software, usually consisting of a standard program or suite of programs. Benchmarks can indicate whether a computer is powerful enough to perform a particular task, and so enable machines to be compared. However, they provide only a very rough guide to practical performance, and may lead manufacturers to design systems that get high scores with the artificial benchmark programs but do not necessarily perform well with day-to-day programs or data.

Berners-Lee Tim(othy) born 1955. English inventor of the World Wide Web 1990. He developed the Web whilst working as a consultant at CERN (Conseil Européen de Recherches Nucléaires). He currently serves as director of the ⮎W3 Consortium, a neutral body that manages the Web. In 1996, the British Computing Society (BCS) gave him a Distinguished Fellow award.

beta pre-release version of a new software program still in development, which is handed out to users for testing. The worst ⮎bugs are usually eliminated at the ⮎alpha stage of development. Beta testers use the software to do real work and report any bugs or badly implemented features they find to the developers, who incorporate this information in refining the product for release. Companies which assist with such testing are known as beta sites.

beta version a pre-release version of ⮎software or an ⮎application program, usually distributed to a limited number of expert users (and often reviewers).

Distribution of beta versions allows user testing and feedback to the developer, so that any necessary modifications can be made before release.

Bezier curve curved line invented by Pierre Bézier that connects a series of points (or 'nodes') in the smoothest possible way. The shape of the curve is governed by a series of complex mathematical formulae. They are used in ⇔computer graphics and ⇔CAD.

Big Blue popular name for ⇔IBM, derived from the company's size and its blue logo.

Big Seven hierarchies on UseNet, the original seven hierarchies of ⇔newsgroups. They are: comp (computing), misc (miscellaneous), news, rec (recreation), sci (science), soc (social issues), and talk (debate). These categories of newsgroups are managed according to specific rules which govern the creation of new groups, in contrast to the ⇔alt hierarchy.

binary file any file that is not plain text. Program (.EXE or .COM), sound, video, and graphics files are all types of binary files. Such files require special treatment for inclusion in e-mail sent across the Internet, which can transmit only ⇔ASCII text and imposes a size limit of 64Kb per message. Several programs have been developed to code binary files into ASCII for transmission, splitting them into smaller parts as necessary. The most commonly used such program is ⇔UUencode, but there are others including base64 and BinHex. See also ⇔MIME.

binary large object (contracted to *BLOB*) any large single block of data stored in a database, such as a picture or sound file. A BLOB does not include record fields, and so cannot be directly searched by the database's search engine.

binary newsgroup any UseNet ⇔newsgroup set up for the transmission of picture and other nontext files. The binary newsgroups have their own sub-⇔ hierarchy, alt.binaries, and include groups such as alt.binaries.pictures.fine-art.digitized and alt.binaries.pictures.erotica.

Because newsgroups are subject to the same restrictions as Internet e-mail for the transmission of ⇔binary files, pictures, programs, and other files posted to these newsgroups are ⇔UUencoded and split into sections. To view the pictures, all the parts must be downloaded and then UUdecoded and stitched back together to form the original file, which can then be viewed using the appropriate graphics program.

Other binary newsgroups distribute sound files (alt.binaries.sound.*) or user-contributed new levels for games such as *Doom* (alt.binaries.doom). These newsgroups take up a lot of ⇔bandwidth and therefore not all sites elect to carry them; blocking software typically bars access to many of these groups.

binary number system system of numbers to base two, using combinations of the digits 1 and 0. Codes based on binary numbers are used to represent instructions and data in all modern digital computers, the values of the binary digits (contracted to 'bits') being stored or transmitted as, for example,

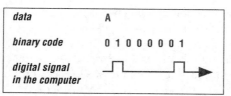

binary number code
*The capital letter A
represented in binary form.*

open/closed switches, magnetized/ unmagnetized discs and tapes, and high/low voltages in circuits.

The value of any position in a binary number increases by powers of 2 (doubles) with each move from right to left (1, 2, 4, 8, 16, and so on). For example, 1011 in the binary number system means $(1 \times 8) + (0 \times 4) + (1 \times 2) + (1 \times 1)$, which adds up to 11 in the decimal system.

binary search a rapid technique used to find any particular record in a list of records held in sequential order. The computer is programmed to compare the record sought with the record in the middle of the ordered list. This being done, the computer discards the half of the list in which the record does not appear, thereby reducing the number of records left to search by half. This process of selecting the middle record and discarding the unwanted half of the list is repeated until the required record is found.

BinHex program for coding ⌐binary files into ⌐ASCII for transmission over the Internet via e-mail.

biometrics biometrics is applied loosely to the measurement of biological (human) data, usually for security purposes, rather than the statistical analysis of biological data. For example, when someone wants to enter a building or cash a cheque, their finger or eyeball may be scanned and compared with a fingerprint or eyeball scan stored earlier. Biometrics saves people from having to remember PINs (personal identification numbers) and passwords.

BIOS (acronym for ***basic input/output system***) the part of the ⌐operating system that handles input and output. The term is also used to describe the programs stored in ⌐ROM (and called ROM BIOS), which are automatically run when a computer is switched on allowing it to ⌐boot. BIOS is unaffected by upgrades to the operating system stored on disc.

bistable circuit or ⌐*flip-flop* simple electronic circuit that remains in one of two stable states until it receives a pulse (logic 1 signal) through one of its inputs, upon which it switches, or 'flips', over to the other state. Because it is a two-state device, it can be used to store binary digits and is widely used in the ⌐integrated circuits used to build computers.

bit (contraction of ***binary digit***) a single binary digit, either 0 or 1. A bit is the smallest unit of data stored in a computer; all other data must be coded into a pattern of individual bits. A ⌐byte represents sufficient computer memory to store a single ⌐character of data, and usually contains eight bits. For example, in the ⌐ASCII code system used by most microcomputers the capital letter A would be stored in a single byte of memory as the bit pattern 01000001.

The maximum number of bits that a computer can normally process at once is called a ***word***. Microcomputers are often described according to how many bits of information they can handle at once. For instance, the first microprocessor, the Intel 4004 (launched 1971), was a 4-bit device. In the 1970s several different 8-bit computers, many based on the Zilog Z80 or Rockwell 6502 processors, came into common use. During the early 1980s, the IBM personal computer (PC) was introduced, using the Intel 8088 processor, which combined a 16-bit processor with an 8-bit ⮑data bus. Business micros of the later 1980s began to use 32-bit processors such as the Intel 80386 and Motorola 68030. Machines based on the first 64-bit microprocessor appeared 1993.

The higher the number of bits a computer can process simultaneously, the more powerful the computer is said to be. However, other factors influence the overall speed of a computer system, such as the ⮑clock rate of the processor and the amount of ⮑RAM available. Tasks that require a high processing speed include sorting a database or doing long, complex calculations in spreadsheets. A system running slowly with a ⮑graphical user interface may benefit more from the addition of extra RAM than from a faster processor.

In the PC industry software development lags behind hardware development, so that Windows 3.1, a 16-bit operating system, runs best on the 32-bit microprocessors and upwards, while Windows 95, OS/2, and Windows NT are all 32-bit operating systems and run best on the 64-bit microprocessors and upwards.

bit map a pattern of ⮑bits used to describe the organization of data. Bit maps are used to store typefaces or graphic images (bit-mapped or ⮑raster graphics), with 1 representing black (or a colour) and 0 white.

Bit maps may be used to store a typeface or ⮑font, but a separate set of bit maps is required for each typesize. A vector font, by contrast, can be held as one set of data and scaled as required. Bit-mapped graphics are not recommended for images that require scaling (compare ⮑vector graphics – those stored in the form of geometric formulas).

bit map
The difference in close-up between a bit-mapped and vector font. As separate sets of bit maps are required for each different type size, scaleable vector graphics(outline) is the preferred medium for fonts.

vector font

bit-mapped font

bit-mapped font ⮑ font held in computer memory as sets of bit maps.

Bitnet (acronym for *Because It's Time Network*) news ⟳network developed 1983 at the City University of New York, USA. Bitnet operates as a collection of mailing lists using ⟳Listserv, which was picked up by the rest of the Internet and is widely used, although Bitnet itself is falling into disuse.

bit pad computer input device; see ⟳graphics tablet.

bits per second (bps) commonly used measure of the speed of transmission of a ⟳modem. In 1996 the fastest modems readily available were rated at 28,800bps, with a few advanced models running at 33,600bps. These speeds must conform to standards, known as ⟳V numbers, laid down by the ⟳Comité Consultatif International Téléphonique et Télégraphique (CCITT) so that modems from different manufacturers can connect to each other. Many modems run much faster than their nominal speeds via techniques such as ⟳data compression.

blind carbon copy e-mail message sent to multiple recipients who do not know each other's identities. The facility for blind carbon copies is built into some e-mail software, and is useful in eliminating long lists of recipients which clutter up a mass-distribution message; it also protects the confidentiality of a particular user's contact list.

blind signature encryption technique that authenticates a message without revealing any information about the sender. Blind signatures are one element in the attempt to develop technology that protects individual privacy as more and more transactions take place over public networks where users' activities can be tracked.

blink in communications, to ⟳log on using an off-line reader or other software that uses automated ⟳scripts. Blinking saves on communications and telephone charges, but it changes the nature of on-line interaction because users cannot use chat facilities. Blinking also encourages repetition, since users replying off-line are unlikely to realize they are echoing each others' comments.

block a group of records treated as a complete unit for transfer to or from ⟳backing storage. For example, many disc drives transfer data in 512-byte blocks.

blocking software any of various software programs that work on the World Wide Web to block access to categories of information considered offensive or dangerous. Typically used by parents or teachers to ensure that children do not see pornographic or other adult material, some blocking products additionally allow the blocking of personal information such as home addresses and telephone numbers; some people regard this as ⟳censorship.

Blocking software became even more controversial in mid-1996 when Washington DC-based reporters Brock Meeks and Declan McCullagh revealed that the list of banned sites in some popular products included political material and that some sites were blocked indiscriminately.

Popular blocking software products include Net Nanny, SurfWatch, CyberPatrol, and CyberSitter.

blue-ribbon campaign campaign for free speech on the Internet. It was launched to protest against various international moves towards ⌐censorship on the Internet, especially the ⌐Communications Decency Act 1996. Participation in the campaign is indicated by the small graphic of a looped blue ribbon displayed on many sites on the World Wide Web and available from the campaign's Web site http://www.eff.org/blueribbon.html.

BMP in Windows, a file extension indicating a graphics file in ⌐bit-map format. Bit-mapped files are commonly used for icons and wallpaper.

bookmark facility for marking a specific place in electronic documentation to enable easy return to it. It is used in several types of software, including electronic help files and tutorials. Bookmarks are especially important on the World Wide Web, where it can be difficult to remember a ⌐URL (uniform resource locator) in order to return to it. Most Web browsers therefore have built-in bookmark facilities, whereby the browser stores the URL with the page name attached. To return directly to the site, the user picks the page name from the list of saved bookmarks.

Boole George 1815–1864. English mathematician. His work *The Mathematical Analysis of Logic* 1847 established the basis of modern mathematical logic, and his *Boolean algebra* can be used in designing computers.

Boole's system is essentially two-valued. By subdividing objects into separate classes, each with a given property, his algebra makes it possible to treat different classes according to the presence or absence of the same property. Hence it involves just two numbers, 0 and 1 – the binary system used in the computer.

Boole was born in Lincoln and was largely self-taught. In 1849 he was appointed professor of mathematics at Queen's College in Cork, Ireland.

In 1847 he announced that logic was more closely allied to mathematics than to philosophy. He argued not only that there was a close analogy between algebraic symbols and those that represented logical forms but also that symbols of quantity could be separated from symbols of operation. These ideas received fuller treatment in *An Investigation of the Laws of Thought on which are Founded the Mathematical Theories of Logic and Probabilities* 1854.

Boolean algebra set of algebraic rules, named after mathematician George Boole, in which TRUE and FALSE are equated to 0 and 1. Boolean algebra includes a series of operators (AND, OR, NOT, NAND (NOT AND), NOR, and XOR (exclusive OR)), which can be used to manipulate TRUE and FALSE values (see ⌐truth table). It is the basis of computer logic because the truth values can be directly associated with ⌐bits.

These rules are used in searching databases either locally or across the ⌐Internet via services like Altavista to limit the number of hits to those which most closely match a user's requirements. A search instruction such as 'tennis NOT table' would retrieve articles about tennis and reject those about ping-pong.

BOOT DISC

TIP: Always have a boot disc to hand and keep it up-to-date; before using it to restart your computer after a virus attack, make sure it is write-protected.

BOUNCE

TIP: If e-mail bounces, check that the address is correct and try sending it again; if it bounces a second time, try sending an e-mail message with the user ID replaced with the word 'postmaster', asking if the user ID is valid.

boot or *bootstrap* in computing, the process of starting up a computer. Most computers have a small, built-in boot program that starts automatically when the computer is switched on – its only task is to load a slightly larger program, usually from a hard disc, which in turn loads the main ⌐operating system.

In microcomputers the operating system is often held in the permanent ⌐ROM memory and the boot program simply triggers its operation.

boot disc (also known as an *emergency disc*) floppy disc containing the necessary files to ⌐boot a computer without needing to access its hard disc. Boot discs are vital in recovering from virus attacks, when it is not known which files on a computer's hard disc may be infected; in recovering from a system crash which has corrupted existing files; or in correcting mistakes introduced into files necessary for starting up the computer by newly installed software programs.

'bot (short for *robot*) on the Internet, automated piece of software that performs specific tasks. 'Bots are commonly found on multi-user dungeons (⌐ MUDs) and other multi-user role-playing game sites, where they maintain a constant level of activity even when few human users are logged on. On the World Wide Web, 'bots automate maintenance tasks such as indexing Web pages and tracing broken links.

bounce system by which an electronic mail message that cannot be delivered to its addressee is returned ('bounced back') to the sender, with a note advising of its failure to reach its destination. Failed delivery is usually due to an incorrect e-mail address or a network problem.

bozo filter facility to eliminate messages from irritating users. It is also known as a ⌐killfile.

bps abbreviation for *bits per second*, measure used in specifying data transmission rates.

Brand Stewart born 1938. US founder of the *Whole Earth Catalog* 1968 and the ⌐WELL 1984. He founded, edited, and published the *Whole Earth Catalog* 1968–85 as well as the *CoEvolution Quarterly* (now known as the *Whole Earth Review*) 1973–84. He is the author of *The Media Lab* 1987, an account of research work carried out at the ⌐MIT Media Lab.

Born in Rockford, Illinois, Brand graduated from Stanford University 1960 and worked as a photojournalist and multimedia artist.

bridge a device that connects two similar local area networks (LANs). Bridges transfer data in packets between the two networks, without making any changes or interpreting the data in any way. See also ⌐router and ⌐brouter.

broadband term indicating a high ⌐bandwidth.

brouter device for connecting computer networks that incorporates the facilities of both a ⌐bridge and a ⌐router. Brouters usually offer routing over a limited number of ⌐protocols, operating by routing where possible and bridging the remaining protocols.

browse to explore a computer system or network for particular files or information. To browse in Windows is to search for a particular file to open or run. On the World Wide Web, browsing is the activity of moving from site to site to view information. This is sometimes also called 'surfing'.

browser any program that allows the user to search for and view data. Browsers are usually limited to a particular type of data, so, for example, a graphics browser

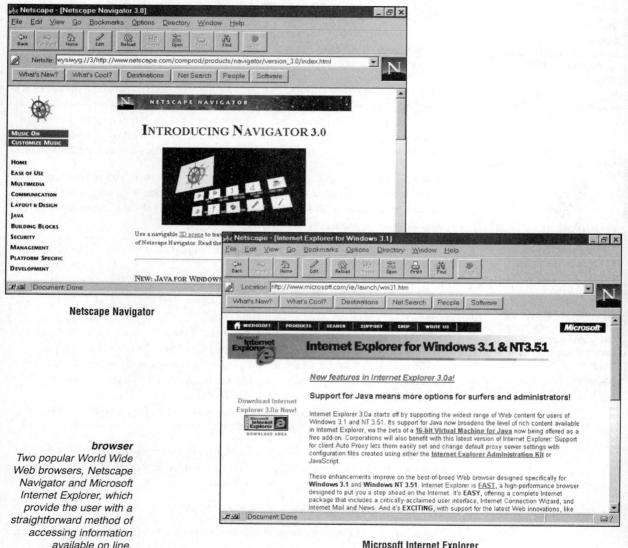

Netscape Navigator

browser
Two popular World Wide Web browsers, Netscape Navigator and Microsoft Internet Explorer, which provide the user with a straightforward method of accessing information available on line.

Microsoft Internet Explorer

will display graphics files stored in many different file formats. Browsers do not permit the user to edit data, but are sometimes able to convert data from one file format to another.

Web browsers allow access to the ⌐World Wide Web. ⌐Netscape and Microsoft's Internet Explorer were the leading Web browsers in 1996. They act as a graphical interface to information available on the Internet – they read ⌐HTML (hypertext markup language) documents and display them as graphical documents which may include images, video, sound, and ⌐hypertext links to other documents.

The first widespread browser for personal computers (PCs) was the text-based program Lynx, which is still used via ⌐gateways from text-based on-line systems such as Delphi and CIX. Browsers using ⌐graphical user interfaces became widely available from 1993 with the release of ⌐Mosaic, written by Marc ⌐Andreessen. For some specialist applications such as viewing the virtual reality sites beginning to appear on the Web, a special ⌐virtual reality modelling language (VRML) browser is needed.

bubble-jet printer an ⌐ink-jet printer in which the ink is heated to boiling point so that it forms a bubble at the end of a nozzle. When the bubble bursts, the ink is transferred to the paper.

bubble memory a memory device based on the creation of small 'bubbles' on a magnetic surface. Bubble memories typically store up to 4 megabits (4 million ⌐bits) of information. They are not sensitive to shock and vibration, unlike other memory devices such as disc drives, yet, like magnetic discs, they are nonvolatile and do not lose their information when the computer is switched off.

bubble sort a technique for ⌐sorting data. Adjacent items are continually exchanged until the data are in sequence.

buffer a part of the ⌐memory used to store data temporarily while it is waiting to be used. For example, a program might store data in a printer buffer until the printer is ready to print it.

bug an ⌐error in a program. It can be an error in the logical structure of a program or a syntax error, such as a spelling mistake. Some bugs cause a program to fail immediately; others remain dormant, causing problems only when a particular combination of events occurs. The process of finding and removing errors from a program is called *debugging*.

bulletin board a centre for the electronic storage of messages, usually accessed over the telephone network via a ⌐modem but also sometimes accessed via ⌐Telnet across the Internet. Bulletin board systems (often abbreviated to BBSs) are usually dedicated to specific interest groups, and may carry public and private messages, notices, and programs.

bundling computer industry practice of selling different, often unrelated, products in a single package. Bundles may consist of hardware or software or

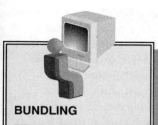

BUNDLING

TIP: Examine bundles carefully for out-of-date or discontinued components to make sure that the bundle really adds value to the overall purchase.

mailer's name and address

newsgroup to which message is sent

message

bulletin board
A typical bulletin board user interface, which enables the user to post a message to specific groups on the Internet. Users may also download messages and programs from a bulletin board.

both; for example, a modem or a selection of software may be bundled with a personal computer to make the purchase of the computer seem more attractive.

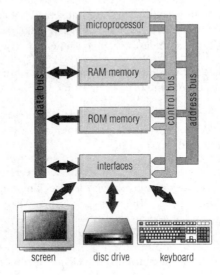

screen   disc drive   keyboard

bus
The communication path used between the component parts of a computer.

bus the electrical pathway through which a computer processor communicates with some of its parts and/or peripherals. Physically, a bus is a set of parallel tracks that can carry digital signals; it may take the form of copper tracks laid down on the computer's ⮑printed circuit boards (PCBs), or of an external cable or connection.

A computer typically has three internal buses laid down on its main circuit board: a **data bus**, which carries data between the components of the computer; an **address bus**, which selects the route to be followed by any particular data item travelling along the data bus; and a **control bus**, which is used to decide whether data is written to or read from the data bus. An external **expansion bus** is used for linking the computer processor to peripheral devices, such as modems and printers.

Byron (Augusta) Ada, Countess of Lovelace 1815–1852. English mathematician, a pioneer in writing programs for Charles ⮑Babbage's analytical engine. In 1983 a new, high-level computer language, Ada, was named after her. She was the daughter of the poet Lord Byron.

byte sufficient computer memory to store a single ᴗcharacter of data. The character is stored in the byte of memory as a pattern of ᴗbits (binary digits), using a code such as ᴗASCII. A byte usually contains eight bits – for example, the capital letter F can be stored as the bit pattern 01000110.

A single byte can specify 256 values, such as the decimal numbers from 0 to 255; in the case of a single-byte ᴗpixel (picture element), it can specify 256 different colours. Three bytes (24 bits) can specify 16,777,216 values. Computer memory size is measured in *kilobytes* (1,024 bytes) or *megabytes* (1,024 kilobytes).

C a high-level, general-purpose programming language popular on minicomputers and microcomputers. Developed in the early 1970s from an earlier language called BCPL, C was first used as the language of the operating system ⌐UNIX, though it has since become widespread beyond UNIX. It is useful for writing fast and efficient systems programs, such as operating systems (which control the operations of the computer).

C++ a high-level programming language used in ⌐object-oriented applications. It is derived from the language C.

cable modem box supplied by cable companies to provide television and telephone services, including Internet connections; it is not yet available, though much talked about. The potential advantages of cable modems over traditional ⌐modems, which operate over standard telephone lines, are greatly increased speed of communications as well as the ability to transmit video and two-way audio, and lower costs.

cache memory a reserved area of the ⌐immediate access memory used to increase the running speed of a computer program.

The cache memory may be constructed from ⌐SRAM, which is faster but more expensive than the normal ⌐DRAM. Most programs access the same instructions or data repeatedly. If these frequently used instructions and data are stored in a fast-access SRAM memory cache, the program will run more quickly. In other cases, the memory cache is normal DRAM, but is used to store frequently used instructions and data that would normally be accessed from ⌐backing storage. Access to DRAM is faster than access to backing storage so, again, the program runs more quickly. This type of cache memory is often called a *disc cache*.

CAD (acronym for *computer-aided design*) the use of computers in creating and editing design drawings. CAD also allows such things as automatic testing of designs and multiple or animated three-dimensional views of designs. CAD systems are widely used in architecture, electronics, and engineering, for example in the motor-vehicle industry, where cars designed with the assistance of computers are now commonplace.

A related development is ⌐CAM (computer-assisted manufacturing).

CAL (acronym for *computer-assisted learning*) the use of computers in education and training: the computer displays instructional material to a student and asks questions about the information given; the student's answers determine the sequence of the lessons.

call for votes on ⌐USENET, process by which the nature and scope of a new ⌐newsgroup is determined. Calls for votes are posted to news.announce.newgroups. In the case of the ⌐Big Seven hierarchies, the call for votes is a requirement; it is recommended but not compulsory for ⌐alt hierarchy groups. The point is to ensure that newsgroup names follow a consistent pattern and that new newsgroups are formed in response to genuine interest.

CAM (acronym for *computer-aided manufacturing*) the use of computers to control production processes; in particular, the control of machine tools and robots in factories. In some factories, the whole design and production system has been automated by linking ⌐CAD (computer-aided design) to CAM.

Linking flexible CAD/CAM manufacturing to computer-based sales and distribution methods makes it possible to produce semicustomized goods cheaply and in large numbers.

campus-wide information system (CWIS) computerized information service used on US university campuses, often hooked to the Internet. These systems typically include local events listings, general campus information, access to the library catalogue, weather reports, directories, and even ⌐bulletin-board and messaging services.

One of the first such systems was Cornell University's CUINFO, developed by a team led by technical administrator Steve Worona 1982. The development of ⌐Gopher servers 1991 made these systems much easier to navigate, and many systems were redesigned to take advantage of the new technology. In the mid-1990s these systems began moving to the World Wide Web.

cancelbot automated software program (see ⌐bot) that cancels messages on UseNet. The arrival of ⌐spamming (advertising) on the Net prompted the development of technology to use features built into UseNet to cancel messages. While single messages are easily cancelled manually, an automated routine is needed to handle mass postings, which may go out to more than 14,000 newsgroups. Cancelbot is activated by the ⌐CancelMoose.

CancelMoose anonymous individual who fires off the ⌐cancelbot. The CancelMoose (usually written as 'CancelMoose [TM]' on the Net) monitors newsgroups such as `alt.current-events.net-abuse` and `news.admin.net-abuse` for complaints about ⌐spamming (advertising), usually defined as messages posted to more than 25 newsgroups of widely varying content. The CancelMoose's identity is kept secret for reasons of personal safety.

Capstone long-term US government project to develop a set of standards for publicly available cryptography as authorized by the Computer Security Act 1987. The initiative has four elements: a data encryption ⌐algorithm (Skipjack), a ⌐hash function, a key exchange protocol, and a ⌐digital signature algorithm (DSS).

The project is managed primarily by the National Security Agency (NSA) and the National Institute of Standards and Technology (NIST).

capture saving of user actions as digital data that can be read by a computer. In real-time data communications, it refers to using software to log a session so that the session can be saved to a file. The term is also used with reference to screens, where the graphical material displayed on a computer screen may be saved as a picture file. In the study of ⌐human-computer interaction, the data captured are user keystrokes, mouse movements, and even facial expressions and muttered complaints so that developers can replay the session to help them design better ⌐user interfaces.

carbon copy in e-mail, a duplicate copy of a message sent to multiple recipients; a nod to traditional office systems. It is often abbreviated in software and on line to 'cc'.

carriage return (CR) a special code (↝ASCII value 13) that moves the screen cursor or a print head to the beginning of the current line. Most word processors and the ↝MS-DOS operating system use a combination of CR and line feed (LF – ASCII value 10) to represent a hard return. The ↝UNIX system, however, uses only LF and therefore files transferred between MS-DOS and UNIX require a conversion program.

case-sensitive term describing a system that distinguishes between capitals and lower-case letters. Domain names and Internet addresses are typically not case-sensitive; however, a particular system may be case-sensitive for user IDs.

CCITT abbreviation for ↝*Comité Consultatif International Téléphonique et Télégraphique*, an organization that sets international communications standards.

CD-I (abbreviation for *compact disc-interactive*), compact disc developed by Philips for storing a combination of video, audio, text, and pictures. It is intended principally for the consumer market to be used in systems using a combination of computer and television. An alternative format is ↝DVI (digital video interactive).

CD-quality sound digitized sound at 44.1 KHz and 16 bits, the standard defined in ISO 10149, known as the Red Book. CD-quality sound was designed to be the minimum standard required to reproduce every sound the human ear can hear. Most audio CDs are recorded to this level.

CD-R (abbreviation for *compact disc-recordable*) compact disc on which data can be overwritten (compare ↝CD-ROM, compact disc read-only memory). The disc combines magnetic and optical technology: during the writing process, a laser melts the surface of the disc, thereby allowing the magnetic elements of the surface layer to be realigned.

CD-ROM (abbreviation for *compact-disc read-only memory*) computer storage device developed from the technology of the audio ↝compact disc. It consists of a plastic-coated metal disc, on which binary digital information is etched in the form of microscopic pits. This can then be read optically by passing a light beam over the disc. CD-ROMs typically hold about 650 ↝megabytes of data, and are used in distributing large amounts of text, graphics, audio, and video, such as encyclopedias, catalogues, technical manuals, and games.

Standard CD-ROMs cannot have information written onto them by computer, but must be manufactured from a master. Although recordable CDs, called CD-R discs, have been developed for use as computer discs, they are as yet too expensive for widespread use. A compact disc that can be overwritten repeatedly by a computer has also been developed; see ↝optical disc. The compact disc, with its enormous storage capability, may eventually replace the magnetic disc as the most common form of backing store for computers.

CD-ROM future

the rise The growing size of popular computer programs has made the CD-ROM (Compact Disc, Read Only Memory) the distribution medium of choice for software. A single CD can hold more than 600 megabytes of data, the equivalent of more than 400 standard 3.5 in floppy discs. Thanks to high volume production of audio CDs, CD-ROMs are also very cheap to produce, and it is not unusual to find them given away free with computer magazines. The CD-ROM has thus become the standard format for operating systems (Microsoft Windows 95 and Windows NT), for suites of programs (Microsoft Office, Corel Office), for large books and encyclopedias (Oxford English Dictionary, Microsoft's *Encarta*), and for computer games. Even the games console business is moving from cartridges to CD-ROMs. Cartridges were used by all the early machines from the Atari VCS through the Sega Master and MegaDrive to the Super Nintendo Entertainment System (SNES). But most third-generation consoles – including the Sega Saturn and Sony PlayStation – use CDs instead.

hybrids But the CD-ROM's advantage – that it stores a large, fixed mass of data – can also be a disadvantage. For example, a CD-ROM encyclopedia may be up to date on publication, but become out of date. At best it will be incomplete. The solution is to produce *hybrid CD-ROMs*, where the bulk of the data is delivered on disc then updated via an online communications system such as the Internet.

Even an operating system such as Windows 95 is really a hybrid: most of the code usually comes on a CD, but updates and new versions of software drivers must be downloaded from bulletin boards or World Wide Web sites. Microsoft's *Encarta 97* encyclopedia is also a hybrid: users can download monthly updates, and follow hypertext links from the CD-ROM to various Web sites. Film and music encyclopedias also benefit from similar updates.

Hybrids are now becoming popular in the games world. CD-based titles are bought and played in the usual way on a single computer or games console, but many can also be played in multi-user mode by connecting to other users via an on-line system such as BT's WirePlay. Often, the program code for three-dimensional virtual worlds like 3DO's *Meridian 59* will be delivered on CD-ROM to avoid the costs and time-delays of downloading many megabytes of data, but the game is played over the Internet.

here for now, at least In an ideal world, every computer would be permanently connected to a network that could deliver tens of megabytes of data per second; hard drives and CD-ROMs would then be unnecessary. However, outside of large corporations, most people have very slow dial-up connections via modems and ordinary phone lines, and they have to pay for every second they spend online. Under these circumstances, hybrid CD-ROMs have a useful part to play, and seem unlikely to disappear in the near future.

Jack Schofield

The technology is being developed rapidly: a standard CD-ROM disc spins at between 240–1170 rpm, but faster discs have been introduced which speed up data retrieval to many times the standard speed. Research is being conducted into high density CDs capable of storing many ⸱gigabytes of data, made possible by using multiple layers on the surface of the disc, and by using double-sided discs. Such improved storage capacity would make products such as interactive movies a possibility.

PhotoCD, developed by Kodak and released in 1992, transfers ordinary still photographs onto CD-ROM discs.

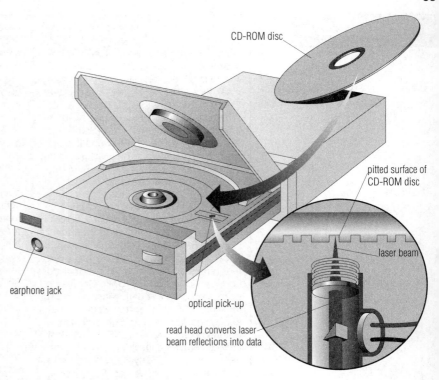

CD-ROM disc

pitted surface of
CD-ROM disc

laser beam

earphone jack

optical pick-up

read head converts laser
beam reflections into data

CD-ROM drive
*Data is obtained by the
CD-ROM drive by
converting the reflections
from a disc's surface into
digital form.*

*CD-ROM and multimedia
CD publishers by major
countries of origin*

	1994	%	1995	%	1996	%
USA	554	45	863	46	1,326	49
UK	206	17	321	17	465	17
Germany	102	8	173	9	201	7
France	80	7	96	5	175	7
Japan	55	4	84	5	124	5
Benelux	80	7	89	5	107	4
Canada	44	4	74	4	95	4
Italy	44	4	53	3	62	2
Australia	29	2	42	2	58	2
Switzerland	16	1	36	2	39	1
Spain	19	2	25	1	38	1
Total	1,229		1,856	.	2,690	

CD-ROM drive a disc drive for reading CD-ROM discs. The vast majority of CD-ROM drives conform to the Yellow Book standard, defined by Philips and Sony. Because of this, all drives are essentially interchangeable. CD-ROM drives are available either as stand-alone or built-in units with a variety of interfaces (connections) and access times.

CD-ROM XA (CD-ROM *ex*tended *a*rchitecture) a set of standards for storing multimedia information on CD-ROM. Developed by Philips, Sony, and Microsoft, it is a partial development of the ⌐CD-I standard. It interleaves data (as in CD-I) so that blocks of audio data are sandwiched between blocks of text, graphics, or video. This allows parallel streams of data to be handled, so that information can be seen and heard simultaneously.

CDTV (abbreviation for ***Commodore Dynamic Total Vision***) multimedia computer system developed by Commodore. It is designed for the home and is a direct rival to ⌐CD-I. It consists of a box about the size of a home video recorder, containing an Amiga 500 computer and a ⌐CD-ROM drive. CDTV discs can store a combination of text, pictures, sound, and video. Like CD-I, CDTV plugs into a TV set and stereo system. CDTV cannot play CD-ROM or CD-I discs.

Ceefax ('see facts') one of Britain's two ⌐teletext systems (the other is Teletext), or 'magazines of the air', developed by the BBC and first broadcast 1973.

   In 1995 the BBC began testing a scheme to allow Ceefax (repackaged in ⌐HTML to enable it to behave like Web pages) to be viewed on a PC by connecting a DAB (digital audio broadcasting) radio to the PC like a modem.

cellular modem type of ⌐modem that connects to a cellular phone for the wireless transmission of data.

cellular phone wireless phone that operates over radio frequencies and links calls to the public telephone system via a base station; the area covered by each base station is called a cell. Unlike phones connected up by telephone lines, cellular phones allow mobility, as calls can be made while moving from one radio cell to another. A network of connected base stations and exchanges connects the cellular calls to the public telephone system.

   In the UK, the two main networks are Cellnet and Vodafone, both covering more than 90% of the country. Older analogue cellular phones are easily tapped via commonly available scanners. Although this practice is illegal, in the early 1990s transcriptions of several phone calls made to or from members of the British royal family found their way into newspapers around the world. Newer digital phones use encryption to protect the confidentiality of phone conversations.

   In Europe, the newer digital standard, GSM (Groupe Spécial Mobile), has been adopted by many countries, enabling travellers to use a single phone throughout Europe.

censorship banning of certain types of information from public access. Concerns over the ready availability of material such as bomb recipes and pornography have led a number of countries to pass laws attempting to censor the Internet. The best known of these is the US ⌐Communications Decency Act 1996, but initiatives have been taken in other countries, for example Singapore, which announced 1996 new regulations bringing the Internet under the Singapore Broadcasting Authority and requiring all access providers and users to

CENSORSHIP

TIP: More information about censorship on the Internet is available from the Fight-Censorship archive http://fight-censorship.dementia.org/top/ and from the Electronic Frontier Foundation.

Censorship of the Internet

worldwide concern Most governments, and many citizens, are alarmed by the free flow of information, so it is hardly surprising if they are alarmed by the Internet, which is the largest free information system the world has ever seen. In very recent years (1994–96) there have been dozens of attempts to limit the free flow of information – not just in 'restrictive' countries such as Singapore and China, but in more liberal ones including Germany, France, Australia, and the UK. Even in the USA, where information is most highly valued, the Communications Decency Act was passed to try to 'clean up' free speech, though after judicial examination, the Act's provisions were found to be unconstitutional.

unstoppable information super-highway The Internet is hard to censor for a number of pragmatic and practical reasons. The first is that it is not a tangible thing, like a road, but a concept, like a transportation system. The Internet is simply a network of networks. While it is usually possible to close down a single computer network, just as it is possible to block a particular road, it is impossible to close down the whole system.

Also, in general terms, if users can connect to part of the Internet, they can find a route to any other part of the Internet. This is like saying that if a driver can get onto one road then in principle he or she can reach any other road anywhere in the world. The difference with the Internet is the speed at which information travels: a message can be sent to Antarctica and back in less than a second. The Internet is a global system, and does not stop at national boundaries.

how do you want to travel? A second problem with the Internet is that, like other transportation systems, it does not carry a single type of traffic. One type of Internet traffic, for example, consists of ***World Wide Web pages***. These combine text and graphics in a way that is very similar to a magazine or newspaper. Another type of traffic is ***electronic mail*** (e-mail), which consists of (mostly) private messages of the sort that could otherwise be sent by post. A third type of traffic consists of ***Internet Relay Chat*** messages, which are typed in real time: this is the computer equivalent of CB radio. There are numerous other types of traffic including video conferencing, radio broadcasts, and computer file transfers.

The problem is that the same type and level of censorship cannot possibly be applied to all the different types of traffic. No sensible person would attempt to impose the same standards on, say, television broadcasts, private letters, and telephone conversations, and the same sensitivity must apply to the Internet. It might, for example, be reasonable to hold a publisher responsible for articles published on a Web site, because the publisher has control of the content, but not to messages posted on an open ***bulletin board***.

whose values? It must also be observed that censoring the Internet is, in principle, dangerous: whose standards, whose laws, apply to something that is written in the US, held on a US-registered Internet server sited in Sweden, and read in Japan? This kind of problem has been highlighted by German attempts to block access to pro-white propaganda held on a server in Canada.

There is undoubtedly material on the Internet that is considered objectionable in the UK, for example, but almost every type of information is considered objectionable by someone somewhere. If one group can ban pro-Nazi material, another can ban pro-Capitalist tracts, or birth control information, or the discussion of evolution, or recipes for cooking and eating certain animals.

no roadblocks yet So far, the separate acts of individual governments to restrict information on the Internet have mainly resulted in increased publicity and the more widespread dissemination of whatever they have tried to ban. This seems likely to remain the case until there is international agreement about what can be controlled, and some means are devised to do it.

Jack Schofield

41

be registered and licensed. Less formal pressures have been applied against
⌐Internet Service Providers in Germany and the UK to block specific types of
material.

central processing unit (CPU) main component of a computer, the part that
executes individual program instructions and controls the operation of other
parts. It is sometimes called the central processor or, when contained on a single integrated circuit, a microprocessor.

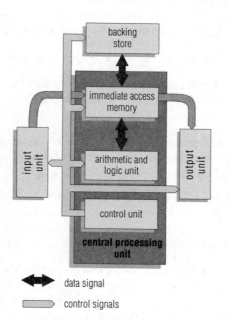

The CPU has three main components: the ***arithmetic and logic unit*** (ALU), where all calculations and logical operations are carried out; a ***control unit***, which decodes, synchronizes, and executes program instructions; and the ***immediate access memory***, which stores the data and programs on which the computer is currently working. All these components contain ⌐registers, which are memory locations reserved for specific purposes.

*central processing unit
The relationship between
the three main areas of a
computer's central
processing unit. The
arithmetic and logic unit
(ALU) does the arithmetic,
using the registers to store
intermediate results,
supervised by the control
unit. Input and output
circuits connect the ALU to
external memory, input, and
output devices.*

data signal

control signals

Centronics interface standard type
of computer ⌐interface, used to
connect computers to ⌐parallel devices, usually printers. (Centronics was an
important printer manufacturer in the early days of microcomputing.)

Cerf Vinton. US inventor of part of the ⌐TCP/IP protocols on which the Internet
is based. Known throughout the industry as the 'Father of the Internet', Cerf is
president of the ⌐Internet Society and was a principal developer of the
⌐ARPANET.

Formerly assistant professor of electrical engineering and computer science at
Stanford University, Cerf is senior vice president of data architecture for MCI
Telecommunications Corporation's Data Services Division in Reston, Virginia.

CERT abbreviation for ⌐Computer Emergency Response Team.

CGA (abbreviation for ***colour graphics adapter***) first colour display system for
IBM PCs and compatible machines. It has been superseded by ⌐EGA, ⌐VGA,
⌐SVGA, and ⌐XGA.

CGI abbreviation for ⌐common gateway interface.

chain letter mass-distributed letter that promises the recipient great riches if
he/she distributes the letter further. Chain letters have been sent via postal

services for decades and began to appear on the Internet 1994. They are a type of pyramid scheme, and as such are illegal for distribution via the US postal service; users are advised not to participate.

channel path connecting a computer to peripheral devices along which data can be transferred.

character one of the symbols that can be represented in a computer. Characters include letters, numbers, spaces, punctuation marks, and special symbols.

character printer computer ↜printer that prints one character at a time.

character set the complete set of symbols that can be used in a program or recognized by a computer. It may include letters, digits, spaces, punctuation marks, and special symbols.

extended character set in PC-based computing, the set of 254 characters stored in ↜ROM. Besides the 128 ↜ASCII characters, the set includes block graphics and foreign language characters.

character type check a ↜validation check to ensure that an input data item does not contain invalid characters. For example, an input name may be checked to ensure that it contains only letters of the alphabet or an input six-figure date may be checked to ensure it contains only numbers.

chat real-time exchange of messages between users of a particular system. Chat allows people who are geographically far apart to type messages to each other which are sent and received instantly. On a system like ↜America Online, users may chat while playing competitive games or while reading messages, as well as joining public or private 'rooms' to talk with a variety of other users. The biggest chat system is ↜Internet Relay Chat (IRC), which is used for the exchange of information and software as well as for social interaction.

check box small, square box used as a control in ↜dialog boxes. Check boxes ↜toggle functions and are operated by moving the cursor over the box and clicking the mouse button to check or clear the box.

check digit a digit attached to an important code number as a ↜validation check.

checksum a ↜control total of specific items of data. A checksum is used as a check that data have been input or transmitted correctly. It is used in communications and in, for example, accounts programs. See also ↜validation.

chip or ↜*silicon chip* another name for an ↜*integrated circuit*, a complete electronic circuit on a slice of silicon (or other semiconductor) crystal only a few millimetres square.

chip-set group of ↜chips that work together to perform a particular set of functions. Standard chip-sets, for example, manage graphics or form the working parts of a modem.

chroma key in television, technique for substituting backgrounds. For example, the empty studio behind a newscaster may be replaced with an outdoor scene or a frame of video footage. This technique is commonly used on news programmes and other shows that feature 'talking heads'.

A computer analyses the image of the newscaster, who is placed in front of a plain background, usually blue, to identify the exact ↩pixels where the talking figure begins and ends. It can then substitute a new image for just the area specified. The technique allows broadcasters to add visual interest while keeping costs down.

CinePak software method of compressing and decompressing ↩QuickTime 'movies', also called a software codec. CinePak takes a recorded QuickTime file and reduces it in size, frame by frame. This is a slow process, but the result is a file that can be played back efficiently by computers with QuickTime installed.

CIS, CI$ abbreviations for *CompuServe Information Service*; see ↩CompuServe.

CISC (acronym for *complex instruction-set computer*) a microprocessor (processor on a single chip) that can carry out a large number of ↩machine code instructions – for example, the Intel 80386. The term was introduced to distinguish them from the more rapid ↩RISC (reduced instruction-set computer) processors, which handle only a smaller set of instructions.

CIX abbreviation for ↩Compulink Information eXchange.

ClariNet commercial news service distributed via ↩USENET. It is not available on all sites since companies must pay to receive ClariNet, which is owned by Clarinet Communications Corp. Under the service's terms and conditions, professional media personnel are banned from using ClariNet news as a source in their work.

CLARINET
TIP: Public access is available via the World Wide Web
`http://www.clarinet.com.`

Clark Jim (James) US founder of ↩Silicon Graphics Inc 1982 and the ↩Netscape Communications Corporation 1994. As an associate professor at Stanford University, California, he and a team of graduate students developed the initial technology upon which Silicon Graphics' first products were built. He resigned as chair of Silicon Graphics early 1994 to start up Netscape, of which he is chair.

cleartext or *plaintext* in encryption, the original, unencrypted message.

click to press down and then immediately release a button on a ↩mouse. The phrase 'to click on' means to select an ↩icon on a computer screen by moving the mouse cursor to the icon's position and clicking a mouse button. See also ↩double click.

clickstream unedited log of mouse-clicks that records visitor actions on a site on the World Wide Web. This data is analysed to create feedback for advertisers, enabling them to check whether their strategies are successful in attracting user attention.

client in ⌕client-server architecture, software that enables a user to access a store of data or programs on a ⌕server. On the Internet, client software is the software that users need to run on home computers in order to be able to use services such as the World Wide Web.

client–architecture in computing, a system in which the mechanics of looking after data are separated from the programs that use the data. For example, the 'server' might be a central database, typically located on a large computer that is reserved for this purpose. The 'client' would be an ordinary program that requests data from the server as needed.

Most Internet services are examples of client-server applications, including the ⌕World Wide Web, ⌕FTP, ⌕Telnet, and ⌕Gopher.

clip art small graphics used to liven up documents and presentations. Many software packages such as word processors and presentation graphics packages come with a selection of clip art.

CLIP ART

TIP: Always check the copyright status before distributing widely.

clipboard a temporary file or memory area where data can be stored before being copied into an application file. It is used, for example, in cut-and-paste operations.

Clipper chip controversial encryption hardware system that contains built-in facilities to allow authorized third parties access to the encrypted data. Adopted as a US government standard 1994, the Clipper chip was a chip that used ⌕public-key cryptography and a proprietary ⌕algorithm called Skipjack, and could be built into any communications device, such as a telephone or modem. It was developed by the US National Security Agency as part of its ⌕Capstone project.

Clipper was instantly unpopular on the Net because of privacy concerns: it contained a system for depositing a copy of the user's private key in escrow (see ⌕key escrow), from where it could be obtained by law enforcement officials equipped with an appropriate court order.

Clipper suffered further defeat when Matt Blaze, a researcher at AT&T Bell Labs cracked the technology 1995. In 1996, the US government proposed the development of a network of trusted third parties to hold keys in escrow; the initiative was dubbed 'Clipper III'.

clock interrupt an ⌕interrupt signal generated by the computer's internal electronic clock.

clock rate the frequency of a computer's internal electronic clock. Every computer contains an electronic clock, which produces a sequence of regular electrical pulses used by the control unit to synchronize the components of the computer and regulate the ⌕fetch-execute cycle by which program instructions are processed.

A fixed number of time pulses is required in order to execute each particular instruction. The speed at which a computer can process instructions therefore depends on the clock rate: increasing the clock rate will decrease the time required to complete each particular instruction.

Clock rates are measured in **megahertz** (MHz), or millions of pulses a second. Microcomputers commonly have a clock rate of 8–50 MHz.

clone copy of hardware or software that may not be identical to the original design but provides the same functions. All personal computers (PCs) except those made by IBM are clones – IBM was the first to define the standard for PC architecture and subsequently licensed the designs to other manufacturers such as Compaq, Dell, and Amstrad. Clones are typically cheaper than the original product, as manufacturers cut costs in order to compete effectively with the original designers.

The process of cloning is endemic in the computer industry. Cloning a disc drive or workstation, however, means making an exact copy of all the files or software so that the new drive or machine functions identically to the original one.

CMOS (abbreviation for **complementary metal-oxide semiconductor**) family of integrated circuits (chips) widely used in building electronic systems.

CMYK (abbreviation for **cyan–magenta–yellow–black**) four-colour separation used in most (subtractive) colour printing processes. Representation on computer screens normally uses the additive ⪰RGB method and so conversion is usually necessary on output for printing either on colour printers or as separations.

CNC abbreviation for ⪰**computer numerical control**.

COBOL (acronym for **common business-oriented language**) high-level computer-programming language, designed in the late 1950s for commercial data-processing problems; it has become the major language in this field. COBOL features powerful facilities for file handling and business arithmetic. Program instructions written in this language make extensive use of words and look very much like English sentences. This makes COBOL one of the easiest languages to learn and understand.

code the expression of an ⪰algorithm in a ⪰programming language. The term is also used as a verb, to describe the act of programming.

codec device that codes and decodes an ⪰analogue stream to or from ⪰digital data. It is used in applications such as remote broadcast-quality voiceovers recorded in a remote studio and transmitted via codecs and ⪰Integrated Services Digital Network (ISDN) lines to a central studio for final mixing.

coffee machine on the Internet, the coffee machine at Cambridge University, England, whose supplies may be monitored via the World Wide Web. It derives from an idea originally developed at a US university, where the Coke machine was some distance from the programming lab. A system of switches was installed so that a programmer could check the machine's supply of Cokes and their temperature before going to collect a drink.

COFFEE MACHINE

TIP: The Cambridge University machine is at http://www.cl.cam.ac.uk/coffee/coffee.html

collision detection in ↩virtual reality, the ability of software to detect when two on-screen objects make contact.

colour depth the maximum number of colours that can be displayed simultaneously in an image by a particular computer system.

The most common modes are 16, 256, 32K, 64K and 16.7 million (true colour). The greater the colour depth, the larger the size of the picture file but the more detailed and realistic the quality of the picture.

COM acronym for ↩*computer output on microfilm/microfiche*.

Comité Consultatif International Téléphonique et Télégraphique (CCITT) international organization that determines international communications standards and protocols for data communications, including ↩fax. It was subsumed into the International Telecommunications Union (ITU) 1993.

command language a set of commands and the rules governing their use, by which users control a program. For example, an ↩operating system may have commands such as SAVE and DELETE, or a payroll program may have commands for adding and amending staff records.

command-line interface (CLI) in computing, a character-based interface in which a prompt is displayed on the screen at which the user types a command, followed by ↩carriage return, at which point the command, if valid, is executed.

Commercial Internet eXchange (CIX) US-based international non-profit-making organization of ↩Internet Service Providers and other data network suppliers. It is part of the Internet's US ↩backbone funded by commercial service providers.

common gateway interface (CGI) on the World Wide Web, a facility for adding scripts to handle user input. It allows a Web ↩server to communicate with other programs running on the same server in order to process data input by visitors to the Web site. CGI scripts 'parse' the input data, identifying each element and feeding it to the correct program for action, normally a ↩search engine or e-mail program. The results are then fed back to the user in the form of search results or sent e-mail.

comms program contraction of ↩communications program.

communications see ↩data communications.

Communications Decency Act 1996 rider (supplement) to the US Telecommunications Bill seeking to prohibit the transmission of indecent material to minors via the Internet.

Within hours of the bill's passage into law on 8 Feb 1996, suits were filed by 46 plaintiffs including the American Civil Liberties Union, Voter Telecom Watch, the Electronic Frontier Foundation, and the Center for Democracy and Technology to block the law's enforcement. On 12 June the Philadelphia federal court struck the law down with a judgment that read in part: 'Just as the strength of the Internet is chaos, so the strength of our liberty depends upon the chaos and cacophony of the unfettered speech the First Amendment (to the US Constitution) protects'. A second judgment from a New York court agreed. The government was expected to appeal both rulings to the Supreme Court.

communications program or *comms program* general-purpose program for accessing older ⟿on-line systems and ⟿bulletin board systems which use a ⟿command-line interface; also known as a terminal emulator.

Most operating systems include a trimmed-down comms program, but full-featured programs include facilities to store phone numbers and settings for frequently called services, address books, and the ability to write scripts to automate logging on. Popular comms programs include ProComm, Smartcom, Qmodem, and Odyssey.

compiler computer program that translates programs written in a ⟿high-level language into machine code (the form in which they can be run by the computer). The compiler translates each high-level instruction into several machine-code instructions – in a process called *compilation* – and produces a complete independent program that can be run by the computer as often as required, without the original source program being present.

Different compilers are needed for different high-level languages and for different computers. In contrast to using an ⟿interpreter, using a compiler adds slightly to the time needed to develop a new program because the machine-code program must be recompiled after each change or correction. Once compiled, however, the machine-code program will run much faster than an interpreted program.

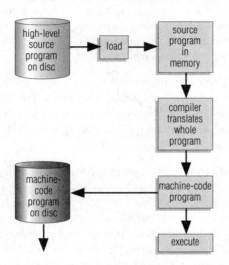

compiler
The process of compilation: a program written in a high-level language is translated into a program that can be run without the original source being present.

complementary metal-oxide semiconductor (CMOS) in electronics, a particular way of manufacturing integrated circuits (chips). The main advantage of CMOS chips is their low power requirement and heat dissipation, which enables them to be used in electronic watches and portable microcomputers. However, CMOS circuits are expensive to manufacture and have lower operating speeds than have circuits of the ⟿transistor–transistor logic (TTL) family.

COM port (contraction of *communication port* on a personal computer (PC), one of the serial ⟿ports through which ⟿data communications take place. PCs may have up to four COM ports. However, these cannot all be used simultaneously as COM1 and COM3 share an ⟿interrupt, as do COM2 and COM4. A modem added to a machine with a mouse on COM1 must be attached to COM2 or COM4.

COM PORT

TIP: In Windows, the mouse must be on COM1 or COM2.

compound document in Windows, a document containing elements that have been created using other programs. Usually managed through a word processor, such a document might include a table created in a spreadsheet and pictures created in a drawing program. These items may be linked using ⌐object linking and embedding (OLE), so that any changes made to the table in the word processor will also be made to the original table developed in the spreadsheet.

Compressed Serial Line Internet Protocol protocol usually abbreviated to ⌐CSLIP.

compression elimination of wasted repetition within a file so that it takes up less space. Compression is necessary for the many applications imagined for the future of the Internet, such as ⌐video-on-demand. The text files which first filled the Internet were relatively small and compact, but graphics take more space to describe, and audio and video require more space again. Compressed files take up less storage space and can be transmitted across the Net much faster.

Most modems include facilities for compressing data while in transmission. The most popular compression program is ⌐PKZIP, widely available as ⌐shareware. New standards of compression have been developed for audio and video, such as DVI (⌐digital video interactive) and ⌐MPEG.

Compulink Information eXchange (CIX) London-based electronic conferencing system founded 1987. Owned by Frank and Sylvia Thornley, CIX is the oldest and largest native British conferencing system. In 1996 it had approximately 16,000 users, including most of the country's technology journalists.

CompuServe large (US-based) public on-line information service. It is widely used for ⌐electronic mail and ⌐bulletin boards, as well as ⌐gateway access to large periodical databases.

CompuServe was established 1979. It is easier to use than the Internet and most computer hardware and software suppliers provide support for their products on CompuServe. Worldwide subscribers to CompuServe had risen from half a million 1988 to nearly 5.5 million 1996. CompuServe announced 1996 that its service would integrate with the ⌐World Wide Web.

There were 300,000 members in the UK 1996.

computer programmable electronic device that processes data and performs calculations and other symbol-manipulation tasks. There are three types: the ⌐*digital computer*, which manipulates information coded as binary numbers (see ⌐binary number system); the ⌐*analogue computer*, which works with continuously varying quantities; and the *hybrid computer*, which has characteristics of both analogue and digital computers.

There are four types of digital computer, corresponding roughly to their size and intended use. *Microcomputers* are the smallest and most common, used in small businesses, at home, and in schools. They are usually single-user machines. *Minicomputers* are found in medium-sized businesses and university departments. They may support from 10 to 200 or so users at once. *Mainframes*,

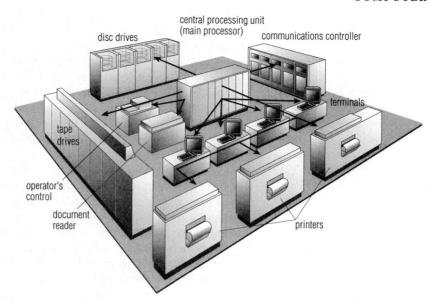

central processing unit
(main processor)

disc drives

communications controller

terminals

tape
drives

operator's
control

document
reader

printers

computer
*A mainframe computer.
Functionally, it has the
same component parts as
a microcomputer, but on a
much larger scale. The
central processing unit is at
the hub, and controls all
the attached devices.*

which can often service several hundred users simultaneously, are found in large organizations, such as national companies and government departments. ***Supercomputers*** are mostly used for highly complex scientific tasks, such as analysing the results of nuclear physics experiments and weather forecasting.

Microcomputers now come in a range of sizes from battery-powered pocket PCs and electronic organizers, notebook and laptop PCs to floor-standing tower systems that may serve local area ⌐networks or work as minicomputers. Indeed, most minicomputers are now built using low-cost microprocessors, and large-scale computers built out of multiple microprocessors are starting to challenge traditional mainframe and supercomputer designs.

PC and modem penetration as a percentage of households		
Country	**PC penetration, % of all households**	**Modem penetration, % of PC households**
USA	37	54
Australia	32	18
Singapore	32	13
Germany	29	14
Sweden	27	17
UK	25	8
Canada	23	n/a
France	15	9
Japan	7	20

*Computers per
household, 1995*

Under the Computer Misuse Act 1990 three new offences were introduced: unauthorized access to computer material (out of curiosity), unauthorized access with intent to facilitate the commission of a crime (for example fraud or blackmail), and unauthorized modification of computer material (to deter the propagation of malicious codes such as viruses and Trojan horses).

history Computers are only one of the many kinds of ↪computing device. The first mechanical computer was conceived by Charles ↪Babbage 1835, but it never went beyond the design stage. In 1943, more than a century later, Thomas Flowers built Colossus, the first electronic computer. Working with him at the time was Alan Turing, a mathematician who seven years earlier had published a paper on the theory of computing machines that had a major impact on subsequent developments. John von Neumann's computer, EDVAC, built 1949, was the first to use binary arithmetic and to store its operating instructions internally. This design still forms the basis of today's computers.

basic components At the heart of a computer is the ↪central processing unit (CPU), which performs all the computations. This is supported by memory, which holds the current program and data, and 'logic arrays', which help move information around the system. A main power supply is needed and, for a mainframe or minicomputer, a cooling system. The computer's 'device driver' circuits control the ↪peripheral devices that can be attached. These will normally be keyboards and ↪VDUs (visual display units) for user input and output, disc drive units for mass memory storage, and printers for printed output.

computer-aided design use of computers to create and modify design drawings; see ↪CAD.

computer-aided manufacturing use of computers to regulate production processes in industry; see ↪CAM.

computer art art produced with the help of a computer. See also ↪computer graphics and ↪animation, computer.

computer-assisted learning use of computers in education and training; see ↪CAL.

computer-assisted reporting use of computers to do journalistic research. At its simplest, computer-assisted reporting involves searching an on-line database for basic information such as addresses and phone numbers. At their most sophisticated, computer systems allow journalists to sift through large quantities of data to find patterns of behaviour or connections that would not be visible by other means.

computer crime broad term applying to any type of crime committed via a computer, including unauthorized access to files. Most computer crime is committed by disgruntled former employees or subcontractors. Examples include the releasing of ↪viruses, ↪hacking, and computer fraud. Many countries, including the USA and the UK, have specialized law enforcement units to supply the technical knowledge needed to investigate computer crime.

Computer Emergency Response Team (CERT) team of engineers based at Carnegie-Mellon University in Pittsburgh, Pennsylvania, USA, that issues security advice and helps resolve emergencies on the Internet by providing technical expertise.

In 1996 the US government announced the formation of a national emergency response team.

computer engineer job classification for ⌐computer personnel. A computer engineer repairs and maintains computer hardware.

computer game or *video game* any computer-controlled game in which the computer (sometimes) opposes the human player. Computer games typically employ fast, animated graphics on a ⌐VDU (visual display unit) and synthesized sound.

Commercial computer games became possible with the advent of the ⌐microprocessor in the mid-1970s and rapidly became popular as amusement-arcade games, using dedicated chips. Available games range from chess to fighter-plane simulations.

Some of the most popular computer games in the early 1990s were ⌐id Software's *Wolfenstein 3D* and *Doom*, which are designed also to be played across networks including the Internet. A whole subculture built up around those particular games, as users took advantage of id's help to create their own additions to the game.

The computer games industry has been criticized for releasing too many violent games with little intellectual content.

Computer games

from simple to 'real' Computer and video games have come a long way since Atari's Pong first appeared in 1972. That was a simplistic version of table tennis (ping pong) without a table or a net. Today's tennis games, like Codemasters' *Sampras' Extreme Tennis* for the Sony PlayStation and PC CD-ROM, show huge advances in realism. The programmers of the Sampras game used *motion capture* to turn video footage into realistic computer graphics, and even the crowd in the game reacts to events on the court.

simulation Simulation – creating computer versions of real-life games – has always been one of the driving forces of the genre. Flight simulators and driving games (*Pole Position*, *Formula 1 Grand Prix*) have long been popular, but all sorts of sports have been simulated including angling, golf, ice hockey, and even swimming. Martial arts are the basis of many popular fighting games, including *Mortal Kombat*. There have also been computer versions of card and board games such as bridge, backgammon, chess, *Monopoly, Risk,* and *Trivial Pursuits*. With a computer, you always have someone to play.

Simulations can be cerebral as well as physical. Management games allow fans to enjoy managing a football or motor racing team through several seasons, or run a railway, a theme park, or a chain of pizza parlours. You can even start with a small tribe of settlers and build a whole civilization, or start with a single space ship and rule the universe. Finish such a game by one means and you can then try others – a flexibility that keeps players coming back for more.

games to win Simulations tend to be open ended, but in other computer games, the player has to solve problems set by the programmers. Examples include puzzle games, adventure games, and so-called **platform games** like the famous *Super Mario* and *Sonic* games. These can take days or months to finish, and once finished, are rarely played again.

Adventures – where you guide a character or 'persona' on an adventure – started as text-based games, where players typed in things like 'kill troll with spear'. Good adventures created imaginary worlds, like good science-fiction and fantasy novels. Today, text is being replaced by three-dimensional graphics, and the persona by an **avatar**.

unseen opponents Many games can be played by more than one person, and some can be played on networks or via on-line services. In football and tennis simulations and martial arts games for example, each side can be controlled by a different player. Adventure games are also played on line, usually in the form of **MUDs** (multi-user dungeons). Often the

human interaction between personae is more fun than the nominal aims such as killing trolls and finding treasure. In some MUDs, players are able to create their own areas or 'rooms', and their on-line characters may have 'virtual sex' with or even marry other personae. All this is done by typing in text, but in the future, graphics-based and 'virtual reality' games may raise this idea to a new level of interest.

shoot'em-up Computer gaming is still strongly associated with 'shoot'em-ups': games that involve death and destruction, and that test the player's speed of reaction. The first really popular game, *Space Invaders*, was one example, but today's titles are much more realistic and contain far more gore. Examples include id Software's series, *Wolfenstein 3D*, *Doom*, and *Quake*, all of which reached huge audiences by being offered as shareware. Whether violent games are beneficial (in being cathartic) or harmful (in being brutalizing) is open to argument, but only the ignorant think all computer games are the same.

Jack Schofield

computer generation any of the five broad groups into which computers may be classified; **first generation** the earliest computers, developed in the 1940s and 1950s, made from valves and wire circuits; **second generation** from the early 1960s, based on transistors and printed circuits; **third generation** from the late 1960s, using integrated circuits and often sold as families of computers, such as the IBM 360 series; **fourth generation** using ⌐microprocessors, ⌐large-scale integration (LSI), and sophisticated programming languages, still in use in the 1990s; and **fifth generation** based on parallel processing and very large-scale integration, currently under development.

computer graphics use of computers to display and manipulate information in pictorial form. Input may be achieved by scanning an image, by drawing with a mouse or stylus on a graphics tablet, or by drawing directly on the screen with a light pen.

The output may be as simple as a pie chart, or as complex as an animated sequence in a science-fiction film (see ⌐animation, computer), three-dimensional engineering blueprint. The drawing is stored in the computer as ⌐raster graphics or ⌐vector graphics. Computer graphics are increasingly used in computer-aided

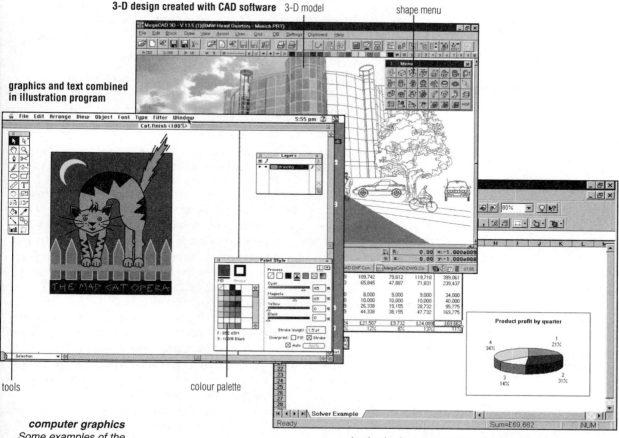

3-D design created with CAD software 3-D model   shape menu

graphics and text combined
in illustration program

tools   colour palette

simple pie chart generared by spreadsheet program

computer graphics
*Some examples of the
kinds of graphic design that
can be achieved using
computers. Text and
graphics may be combined
within an illustration
package, and sophisticated
three-dimensional drawings
can be created using a
computer-aided design
(CAD) system.*

design ($\leftharpoondown$CAD), and to generate models and simulations in engineering, meteorology, medicine and surgery, and other fields of science.

Recent developments in software mean that designers on opposite sides of the world will soon be able to work on complex three-dimensional computer models using ordinary PCs linked by telephone lines rather then powerful graphics workstations.

computer-mediated communication umbrella term for all types of communication via computers, such as $\leftharpoondown$electronic conferencing and $\leftharpoondown$chat.

Computer Misuse Act British law passed 1990 which makes it illegal to hack into computers (see $\leftharpoondown$hacking). The first prosecution under the Act was that of British hacker Paul Bedworth, who in 1993 was acquitted on the grounds that he was addicted to computing.

The law was inspired by the Law Lords' acquittal on appeal of Robert Schifreen and Steve Gold, two journalists who had hacked into Prince Philip's mailbox 1984 on the British Telecom service $\leftharpoondown$Prestel. The Lords ruled that the Forgery Act did not cover deceiving a computer.

computer numerical control control of machine tools, most often milling machines, by a computer. The pattern of work for the machine to follow, which often involves performing repeated sequences of actions, is described using a special-purpose programming language.

computer operator job classification for ⌐computer personnel. Computer operators work directly with the computer, running the programs, changing discs and tapes, loading paper into printers, and ensuring all ⌐data security procedures are followed.

computer output on microfilm/microfiche (COM) technique for producing computer output in very compact, photographically reduced form (⌐microform).

computer personnel people who work with or are associated with computers. In a large computer department the staff may work under the direction of a *data processing manager*, who supervises and coordinates the work performed. Computer personnel can be broadly divided into two categories: those who run and maintain existing ⌐applications programs (programs that perform a task for the benefit of the user) and those who develop new applications.

Personnel who run existing applications programs: *data control staff* receive information from computer users (for instance, from the company's wages clerks), ensure that it is processed as required, and return it to them in processed form; *data preparation staff*, or *keyboard operators*, prepare the information received by the data control staff so that it is ready for processing by computer. Once the information has been typed at the keyboard of a VDU (or at a ⌐key-to-disc or key-to-tape station), it is placed directly onto a medium such as disc or tape; *computer operators* work directly with computers, running the programs, changing discs and tapes, loading paper into printers, and ensuring that all ⌐data security procedures are followed; *computer engineers* repair and maintain computer hardware; *file librarians*, or *media librarians*, store and issue the data files used by the department; an *operations manager* coordinates all the day-to-day activities of these staff. Personnel who develop new applications: *systems analysts* carry out the analysis of an existing system (see ⌐systems analysis), whether already computerized or not, and prepare proposals for a new system; *programmers* write the software needed for new systems.

Country	$	£	Percentage growth 1992–96
USA	2,021	1,296	8
Japan	1,565	1,003	4
Sweden	1,521	975	7
France	1,243	797	3
UK	1,075	689	6
Germany	1,056	677	4

Investment in IT per employee, 1996 est.

Computer Professionals for Social Responsibility (CPSR) US organization advocating the responsible use of computers. Based in Washington DC, it was one of the first organizations to oppose President Reagan's Strategic Defense Initiative on the grounds that the many billions of lines of code it would take to program it could never be debugged successfully.

computer program coded instructions for a computer; see ⌇program.

computer simulation representation of a real-life situation in a computer program. For example, the program might simulate the flow of customers arriving at a bank. The user can alter variables, such as the number of cashiers on duty, and see the effect.

More complex simulations can model the behaviour of chemical reactions or even nuclear explosions. The behaviour of solids and liquids at high temperatures can be simulated using quantum simulation. Computers also control the actions of machines – for example, a ⌇flight simulator models the behaviour of real aircraft and allows training to take place in safety. Computer simulations are very useful when it is too dangerous, time consuming, or simply impossible to carry out a real experiment or test.

computer-supported collaborative work (CSCW) work undertaken by individuals who, using computers, are able to function together as a group on a project despite being geographically separated. The technology to facilitate CSCW is still under development. Early initiatives include video and data conferencing so that two users can talk on the telephone while simultaneously viewing a document in progress. Changes made by either participant affect both participants' displays.

computer terminal the device whereby the operator communicates with the computer; see ⌇terminal.

Computer Underground Digest widely distributed ⌇e-zine covering such issues as ⌇hacking, freedom of speech, and security risks.

COMPUTER UNDER GROUND DIGEST

TIP: It is available via USENET in the newsgroup comp.soc.cu-digest.

computing device any device built to perform or help perform computations, such as the abacus, slide rule, or ⌇computer.

The earliest known example is the abacus. Mechanical devices with sliding scales (similar to the slide rule) date from ancient Greece. In 1642, French mathematician Blaise Pascal built a mechanical adding machine and, in 1671, German mathematician Gottfried Leibniz produced a machine to carry out multiplication. The first mechanical computer, the ⌇analytical engine, was designed by British mathematician Charles Babbage 1835. For the subsequent history of computing, see ⌇computer.

config.sys the ⌇configuration file used by the MS-DOS and OS/2 ⌇operating systems. It is read when the system is ⌇booted.

configuration the way in which a system, whether it be ⌇hardware and/or ⌇software, is set up. A minimum configuration is often referred to for a particular

Computer simulation and ecology and evolution

electronic life One of the problems with studying life sciences is that changes in ecosystems and the evolution of life forms takes place over long periods of time. Scientists have attempted to simulate life processes on computers, so that such changes can be studied with artificial life. Now researchers at the University of Delaware have made significant advances with such computer-generated organisms.

Tierra, **the electronic world** Under the direction of Thomas Ray, an electronic world, known as Tierra, has been created. Life, death, competition, and reproduction are all modelled in computer terms, and the electronic organisms can be viewed as coloured patterns on a computer screen. A simple program, written to replicate itself, will rapidly fill the screen with progeny. More complex programming sets free numerous organisms to reproduce and compete with each other for limited resources.

the soup Tierra uses a concept known as a virtual computer – a software program that models a computer inside the real computer. This is a safety device to prevent any of the electronic organisms getting out of control and behaving like computer viruses. An interesting feature of the virtual computer is a block of memory termed the 'soup'. This is analogous to the 'primordial soup' – the mixture of organic molecules in which life is thought to have evolved. The electronic organisms use this memory to grow and to change.

mutating electronic organisms Changes, or mutations, to the electronic organisms are what makes Tierra such a fascinating environment. Changes come about in two ways – either by random flips in the memory soup (the memory changes from 0 to 1 or vice versa) or by inaccurate copying of the organisms' template during replication, which happens about once in every 2,000 instructions copied. Provided that important instructions are unaltered, the mutant organism can still function. Just as in the evolution of life, the occasional mutation is actually of benefit to the organism, and it can compete with greater success against other Tierran life.

the reaper There is also a monitoring program, known as the *Reaper*. This program comes into operation when over three-quarters of the memory soup is occupied (that is, at high population levels). Its function is to simulate death, and it removes both the oldest creatures and those least efficient at replicating.

running Tierra *Tierra* was first run in 1990 with a single ancestor organism some 80 instructions long. Almost immediately a creature evolved that was only 22 instructions long and could reproduce six times as rapidly as the ancestor. Large creatures – one of 23,000 instructions – also arose, but died out because they could not compete with the smaller, faster-reproducing organisms.

Parasites emerged – programs that could not reproduce themselves, but could use the instructions of other organisms to do so. These programs were at an advantage because they were smaller and reproduced more quickly. However, a 79-instruction creature evolved, which was similar to the ancestor but immune to parasites. This creature dominated Tierra until a new parasite evolved which could evade the dominant creature's defences.

what is the system used for? Fascinating though the Tierran system is, what use is it to life science in general? Thomas Ray suggests that it will be important to two groups in particular. Ecologists and evolutionary biologists will find the interaction of creatures and the emerging population patterns of significance.

Tierra is already a powerful modelling and teaching tool. With its unpredictable and mutating organisms, it will also figure strongly in the debate about what life actually is.

Steve Smyth

application, and this will usually include a specification of processor, disc and memory size, and peripherals required.

console a combination of keyboard and screen (also described as a terminal). For a multiuser system, such as ⮑UNIX, there is only one system console from which the system can be administered, while there may be many user terminals. See also ⮑games console.

content provider organization or individual who creates intellectual property, such as information databases, which may be distributed via traditional media or via the World Wide Web.

context-sensitive help type of help built into software that displays information related to the particular function in use.

contouring in ⮑computer graphics, a technique for enhancing the outline of a particular shape. This technique is used in applications such as mapping (see ⮑animation, computer), where a computer following the contours of an object ⮑pixel by pixel can be much more precise than a human.

control bus the electrical pathway, or ⮑bus, used to communicate control signals.

control character any character produced by depressing the control key (Ctrl) on a keyboard at the same time as another (usually alphabetical) key. The control characters form the first 32 ⮑ASCII characters and most have specific meanings according to the operating system used. They are also used in combination to provide formatting control in many word processors, although the user may not enter them explicitly.

control total a ⮑validation check in which an arithmetic total of a specific field from a group of records is calculated. This total is input together with the data to which it refers. The program recalculates the control total and compares it with the one entered to ensure that no entry errors have been made.

control unit the component of the ⮑central processing unit that decodes, synchronizes, and executes program instructions.

cookie formerly, on-line aphorism (short witty saying) named after fortune cookies; on the World Wide Web, a cookie is a user profile stored for a particular site. On many older systems, typing 'cookie' at the main system prompt retrieves a fortune-cookie style thought for the day from a randomized database.

cookie recipe urban legend that circulates around the Net. The story is about a protagonist who ate some delicious cookies for dessert after a meal in a fancy department store or restaurant. When asked for the recipe, the waiter refuses, but finally relents saying it will cost 'two fifty'. When the bill comes, the protagonist discovers the restaurant has charged $250. Feeling stung, he/she posts the recipe to the Net to ensure the maximum distribution (and therefore revenge) possible. A cookie recipe is attached.

COOKIE RECIPE

TIP: You can bake the cookies (the recipe is usually good), but DO NOT repost the article; millions of users have already seen it too many times before and you will be flamed to death.

coprocessor an additional ⌒processor that works with the main ⌒central processing unit to carry out a specific function. The two most common coprocessors are the *mathematical coprocessor*, used to speed up calculations, and the *graphic coprocessor*, used to improve the handling of graphics.

copy protection techniques used to prevent illegal copying of computer programs. Copy protection is not used as frequently as it used to be because it also prevents legal copying (for backup purposes). Alternative techniques to prevent illegal use include ⌒dongles, ⌒passwords and the need to uninstall a program before it can be installed on another machine.

Corba (acronym for *common object request broker architecture*) agreed specification that enables software components or 'objects' from different suppliers running on different computers using different operating systems to interoperate with one another. Corba has been extended via the Internet Inter-Orb Protocol (IIOP) to work over the Internet. Corba is promulgated as a standard by the Object Management Group (OMG).

Corel Canadian software company, second only to Microsoft for business applications in 1996. Corel was founded 1983 by British citizen Michael Cowpland. Its drawing program *Corel Draw* led the market from its first release. Corel bought the desktop publishing package Ventura Publisher 1995 and then the word processor WordPerfect 1996.

corruption of data introduction or presence of errors in data. Most computers use a range of ⌒verification and ⌒validation routines to prevent corrupt data from entering the computer system or detect corrupt data that are already present.

CoSy (contraction of *conferencing system*) ⌒command-line interface electronic conferencing software developed at the University of Guelph in the Canadian province of Ontario. It is used on London's ⌒Compulink Information eXchange (CIX) service and for the Open University's conferencing, as well as many others worldwide.

CP/M (abbreviation for *control program/monitor* or *control program for microcomputers*) one of the earliest ⌒operating systems for microcomputers. It was written by Gary Kildall, who founded Digital Research, and became a standard for microcomputers based on the Intel 8080 and Zilog Z80 8-bit microprocessors. In the 1980s it was superseded by Microsoft's ⌒MS-DOS, written for 16-bit microprocessors.

CPSR abbreviation for ⌒Computer Professionals for Social Responsibility.

CPU abbreviation for ⌒central processing unit.

cracker a hacker (see ⌒hacking); the term distinguishes criminal hacking ('cracking') from those who explore to satisfy their intellectual curiosity. The term is used much less than most hackers would like.

crawler on the World Wide Web, automated indexing software that scours the Web for new or updated sites. See also ↝'bot, ↝spider, and ↝agent.

Cray Seymour Roger 1925–1996. US computer scientist and pioneer in the field of supercomputing. He designed one of the earliest computers to contain transistors 1960. In 1972 he formed Cray Research to build the first ↝supercomputer, the Cray-1, released 1976. Its success led to the production of further supercomputers, including the Cray-2 1985, the Cray Y-MP, a multiprocessor design 1988, and the Cray-3 1989.

Creative Labs name of the US and British subsidiaries of the parent computing company Creative Technology, which was founded in Singapore in 1981. Creative Labs manufacture the leading ↝soundcard, the SoundBlaster, which they market alongside the Internet telephony, video, and multimedia products that make up the company's product range.

By 1996, the company claimed 20 million users of its products and had 4,400 staff worldwide, 400 of them in research and development.

critical path analysis procedure used in the management of complex projects to minimize the amount of time taken. The analysis shows which subprojects can run in parallel with each other, and which have to be completed before other subprojects can follow on.

By identifying the time required for each separate subproject and the relationship between the subprojects, it is possible to produce a planning schedule showing when each subproject should be started and finished in order to complete the whole project most efficiently. Complex projects may involve hundreds of subprojects, and computer ↝applications packages for critical path analysis are widely used to help reduce the time and effort involved in their analysis.

crop to cut away unwanted portions of a picture. The term comes from traditional manual methods of layout and paste-up; cropping is an option made available via photo-finishing and graphics software.

cross-posting on ↝USENET, the practice of sending a message to more than one ↝newsgroup. A small amount of cross-posting is acceptable if the message is on a topic that is relevant to more than one newsgroup. For example, a message about top tennis player André Agassi's personal life might be posted to both rec.sport.tennis and alt.showbiz.gossip.

CSCW abbreviation for ↝computer-supported collaborative work.

CSLIP (abbreviation for *Compressed Serial Line Internet Protocol*) in computing, newer version of ↝SLIP allowing slightly faster dial-up connections to the Internet.

CTS/RTS (abbreviation for *Clear To Send/Ready To Send*) hardware handshaking (see ↝handshake) used in high-speed modems. In most

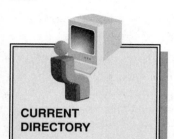

communications software this is an option that can be ⌐toggled on or off. The alternative, software handshaking, is considered less reliable at high speeds.

CUA (abbreviation for *common user access*) standard designed by ⌐Microsoft to ensure that identical actions, such as saving a file or accessing help, can be carried out using the same keystrokes in any piece of software. For example, in programs written to the CUA standard, help is always summoned by pressing the F1 function key. New programs should be easier to use because users will not have to learn new commands to perform standard tasks.

current directory in a computer's file system, the ⌐directory in which the user is positioned. As users move around a computer system, opening, reading, writing, and storing files, they navigate through that computer's directory structure, often unconsciously. Most file commands are assumed to apply to the files in the current directory.

In ⌐DOS, adding the command 'prompt pg' to the ⌐autoexec.bat file sets the computer to display the name and path of the current directory at the system prompt. On an ⌐FTP (file transfer protocol) site, the command 'pwd' will print the name of the current directory on the remote machine.

cursor on a computer screen, the symbol that indicates the current entry position (where the next character will appear). It usually consists of a solid rectangle or underline character, flashing on and off.

CU-SeeMe software that enables ⌐videoconferencing across the Internet. Developed by US computer scientist Richard Cogger, CU-SeeMe was bought 1996 by US videoconferencing specialist White Pine Software of Nashua, New Hampshire, and is now a commercial product.

Early experiments with CU-SeeMe included broadcasts by the North American Space Agency (NASA) of live and prerecorded video footage of shuttle missions, New Year parties held at ⌐cybercafes around the world, and live hook-ups between schools.

CWIS abbreviation for ⌐campus-wide information service.

cybercafe coffeehouse equipped with public-access Internet terminals. Typically, users pay a small sum to use the terminals for short periods. Cafes usually supply brief tutorials for newcomers. By 1996 many major cities around the world had such cafes. There were an estimated cybercafes 250 worldwide in 1996.

Britain's first cybercafe was Cyberia, set up in Whitfield Street, London 1994. The first W African cybercafe went on line in Dakar, Senegal in Oct 1996. It is Africa's seventh, the other six being in the south.

CyberCash one of several schemes for electronic money that can be used to trade on the Internet. Founded in Aug 1994, CyberCash uses the RSA encryption ⌐algorithm to protect customer financial information in transit.

The system stores customers' payment information, such as credit card numbers, in an electronic wallet, software which is downloaded from the

company's site on the World Wide Web. When a customer wishes to buy something at a commercial Web site, the site generates a payment request, the customer adds a payment method, and the CyberCash server authenticates the transaction. Future plans are to add electronic cheques and cash or debit cards to the choice of payment instruments. See also ⌐DigiCash.

cyberlaw relatively new field of Internet and computer law. Still being defined, the field includes new areas such as the responsibility of ⌐Internet Service Providers and ⌐bulletin-board system operators for the material that passes through or is stored on their systems and the framework for international electronic commerce, and a new look at traditional areas such as ⌐intellectual property rights and copyright and ⌐censorship.

cyberpunk term coined by US science-fiction writer and editor Gardner Dozois for a particular type of modern science fiction that combines high-technology landscapes with countercultural social and political ideas. Leading writers in this genre include William Gibson, Bruce Sterling, Pat Cadigan, Greg Bear, and Rudy Rucker.

cybersex online sexual fantasy spun by two or more participants via live, on-line ⌐chat. Futurists hypothesize about a future where 'virtual' sex will take place in ⌐virtual reality via body suits and other hardware input devices. In 1996, however, cybersex is limited to text-based systems such as IRC (⌐Internet Relay Chat) or the shared worlds created in ⌐MUDs (Multiuser dungeons) and ⌐MOOs (Multiuser object orienteds), both shared role-playing game worlds.

cyberspace the imaginary, interactive 'worlds' created by networked computers; often used interchangeably with 'virtual world'. The invention of the word 'cyberspace' is generally credited to US science-fiction writer William Gibson (1948–   ) and his first novel *Neuromancer* 1984.

As well as meaning the interactive environment encountered in a virtual reality system, cyberspace is 'where' the global community of computer-linked individuals and groups lives. From the mid-1980s, the development of computer networks and telecommunications, both international (such as the ⌐Internet) and local (such as the services known as 'bulletin board' or conferencing systems), made possible the instant exchange of messages using ⌐electronic mail and electronic conferencing systems directly from the individual's own home.

cylinder combination of the tracks on all the platters making up a fixed disc that can be accessed without moving the read/write heads.

cypherpunk (contraction of 'cipher' and 'cyberpunk') a passionate believer in the importance of free access to strong encryption on the Net, in the interests of guarding privacy and free speech.

DAC abbreviation for ⌐digital-to-analogue converter.

daemon background process running on a ⌐UNIX computer system that automatically handles tasks such as routing e-mail.

The word derives from medieval spirits deemed to be neutral, that is, neither good (angels) nor evil (devils).

daisywheel printing head in a computer printer or typewriter that consists of a small plastic or metal disc made up of many spokes (like the petals of a daisy). At the end of each spoke is a character in relief. The daisywheel is rotated until the spoke bearing the required character is facing an inked ribbon, then a hammer strikes the spoke against the ribbon, leaving the impression of the character on the paper beneath.

The daisywheel can be changed to provide different typefaces; however, daisywheel printers cannot print graphics nor can they print more than one typeface in the same document. For these reasons, they are rapidly becoming obsolete.

DARPANET early US computer network. See ⌐ARPANET.

data (singular *datum*) facts, figures, and symbols, especially as stored in computers. The term is often used to mean raw, unprocessed facts, as distinct from information, to which a meaning or interpretation has been applied.

database a structured collection of data, which may be manipulated to select and sort desired items of information. For example, an accounting system might be built around a database containing details of customers and suppliers. In larger computers, the database makes data available to the various programs that need

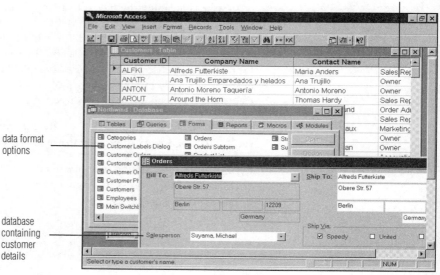

database
An example of the type of information that may be stored on a database. The information may be stored in various formats, enabling it to be sorted and output to other software programs.

Software description	Manufacturer	Description
Access	Microsoft	features wizards and macros; included in Microsoft Office Professional
Approach	Lotus	easy to use; requires no programming; with multiple database formats
dBASE	Borland	powerful and flexible relational database
Filemaker Pro	Claris	versatile and easy-to-use application with relational features
FoxPro	Microsoft	relational database with programming language

Some major database programs

it, without the need for those programs to be aware of how the data are stored. The term is also sometimes used for simple record-keeping systems, such as mailing lists, in which there are facilities for searching, sorting, and producing records.

There are three main types (or 'models'): hierarchical, network, and ↪relational, of which relational is the most widely used. A *free-text database* is one that holds the unstructured text of articles or books in a form that permits rapid searching.

A collection of databases is known as a *databank*. A database-management system (DBMS) program ensures that the integrity of the data is maintained by controlling the degree of access of the ↪applications programs using the data. Databases are normally used by large organizations with mainframes or minicomputers.

A telephone directory stored as a database might allow all the people whose names start with the letter B to be selected by one program, and all those living in Chicago by another.

data bus the electrical pathway, or ↪bus, used to carry data between the components of the computer.

data capture collecting information for computer processing and analysis. Data may be captured automatically – for example, by a ↪sensor that continuously monitors physical conditions such as temperature – or manually, for example, by reading electricity meters.

data communications sending and receiving data via any communications medium, such as a telephone line. The term usually implies that the data are digital (such as computer data) rather than analogue (such as voice messages). However, in the ISDN (↪Integrated Services Digital Network) system, all data – including voices and video images – are transmitted digitally.

data compression techniques for reducing the amount of storage needed for a given amount of data. They include word tokenization (in which frequently used words are stored as shorter codes), variable bit lengths (in which common characters are represented by fewer ↪bits than less common ones), and run-length encoding (in which a repeated value is stored once along with a count).

In *lossless compression* the original file is retrieved unchanged after decompression. Some types of data (sound and pictures) can be stored by *lossy compression* where some detail is lost during compression, but the loss is not noticeable. Lossy compression allows a greater level of compression.

data dictionary a file that holds data about data – for example, lists of files, number of records in each file, and types of fields. Data dictionaries are used by database software to enable access to the data; they are not normally accessible to the user.

Data Encryption Standard (DES) in computing, widely used US government standard for encryption, adopted 1977 and recertified for five more years 1993. DES was developed by IBM and adopted as a government standard by the National Security Agency. It is a private-key system, so that the sender and recipient encrypt and decrypt the message using the same key.

This means that a secure way has to be found to send the key from one party to the other; any third party who has the key can decrypt the encoded transmissions. Concerns over the long-term security of DES in the face of increasingly available cheap hardware have been somewhat mitigated by new techniques such as triply encrypted DES.

data flow chart diagram illustrating the possible routes that data can take through a system or program; see ⌒flow chart.

DataGlove in ⌒virtual reality, a glove wired to the computer that allows it to take input from a user's hand gestures. Sensors in the glove detect the wearer's hand movements, and transmit these to the computer in a digital format which the computer can interpret.

DataGlove is a trademark of VPL Research; the general term for such devices is *wired glove*.

data logging the process, usually automatic, of capturing and recording a sequence of values for later processing and analysis by computer. For example, the level in a water-storage tank might be automatically logged every hour over a seven-day period, so that a computer could produce an analysis of water use.

data preparation preparing data for computer input by transferring it to a machine-readable medium. This usually involves typing the data at a keyboard (or at a ⌒key-to-disc or key-to-tape station) so that it can be transferred directly to tapes or discs. Various methods of direct data capture, such as ⌒bar codes, ⌒optical mark recognition (OMR), and ⌒optical character recognition (OCR), have been developed to reduce or eliminate lengthy data preparation before computer input.

data processing (DP) or *electronic data processing* (EDP) use of computers for performing clerical tasks such as stock control, payroll, and dealing with orders. DP systems are typically ⌒batch systems, running on mainframe computers.

A large organization usually has a special department to support its DP activities, which might include the writing and maintenance of software

DATA RECOVERY

TIP: If files on your hard drive are missing or corrupted *do not* install any new software onto the hard drive as it will probably overwrite the data you are trying to recover. Run a program like Norton Utilities from a floppy disc. If the damage is too serious for Norton (or your technical ability), call a specialist for advice. Do not let anyone install software on that disc – even reinstalling existing software – until a specialist has agreed the data is irretrievable.

(programs), control and operation of the computers, and an analysis of the organization's information requirements.

data protection safeguarding of information about individuals stored on computers, to protect privacy.

The Council of Europe adopted, in 1981, a Data Protection Convention, which led in the UK to the Data Protection Act 1984. This requires computer databases containing personal information to be registered, and users to process only accurate information and to retain the information only for a necessary period and for specified purposes. Subject to certain exemptions, individuals have a right of access to their personal data and to have any errors corrected.

data recovery any of several possible procedures for restoring a computer system and its data after a system crash, burglary, or other damage. The first line of defence in any computer system is ⮌backups.

Every system fails at some point, and typically the data on the system is more valuable than the hardware on which it resides. The best course of action depends on the cause of the damage, which may be due to an outside agent, such as a virus, or a simple mistake, such as accidentally deleting important files. Some antivirus software comes with tools to assist users to clean up their systems; for deleted files, utility software such as Norton Utilities may be able to restore ('undelete') the data. In worse cases, specialists may still be able to restore the information by reading the hard disc's platters directly.

data security precautions taken to prevent the loss or misuse of data, whether accidental or deliberate. These include measures that ensure that only authorized personnel can gain entry to a computer system or file, and regular procedures for storing and 'backing up' data, which enable files to be retrieved or recreated in the event of loss, theft, or damage.

A number of ⮌verification and ⮌validation techniques may also be used to prevent data from being lost or corrupted by misprocessing.

Encryption involves the translation of data into a form that is meaningless to unauthorized users who do not have the necessary decoding software.

Passwords can be chosen by, or issued to, individual users. These secret words (or combinations of alphanumeric characters) may have to be entered each time a user logs on to a computer system or attempts to access a particular protected file within the system.

Physical access to the computer facilities can be restricted by locking entry doors and storage cabinets.

Master files (files that are updated periodically) can be protected by storing successive versions, or *generations*, of these files and of the transaction files used to update them. The most recent version of the master file may then be recreated, if necessary, from a previous generation. It is common practice to store the three most recent versions of a master file (often called the grandfather, father, and son generations).

Direct-access files are protected by making regular *dumps*, or back-up copies. Because the individual records in direct-access files are constantly being accessed and updated, specific generations of these files cannot be said to exist.

The files are therefore dumped at fixed time intervals onto a secure form of backing store. A record, or log, is also kept of all the changes made to a file between security dumps.

Fireproof safes are used to store file generations or sets of security dumps, so that the system can be restarted on a new computer in the event of a fire in the computer department.

Write-protect mechanisms on discs or tapes allow data to be read but not deleted, altered, or overwritten. For example, the protective case of a $3\frac{1}{2}$-inch floppy disc has a write-protect tab that can be slid back with the tip of a pencil or pen to protect the disc's contents.

data terminator or *rogue value* a special value used to mark the end of a list of input data items. The computer must be able to detect that the data terminator is different from the input data in some way – for instance, a negative number might be used to signal the end of a list of positive numbers, or 'XXX' might be used to terminate the entry of a list of names.

daughterboard small printed circuit board that plugs into a ⌐motherboard to give it new capabilities.

dBASE family of microcomputer programs used for manipulating large quantities of data; also, a related ⌐fourth-generation language. The first version, dBASE II, appeared in 1981; it has since become the basis for a recognized standard for database applications, known as Xbase.

DBS abbreviation for ⌐direct broadcast system.

DCE (abbreviation for *Data Communications Equipment*) another name for a ⌐modem.

DDE abbreviation for ⌐dynamic data exchange, a form of communication between processes used in Microsoft Windows.

debugging finding and removing errors, or ⌐bugs, from a computer program or system.

DEC (acronym for *Digital Equipment Corporation*) US computer manufacturer. DEC was founded by US computer engineers, Kenneth Olsen and Harlan Anderson, and was the first ⌐minicomputer manufacturer. It became the world's second largest computer manufacturer, after ⌐IBM, but made huge losses in the early 1990s. DEC's most successful computers were the PDP-11 and the VAX (Virtual Address eXtension). The former was used in the creation of the ⌐UNIX operating system.

The original aim was to make the first small computers for engineering and departmental use, and the PDP (Programmed Data Processor) range became known as minicomputers to contrast them with giant mainframes. The success of its 32-bit VAX minis in the 1980s made DEC one of the world's largest computer manufacturers. The company – now called *Digital* – has still to recover, but makes the world's fastest microprocessor, the Alpha chip, and has a popular search engine called ⌐AltaVista on the Internet's World Wide Web.

decimal number system or *denary number system* the most commonly used number system, to the base ten. Decimal numbers do not necessarily contain a decimal point; 563, 5.63, and –563 are all decimal numbers. Other systems are mainly used in computing and include the ⌐binary number system, ⌐octal number system, and ⌐hexadecimal number system.

Decimal numbers may be thought of as written under column headings based on the number ten. For example, the number 2,567 stands for 2 thousands, 5 hundreds, 6 tens, and 7 ones. Large decimal numbers may also be expressed in ⌐floating-point notation.

decision table a method of describing a procedure for a program to follow, based on comparing possible decisions and their consequences. It is often used as an aid in systems design.

The top part of the table contains the conditions for making decisions (for example, if a number is negative rather than positive and is less than 1), and the bottom part describes the outcomes when those conditions are met. The program either ends or repeats the operation.

declarative programming computer programming that does not describe how to solve a problem, but rather describes the logical structure of the problem. It is used in the programming language ⌐PROLOG. Running such a program is more like proving an assertion than following a ⌐procedure.

decoder an electronic circuit used to select one of several possible data pathways. Decoders are, for example, used to direct data to individual memory locations within a computer's immediate access memory.

dedicated computer computer built into another device for the purpose of controlling or supplying information to it. Its use has increased dramatically since the advent of the ⌐microprocessor: washing machines, digital watches, cars, and video recorders all now have their own processors.

A dedicated system is a general-purpose computer system confined to performing only one function for reasons of efficiency or convenience. A word processor is an example.

Deep Blue name given to the IBM chess-playing computer that first defeated a human grandmaster, the Russian Gary Kasparov, 1996.

The architect and principal designer of Deep Blue is Feng-Hsiung Hsu, who joined IBM 1989. Deep Blue's precursor, Deep Thought, for which Hsu won several awards, was the first computer to achieve a grandmaster rating 1988.

default a factory setting for user-configurable options. Default settings appear in all areas of computing, from the on-screen colour scheme in a ⌐graphical user interface to the directories where software programs store data.

defragmentation program or *disc optimizer* a program that rearranges data on disc so that files are not scattered in many small sections. See also ⌐fragmentation.

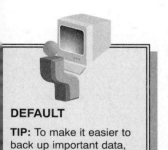

DEFAULT

TIP: To make it easier to back up important data, change the default settings so that programs store data in a common directory or directory tree of your own choosing.

delete remove or erase. In computing, the deletion of a character removes it from the file; the deletion of a file normally means removing its directory entry, rather than actually deleting it from the disc. Many systems now have an ⬎undelete facility that allows the restoration of the directory entry.

Delphi text-based UK and US national on-line information service. In Nov 1992, Delphi was the first national US service to open a ⬎gateway to the Internet. Founded 1982 as the world's first on-line encyclopedia, Delphi was bought by News International 1993, and launched its UK service 1994. In 1996 the US arm of Delphi was sold back to one of its original owners. The UK service continues in the hands of News International.

demo or *demonstration software* preview version of software that allows users to try out the main features of a particular program before buying it. Especially common among ⬎shareware producers, demo software usually blocks some features of the full version, so that a demo database might be able to handle only a small number of records.

The word 'demo' is also used to refer to fancy graphics and sound routines which are created by young programmers to demonstrate their skills to friends, admirers, and potential employers such as computer game publishers.

Demon Internet Britain's first and largest mass-market ⬎Internet Service Provider. Founded 1992 by English hardware salesman Cliff Stanford with 200 founding subscribers who each paid £120 in advance for a year's service, Demon set the price (£10 a month plus VAT) for Internet access in the UK. By 1996, Demon Internet had 65,000 customers.

demonstration software in computing, see ⬎demo.

DES abbreviation for ⬎Data Encryption Standard.

desktop a graphical representation of file systems, in which applications and files are represented by pictures (icons), which can be triggered by a single or double click with a ⬎mouse button. Such a ⬎graphical user interface can be compared with the ⬎command-line interface, which is character-based.

desktop publishing (DTP) use of microcomputers for small-scale typesetting and page makeup. DTP systems are capable of producing camera-ready pages

Software	Manufacturer	Description
FrameMaker	Frame Technologies	strong on technical reports and book production
PageMaker	Adobe	powerful professional tool; strong layout and colour capabilities
PagePlus	Serif	good value; includes vector drawing program and bitmap editor
Publisher	Microsoft	low-level for beginners; provides wizards and clip art gallery.
QuarkXpress	Quark	industry standard; numerous enhancement modules available

Some major desktop publishing software programs

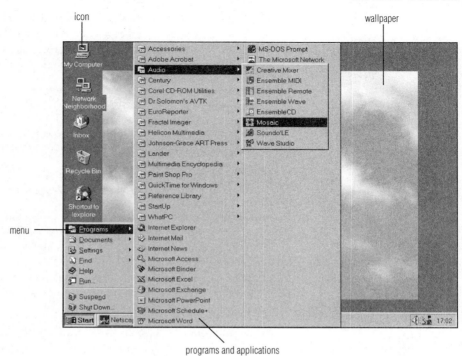

icon   wallpaper

menu

programs and applications

desktop
A typical graphical desktop, showing the menu system, icons, programs, and applications available to the user.

(pages ready for photographing and printing), made up of text and graphics, with text set in different typefaces and sizes. The page can be previewed on the screen before final printing on a laser printer.

desktop video a ↪videoconferencing system that can be used by an individual from a desktop computer. A desktop conferencing system needs a computer, an attached video camera, microphone, and speakers, and a telephone or network connection.

Early videoconferencing systems required such expensive equipment that participants had to gather in the room where the equipment was kept. Systems introduced in the mid-1990s, however, made videoconferencing as convenient, private, and easy to use as ordinary telephone calls.
The first desktop videoconferencing system on the Internet was ↪CU-SeeMe.

destination page page designated by a ↪hypertext link.

developer designer of a computer system.

device driver small piece of software required to tell the operating system how to interact with a particular input or output device or peripheral.
Much work has been done to standardize devices and their interfaces to eliminate the need for individual device drivers. Peripherals such as CD-ROM drives, for example, work with a single standard device driver (in Microsoft Windows, MSCDEX.EXE). Other devices, such as modems and printers, still need an individual driver tailored to work with that specific model.

dialler element of an Internet software package that makes the connection to the ↶on-line service or ↶Internet Service Provider. In Windows systems, this is usually the WINSOCK.DLL file, with or without a front end (part of the program that interacts with the user) to make configuration easier.

dialog box in ↶graphical user interfaces, a small on-screen window with blanks for user input.

dial-up connection connection to an ↶on-line system or ↶Internet Service Provider made by dialling via a ↶modem over a telephone line.

DIANE (acronym for *direct information access network for Europe*) collection of information suppliers, or 'hosts', for the European computer network.

difference engine mechanical calculating machine designed (and partly built 1822) by the British mathematician Charles ↶Babbage to produce reliable tables of life expectancy. A precursor of the ↶analytical engine, it was to calculate mathematical functions by solving the differences between values given to variables within equations. Babbage designed the calculator so that once the initial values for the variables were set it would produce the next few thousand values without error.

Diffie-Hellman key exchange system the basis of ↶public-key cryptography, proposed by researchers Whitfield Diffie and Martin Hellman 1976.

DigiCash one of several competing systems for electronic money suitable for use on the Internet. Invented by Belgian-based US cryptographer David Chaum, DigiCash uses ↶public-key cryptography techniques to assure anonymity. Trials of the system began 1994 using software developed for Windows, UNIX, and the Mac.

digit any of the numbers from 0 to 9 in the decimal system, 0 to 9 and A to F in the ↶hexadecimal system, whereas the binary system has two digits (or ↶bits), 0 and 1.

digital in electronics and computing, a term meaning 'coded as numbers'. A digital system uses two-state, either on/off or high/low voltage pulses, to encode, receive, and transmit information. A *digital display* shows discrete values as numbers (as opposed to an analogue signal, such as the continuous sweep of a pointer on a dial).

   Digital electronics is the technology that underlies digital techniques. Low-power, miniature, integrated circuits (chips) provide the means for the coding, storage, transmission, processing, and reconstruction of information of all kinds.

digital camera camera that uses a charge-coupled device (CCD) to take pictures which are stored as digital data rather than on film. The output from digital cameras can be downloaded onto a computer for retouching or storage, and can be readily distributed as computer files. Leading manufacturers of digital cameras include Canon and Kodak.

DIGICASH

TIP: More information about DigiCash is available at http://www.digicash.com.

DIGITAL CITY

TIP: The best-known digital city is a mirror of Amsterdam, in the Netherlands. It can be reached via the World Wide Web at http://www.dds.nl.

digital city area in ⮑cyberspace, either text-based or graphical, that uses the model of a city to make it easy for visitors and residents to find specific types of information.

digital composition or *compositing* computerized film editing. Some film special effects require shots to be cut together – composited. A sequence showing an actor hanging off the edge of a skyscraper, for example, may be put together out of footage of the actor in a safe location inserted into a shot looking down the side of the skyscraper, which may itself be a model. Traditional techniques for creating such a shot involved photographing the foreground shot with the background shot playing behind it, with an inevitable degradation of quality in the background material. In digital compositing, the same footage is digitized, and the work of merging the two sequences is done by manipulating computer files. The composite image is then transferred back onto film with no loss of quality.

digital computer computing device that operates on a two-state system, using symbols that are internally coded as binary numbers (numbers made up of combinations of the digits 0 and 1); see ⮑computer.

digital data transmission in computing, a way of sending data by converting all signals (whether pictures, sounds, or words) into numeric (normally binary) codes before transmission, then reconverting them on receipt. This virtually eliminates any distortion or degradation of the signal during transmission, storage, or processing.

Digital future

beginnings Computing started with numbers, and computation means calculation. Indeed, it is hard to say where the computer business started because it came out of the continuous development of calculating machines, but the US Army's ENIAC (Electronic Numerator, Integrator, Analyzer and Computer) is commonly regarded as the first 'real computer'. It was designed during the World War II to calculate shell trajectories for firing tables.

When computers were first used in business, it was usually for handling numerical tasks such as stock control and financial calculations, but this was mainly because of their huge cost. No company was going to spend millions of pounds or dollars on a computer and use it for a trivial task such as word processing, which could be done cheaply with mechanical typewriters.

Nonetheless, word processing – or at least, text editing – was an obvious application for the computer. The idea of letting a particular number stand for a particular letter of the alphabet or punctuation mark goes back thousands of years, but a popular electronic system had been invented by Emile Baudot in 1877 for sending messages by telex, and it is still in use today.

If a particular number in a computer's memory could stand for an alphanumeric character, it could just as easily stand for a graphical one, or for a single point on a high-resolution display screen. In other words, computers could also be used to handle line drawings for computer-aided drafting. Thus as computers became cheaper and more powerful, and as video display terminals became more sophisticated, they were used to handle more and more things digitally. Pictures and sounds were followed by moving colour pictures with synchronized sound, until today, no-one finds it strange that a home computer can play back video sequences and films that have been digitally encoded on compact discs.

As computers have become more capable of handling complex analogue data – such as music and photographs – so computers have started to take over the storage and reproduction of these data. The compact disc is a digital (computerized) medium for music, and digital cameras are now starting to replace ones based on films coated with chemicals.

the way ahead In computing, interest is moving on from two-dimensional to three-dimensional representations of reality or 'virtual worlds'. A user, represented by a 'persona' or 'avatar', can put on a virtual reality (VR) headset and move around inside an artificial reality created by one or more computers. The effects are still primitive (in most, the resolution is so low you'd qualify as legally blind) but the rapid growth in processor power and tumbling memory prices will make VR worlds increasingly detailed. Some will be more realistic, though many will simply be more fantastical. Researchers are also developing feedback mechanisms and body suits that will provide some form of touch sensitivity.

The story of computing can be seen as the digitization of more and more things, including words, images, sounds, films, and television signals. This process will certainly continue, and no one can predict where it will end.

Jack Schofield

digital monitor display ⮎monitor using standard cathode-ray tube technology that converts a ⮎digital signal from the computer into an ⮎analogue signal for display.

Digital monitors are unable to display the continuously variable range of colours offered by analogue monitors.

digital recording technique whereby the pressure of sound waves is sampled more than 30,000 times a second and the values converted by computer into precise numerical values. These are recorded and, during playback, are reconverted to sound waves.

This technique gives very high-quality reproduction. The numerical values converted by computer represent the original sound-wave form exactly and are recorded on compact disc. When this is played back by laser, the exact values are retrieved.

When the signal is fed via an amplifier to a loudspeaker, sound waves exactly like the original ones are reproduced.

digital retouching technique for touching up digital photographs, similar to airbrushing in the analogue world. It is commonly used in the film industry to remove scratches or to cover up filming mistakes.

The retoucher points out the error to the computer and the computer calculates new colour values for the affected ⮎pixels from the colours of neighbouring pixels.

digital signal processor (DSP) in computing, special-purpose integrated circuit that handles voice. DSPs are used in voice modems, which add answering machine facilities to a personal computer, and also in computer dictation systems.

digital signature method of using encryption to certify the source and integrity of a particular electronic document. Because all ⮡ASCII characters look the same no matter who types them, methods have to be found to certify the origins of particular messages if they are to be legally binding for electronic commerce or other transactions. One type of digital signature commonly seen on the Net is generated by the program ⮡Pretty Good Privacy (PGP), which adds a digest of the message to the signature.

digital-to-analogue converter electronic circuit that converts a digital signal into an ⮡analogue (continuously varying) signal. Such a circuit is used to convert the digital output from a computer into the analogue voltage required to produce sound from a conventional loudspeaker.

digital versatile disc or *digital video disc* (DVD) disc format for storing digital information. DVDs can hold 14 times the data stored on current CDs. As with CDs, information is etched in the form of microscopic pits onto a plastic disc (though the pits are half the size), the pitted side of which is then coated with aluminium. DVDs have two pitted surfaces whereas CDs have only one. The data is read optically using a laser as the disc rotates. A double layer disc can hold 4 hours of video. The Japanese company TDK produced the rewriteable DVD-RAM, capable of holding 2.6 gigabytes, 1996.

	DVD	CD
pit diameter (microns)	0.4	0.83
distance between data tracks (microns)	0.74	1.6
data spiral length (km/mi)	11/6.8	5/3
type of laser	red	infrared
laser wavelength (nanometres)	635–650	780
data capacity	8.5 gigabytes	680 megabytes

DVDs compared with CDs

digital video interactive powerful compression system used for storing video images on computer; see ⮡DVI.

digitize to turn ⮡analogue signals into the binary data a computer can read. Any type of analogue signal can be digitized, including pictures, sound, video, or film. The result is files that can be manipulated, stored, or transmitted by computers.

digitizer a device that converts an analogue video signal into a digital format so that video images can be input, stored, displayed, and manipulated by a computer. The term is sometimes used to refer to a ⮡graphics tablet.

dingbat non-alphanumeric character, such as a star, bullet, or arrow. Dingbats have been combined into ⮡PostScript and ⮡TrueType fonts for use with word processors and graphics programs.

DIP abbreviation for ⮡document image processing.

DIP switch (abbreviation of *dual in-line package*) tiny switch that controls settings on devices such as printers and modems. The owner's manual will usually specify how DIP switches should be set.

On printers, these switches are typically used to specify which emulation to use; on modems, they set the modem to match the ⇨COM port to which it is connected. They should not need to be changed once the device has been installed and is working properly.

direct access or *random access* type of ⇨file access. A direct-access file contains records that can be accessed by the computer directly because each record has its own address on the storage disc.

direct broadcast system (DBS) in computing, combination of a small satellite dish and receiver which allows consumers to receive television and radio broadcasts from a satellite rather than via terrestrial broadcasting towers and repeaters.

The most common systems in the UK are those that work with the four Astra satellites, which carry a group of channels from British Sky Broadcasting (BSkyB), among others. New plans announced in the UK 1996 include a move to digital direct broadcast systems, which besides allowing the transmission of many more channels will also allow fast access to data from the most popular sites on the World Wide Web.

direct connection connection between two computers via cable to transfer files without the intermediary of a network or on-line service. Each computer must be running communications software using the same protocols for file transfers. If the computers are in the same room, they can be connected using a special type of serial cable known as a null modem cable; if they are connected via telephone lines each must have a modem so that one can dial the other.

There are several software packages designed for this purpose; the market leader is Laplink.

direct memory access (DMA) in computing, a technique used for transferring data to and from external devices without going through the ⇨central processing unit (CPU) and thus speeding up transfer rates. DMA is used for devices such as ⇨scanners.

direct memory access channel in computing, channel used for the fast transfer of data; usually abbreviated as ⇨DMA channel.

Director multimedia software ⇨authoring tool published by Macromedia, a company of multimedia software specialists based in San Francisco, USA.

directory a list of file names, together with information that enables a computer to retrieve those files from ⇨backing storage. The computer operating system will usually store and update a directory on the backing storage to which it refers. So, for example, on each ⇨disc used by a computer a directory file will be created listing the disc's contents.

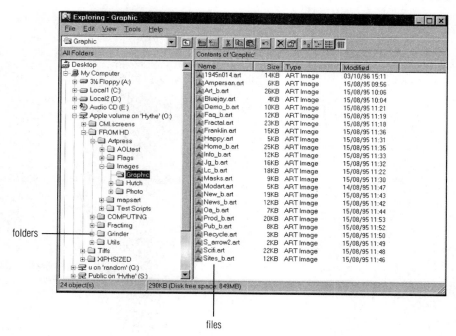

folders —

files

directory

A graphical illustration of the directory filing system on a computer. On the left hand side of the screen are the sub-directories available from the root; on the right are the files contained within the active directory.

directory tree collective name for a ↪directory and all its subdirectories.

disc or **_disk_** in computing, a common medium for storing large volumes of data (an alternative is ↪magnetic tape). A **_magnetic disc_** is rotated at high speed in a disc-drive unit as a read/write (playback or record) head passes over its surfaces to record or read the magnetic variations that encode the data. Recently, **_optical discs_**, such as ↪CD-ROM (compact-disc read-only memory) and ↪WORM (write once, read many times), have been used to store computer data. Data are recorded on the disc surface as etched microscopic pits and are read by a laser-scanning device. Optical discs have an enormous capacity – about 550 megabytes (million ↪bytes) on a compact disc, and thousands of megabytes on a full-size optical disc.

Magnetic discs come in several forms: **_fixed hard discs_** are built into the disc-drive unit, occasionally stacked on top of one another. A fixed disc cannot be removed: once it is full, data must be deleted in order to free space or a complete new disc drive must be added to the computer system in order to increase storage capacity. Large fixed discs, used with mainframe and minicomputers, provide up to 3,000 megabytes. Small fixed discs for use with microcomputers were introduced in the 1980s and typically hold 40–400 megabytes. **_Removable hard discs_** are common in minicomputer systems. The discs are contained, individually or as stacks (disc packs), in a protective plastic case, and can be taken out of the drive unit and kept for later use. By swapping such discs around, a single hard-disc drive can be made to provide a potentially infinite storage capacity. However, access speeds and capacities tend to be lower that those associated with large fixed hard discs. A **_floppy disc_** (or diskette) is the most

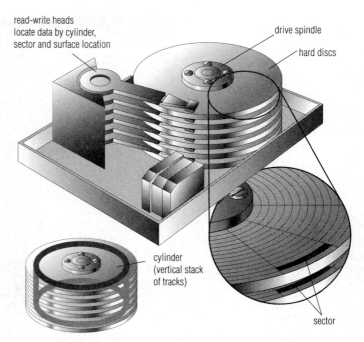

read-write heads
locate data by cylinder,
sector and surface location

drive spindle

hard discs

cylinder
(vertical stack
of tracks)

sector

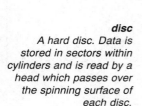

disc
*A hard disc. Data is
stored in sectors within
cylinders and is read by a
head which passes over
the spinning surface of
each disc.*

common form of backing store for microcomputers. It is much smaller in size and capacity than a hard disc, normally holding 0.5–2 megabytes of data. The floppy disc is so called because it is manufactured from thin flexible plastic coated with a magnetic material. The earliest form of floppy disc was packaged in a card case and was easily damaged; more recent versions are contained in a smaller, rigid plastic case and are much more robust. All floppy discs can be removed from the drive unit.

disc compression technique, based on ⌐data compression, that makes hard discs and floppy discs appear to have more storage capacity than is normally available. If the data stored on a disc can be compressed to occupy half the original amount of disc space, it will appear that the disc is twice its original size. The processes of compression (to store data) and decompression (so that data can be used) are hidden from the user by the software.

disc drive mechanical device that reads data from and writes data to a magnetic ⌐disc.

disc formatting preparing a blank magnetic disc in order that data can be stored on it. Data are recorded on a disc's surface on circular tracks, each of which is divided into a number of sectors. In formatting a disc, the computer's operating system adds control information such as track and sector numbers, which enables the data stored to be accessed correctly by the disc-drive unit.

Some floppy discs, called ***hard-sectored discs***, are sold already formatted. However, because different makes of computer use different disc formats, discs

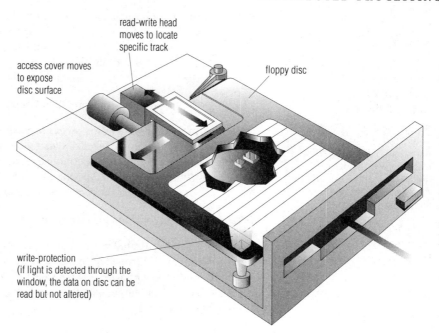

read-write head
moves to locate
specific track

access cover moves
to expose
disc surface

floppy disc

write-protection
(if light is detected through the
window, the data on disc can be
read but not altered)

disc drive
*A floppy disc drive. As the
disc is inserted into the
drive, its surface is
exposed to the read-write
head, which moves over
the spinning disc surface to
locate a specific track.*

are also sold unformatted, or ***soft-sectored***, and computers are provided with the necessary ⮡utility program to format these discs correctly before they are used.

Discman Sony trademark for a portable compact-disc player; the equivalent of a Walkman, it also comes in a model with a liquid-crystal display for data discs.

disc optimizer another name for a ⮡defragmentation program, a program that gathers together files that have become fragmented for storage on different areas of a disc. See also ⮡fragmentation.

display an ⮡output device that looks like a television set and displays commands to the computer and their results.

display control interface in computing, standard developed by Microsoft and Intel for the ⮡device drivers that control ⮡graphics cards.

distance learning form of education using technology to teach pupils who are dispersed geographically. Britain's Open University, founded 1969, is the oldest and most successful distance-learning institution in the world, using a mixture of postal mail, television, electronic conferencing, and the Internet to offer degree courses to students all over the world. Experiments in the 1990s used ⮡videoconferencing and other multimedia techniques to widen the university's range.

distributed processing computer processing that uses more than one computer to run an application. ⮡Local area networks, ⮡client–server architecture, and ⮡parallel processing involve distributed processing.

DMA CHANNEL

TIP: Keep a log book for
your PC listing each
peripheral you have
installed with a note of
the DMA channel number,
interrupt request (IRQ)
lines, and memory
address assigned to it, to
make installing additional
devices easier.

dithering in computer graphics, a technique for varying the patterns of dots in an image in order to give the impression of shades of grey. Each dot, however, is of the same size and the same intensity, unlike grey scaling (where each dot can have a different shade) and photographically reproduced half-tones (where the dot size varies).

DLL the abbreviation for ⬗dynamic link library.

DMA channel (abbreviation for *direct memory access channel*) type of channel used for the fast transfer of data between a computer and peripherals such as CD-ROM drives. Most ISA (industry standard architecture) personal computers (PCs) have eight DMA channels, of which typically six are available for use by add-on peripherals, most of which require dedicated channels.

DNS abbreviation for domain ⬗name server.

document data associated with a particular application. For example, a *text document* might be produced by a ⬗word processor and a *graphics document* might be produced with a ⬗CAD package. An ⬗*OMR* or ⬗*OCR* document is a paper document containing data that can be directly input to the computer using a ⬗document reader.

documentation the written information associated with a computer program or ⬗applications package. Documentation is usually divided into two categories: program documentation and user documentation.

    Program documentation is the complete technical description of a program, drawn up as the software is written and intended to support any later maintenance or development of that program. It typically includes details of when, where, and by whom the software was written; a general description of the purpose of the software, including recommended input, output, and storage methods; a detailed description of the way the software functions, including full program listings and ⬗flow charts; and details of software testing, including sets of ⬗test data with expected results. *User documentation* explains how to operate the software. It typically includes a nontechnical explanation of the purpose of the software; instructions for loading, running, and using the software; instructions for preparing any necessary input data; instructions for requesting and interpreting output data; and explanations of any error messages that the program may produce.

document image processing (DIP) scanning documents for storage on ⬗CD-ROM. The scanned images are indexed electronically, which provides much faster access than is possible with either paper or ⬗microform. See also ⬗optical character recognition.

document reader an input device that reads marks or characters, usually on preprepared forms and documents. Such devices are used to capture data by ⬗optical mark recognition (OMR), ⬗optical character recognition (OCR), and ⬗mark sensing.

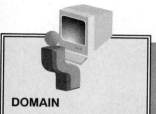

dog reference to a cartoon published in *The New Yorker* that showed a dog poised over a computer keyboard remarking to another dog, 'On the Internet, no one knows you're a dog.' It is used to illustrate the point that the Internet gives users the opportunity to adopt a different persona, for example many women surf using a male identity.

domain on the Internet, segment of an address that specifies an organization, its type, or its country of origin. Domain names are read backwards, starting at the end. All countries except the USA use a final two-letter code such as `ca` for Canada and `uk` for the UK. US addresses end in one of seven 'top-level' domains, which specify the type of organization: `com` (commercial), `mil` (military), `org` (usually a nonprofit-making organization), and so on.

These names are for humans; to enable mail and other messages to be sorted by machine, computers use IP (Internet protocol) numbers. To route a message, the computer looks up the domain name on a domain name server (DNS), which tells the computer the number.

domain name server see ⊸name server.

dongle a device that ensures the legal use of an application program. It is usually attached to the printer port of the computer (between the port and the printer cable) and the program will not run in its absence.

Doom popular computer game released 1994. It is one of a series of games from the Texas-based company id Software, which specializes in 3-D graphics, alien monsters, and complex mazes which players must navigate to find secret treasures and hidden keys along the way. *Doom* can be played competitively over a network as well as on a single computer.

Because the company has encouraged players to create their own additional levels for *Doom* (and its other games) by releasing the necessary source code, a whole culture has grown up around *Doom* and id's other games.

DOS (acronym for *disc operating system*) computer ⊸operating system specifically designed for use with disc storage; also used as an alternative name for a particular operating system, ⊸MS-DOS.

dot full stop that separates ⊸IP addresses, sections of ⊸domain names, and the hierarchies in ⊸newsgroup names, as well as file names and their extensions.

dot matrix printer computer printer that produces each character individually by printing a pattern, or matrix, of very small dots. The printing head consists of a vertical line or block of either 9 or 24 printing pins. As the printing head is moved from side to side across the paper, the pins are pushed forwards selectively to strike an inked ribbon and build up the dot pattern for each character on the paper beneath. It has been largely replaced by the ⊸laser printer.

dot pitch distance between the dots which make up the picture on a computer monitor. The smaller the dot pitch, the better and finer-grained the picture.

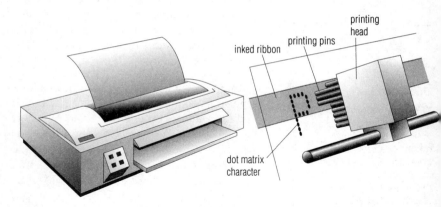

printing head

printing pins

inked ribbon

dot matrix character

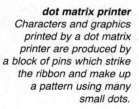

dot matrix printer
Characters and graphics printed by a dot matrix printer are produced by a block of pins which strike the ribbon and make up a pattern using many small dots.

double click to click (press and release a ⌖mouse button) twice in quick succession. Double clicking on an ⌖icon shown on a ⌖graphical user interface (GUI) is used to start an application. In most GUIs it is possible to set the maximum time interval between the two clicks.

double precision a type of floating-point notation that has higher precision, that is, more significant decimal places. The term 'double' is not strictly correct, deriving from such numbers using twice as many ⌖bits as standard floating-point notation.

downtime time when a computer system is unavailable for use, due to maintenance or a system crash. Some downtime is inevitable on almost all systems.

dpi abbreviation for ***dots per inch***, measure of the ⌖resolution of images produced by computer screens and printers.

drag and drop in ⌖graphical user interfaces, feature that allows users to select a file name or icon using a mouse and move it to the name or icon representing a program so that the computer runs the program using that file as input data.
This method is convenient for computer users, as it eliminates unnecessary typing. Moving the name of a text file, for example, to a copy of a word processor will start up the word processor with that file loaded and ready for editing.

DRAM (acronym for ***dynamic random-access memory***) computer memory device in the form of a silicon chip commonly used to provide the ⌖immediate-access memory of microcomputers. DRAM loses its contents unless they are read and rewritten every 2 milliseconds or so. This process is called ***refreshing*** the memory. DRAM is slower but cheaper than ⌖SRAM, an alternative form of silicon-chip memory.

drawing program software that allows a user to draw freehand and create complex graphics. Additional features may include special ⌖fonts, ⌖clip art, or painting facilities that allow a user to simulate on the computer the drawing characteristics of specific real-world implements such as charcoal, watercolours, or pastels. The market-leading drawing package is Corel Draw.

drive bay slot in a computer designed to hold a disc drive such as a hard drive, floppy drive, or CD-ROM drive. Like most computer components, disc drives have decreased in size. Older drives were $5\frac{1}{4}$ inches in size, but most newer drives are $3\frac{1}{2}$ inches. Kits to fit a $3\frac{1}{2}$ inch drive into a $5\frac{1}{4}$ inch bay are readily available.

driver a program that controls a peripheral device. Every device connected to the computer needs a driver program.

The driver ensures that communication between the computer and the device is successful.

For example, it is often possible to connect many different types of printer, each with its own special operating codes, to the same type of computer. This is because driver programs are supplied to translate the computer's standard printing commands into the special commands needed for each printer.

drop-down list in a ⌐graphical user interface, a list of options that hangs down from a blank space in a ⌐dialog box or other on-screen form when a computer awaits user input.

To select one of the choices, highlight it and click. The list will disappear and the selected item will appear in the blank. If the list is longer than the space available, small arrows and a scroll bar will appear on the right-hand side.

DSP abbreviation for ⌐digital signal processor.

DTP abbreviation for ⌐*desktop publishing*.

dumb terminal a ⌐terminal that has no processing capacity of its own. It works purely as a means of access to a main ⌐central processing unit. Compare with a ⌐personal computer used as an intelligent terminal – for example in ⌐client–server architecture.

dump the process of rapidly transferring data to external memory or to a printer. It is usually done to help with debugging (see ⌐bug) or as part of an error-recovery procedure designed to provide ⌐data security. A ⌐screen dump makes a printed copy of the current screen display.

duplex or ⌐*echo* in printing, the ability to print on both sides of the page; in computer communications, setting that ⌐toggles the ability to send and receive signals simultaneously. ⌐*Full duplex* means two-way communication is enabled; ⌐*half duplex* means it is disabled.

DVD abbreviation for ⌐digital versatile disc or *digital video disc*.

DVI (abbreviation for *digital video interactive*) a powerful compression and decompression system for digital video and audio. DVI enables 72 minutes of full-screen, full-motion video and its audio track to be stored on a CD-ROM. Originally developed by the US firm RCA, DVI is now owned by ⌐Intel and has active support from ⌐IBM and ⌐Microsoft. It can be used on the hard disc of a PC as well as on a CD-ROM.

DRIVE BAY

TIP: Having a spare drive bay in a personal computer allows room for expansion when you run out of hard drive space.

DUPLEX

TIP: When connected to a remote computer, if you see two of every letter you type, set your computer to half duplex to disable local echo; if you do not see anything at all, set your computer to full duplex to turn on local echo.

Dvorak keyboard alternative keyboard layout to the normal typewriter keyboard layout (⌐QWERTY). In the Dvorak layout the most commonly used keys are situated in the centre, so that keying is faster.

dynamic data exchange (DDE) in computing, a form of interprocess communication used in Microsoft ⌐Windows, providing exchange of commands and data between two applications. DDE is used principally to include live data from one application in another – for example, spreadsheet data in a word-processed report. In Windows 3.1 DDE is enhanced by ⌐object linking and embedding.

DDE links between files rely on the files remaining in the same locations in the computer's directory.

dynamic IP address a temporary ⌐IP address assigned from a pool of available addresses by an ⌐Internet Service Provider when a customer logs on to begin an on-line session.

Companies and other organizations which have their own networks typically have their own permanent IP addresses. Customers of a dial-up service provider, however, only need addresses for the length of time that they are actually on line. This method allows the finite number of available IP addresses to be used most efficiently.

dynamic link library (DLL) in computing, files of executable functions that can be loaded on demand in Microsoft ⌐Windows and linked at run time. Windows itself uses DLL files for handling international keyboards, for example, and Windows word-processing programs use DLL files for functions such as spelling and hyphenation checks, and thesaurus.

EBCDIC (abbreviation for ***extended binary-coded decimal interchange code***) in computing, a code used for storing and communicating alphabetic and numeric characters. It is an 8-bit code, capable of holding 256 different characters, although only 85 of these are defined in the standard version. It is still used in many mainframe computers, but almost all mini-and microcomputers now use ⮑ASCII code.

e-cash (contraction of ***electronic cash***) generic name for new electronic money systems such as Mondex and ⮑DigiCash.

echo user input that is printed to the screen so the user can read it.

Eckert John Presper Jr 1919–1995. US electronics engineer and mathematician who collaborated with John ⮑Mauchly on the development of the early ENIAC (1946) and UNIVAC 1 (1951) computers.

Eckert was born in Philadelphia, Pennsylvania, and studied at the University of Pennsylvania. During World War II he worked on radar ranging systems and then turned to the design of calculating devices, building the Electronic Numerical Integrator and Calculator (ENIAC) with Mauchly. The Eckert–Mauchly Computer Corporation, formed 1947, was incorporated in Remington Rand 1950 and subsequently came under the control of the Sperry Rand Corporation.

The ENIAC weighed many tonnes and lacked a memory, but could store a limited amount of information and perform mathematical functions. It was used for calculating ballistic firing tables and for meteorological and research problems.

ENIAC was superseded by BINAC, also designed in part by Eckert, and in the early 1950s, Eckert's group began to produce computers for the commercial market with the construction of the UNIVAC 1. Its chief advance was the capacity to store programs.

EcoNet one of several international computer networks dedicated to environmental issues.

edge connector an electrical connection formed by taking some of the metallic tracks on a ⮑printed circuit board to the edge of the board and using them to plug directly into a matching socket.

Edge connectors are often used to connect the computer's main circuit board, or ⮑motherboard, to the ⮑expansion boards that provide the computer with extra memory or other facilities.

EDI abbreviation for ⮑electronic data interchange.

EDIFACT one of a number of systems for handling ⮑EDI (electronic data interchange) transactions.

editing act of creating, changing, and formatting word processor documents or pages for distribution on the World Wide Web.

EDO RAM (abbreviation for ***extended data out random-access memory***) faster type of ⮑RAM introduced in the mid-1990s.

EDP abbreviation for *electronic ⮞data processing*.

Educational Resources Information Center database of resources for education available on the Internet. See ⮞ERIC.

edutainment (contraction of *education and entertainment*) ⮞multimedia-related term, used to describe computer software that is both educational and entertaining. Examples include educational software for children that teaches them to spell or count while playing games, and ⮞CD-ROMs about machines that contain animations showing how the machines work. Compare ⮞infotainment.

EEPROM (acronym for *electrically erasable programmable read-only memory*) computer memory that can record data and retain it indefinitely. The data can be erased with an electrical charge and new data recorded.

Some EEPROM must be removed from the computer and erased and reprogrammed using a special device. Other EEPROM, called ⮞*flash memory*, can be erased and reprogrammed without removal from the computer.

EFF abbreviation for ⮞Electronic Frontier Foundation.

EFTPOS acronym for *electronic funds transfer at point of sale*, a form of electronic funds transfer.

EGA (abbreviation for *enhanced graphics array*) computer colour display system superior to ⮞CGA (colour graphics adapter), providing 16 colours on screen and a resolution of 640 x 350, but not as good as ⮞VGA.

EIS (abbreviation for *executive information systems*) software applications that extract information from an organization's computer applications and data files and present the data in a form required by management.

EISA (abbreviation for *extended industry standard architecture*) in computing, one of several types of ⮞data bus created to improve on the original ⮞ISA (industry standard architecture) design. The EISA bus adds speed and capacity because it is a 32-bit bus (ISA is a 16-bit bus), although it can still accept ISA-compatible expansion cards.

The EISA bus was developed by a consortium of PC manufacturers to counter IBM's proprietary MCA (micro channel architecture) bus, but has been superseded by newer, more efficient standards such as ⮞PCI (peripheral component interconnect) and VESA (Video Electronics Standards Association) buses. See also ⮞local bus.

electronic banking system whereby a user can execute banking transactions via a modem, either directly or through an on-line service or the Internet.

The first bank to offer modem access in the UK was the Royal Bank of Scotland. In 1995, the TSB announced a limited service via CompuServe allowing customers 24-hour access to account statements and current balances.

electronic book software with or without specialized hardware that provides the equivalent of a book's worth of information. The term is used generally to apply even to simple text files created by scanning printed books or manuals such as those created and archived by ⌁Project Gutenberg.

'Electronic Book' refers to a specific product released by Sony, a special player for small-sized CD-ROMs containing educational and reference material.

electronic cash see ⌁e-cash.

electronic commerce business-to-business use of networks such as the Internet to handle legally binding transactions. Traditionally, electronic commerce has required expensive membership of an ⌁electronic data interchange (EDI) service. In the mid-1990s, electronic commerce began to shift to the Internet to take advantage of its global reach and inexpensive connections. By 1996 many legal issues remained to be resolved.

Electronic Communications Privacy Act US law passed 1986 that protects the privacy of e-mail and other electronic communications.

electronic conferencing in computing, public discussions conducted on an on-line service or via ⌁USENET; any participant may log in at any time and read the collected messages and add new ones.

Because of its time-independent, many-to-many nature, electronic conferencing can be used to provide some of the same functions as real-life meetings, classrooms, and unstructured socializing without requiring the participants to meet face-to-face. While electronic conferencing is no substitute for live interaction, it does allow people who are widely geographically separated or might otherwise never meet to exchange ideas.

electronic data interchange (EDI) system for managing business-to-business transactions such as invoicing and ordering to eliminate the wastefulness of paper-based transaction systems.

Traditionally, most EDI systems have relied on proprietary protocols and private data networks, with the disadvantages that individual systems were incompatible. With the growth of the Internet, EDI systems are shifting to open standards and the use of the Internet as a carrier medium, opening the way for global electronic commerce.

Electronic Frontier Foundation (EFF) US organization that lobbies for the extension of civil liberties and constitutional rights into ⌁cyberspace. It was founded by former Grateful Dead lyricist John Perry ⌁Barlow and Lotus founder Mitch ⌁Kapor 1991 after a series of US raids on suspected computer hackers. Its offices are in San Francisco.

electronic mail or *e-mail* private messages sent electronically from computer to computer via network connections such as ⌁Ethernet or the Internet, or via telephone lines to a host system. Messages once sent are stored on the network or by the host system until the recipient picks them up.

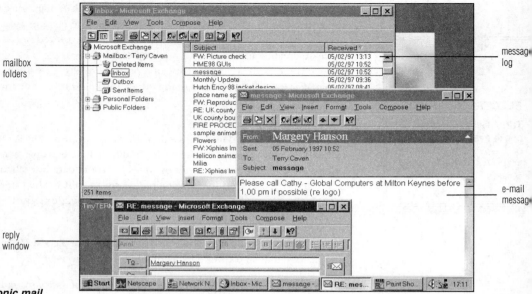

mailbox folders

message log

reply window

e-mail message

electronic mail
A typical e-mail user interface. Because messages can be created 'off-line' and are sent at high speed, line connection time, and therefore costs, can be kept to a minimum.

Subscribers to an electronic mail system type messages in ordinary letter form on a word processor, or microcomputer, and 'drop' the letters into a central computer's memory bank by means of a computer/telephone connector (a ☞modem). The recipient 'collects' the letter by calling up the central computer and feeding a unique password into the system.

electronic publishing the distribution of information using computer-based media such as ☞multimedia and ☞hypertext in the creation of electronic 'books'. Critical technologies in the development of electronic publishing were ☞CD-ROM, with its massive yet compact storage capabilities, and the advent of computer networking with its ability to deliver information instantaneously anywhere in the world.

electronic shopping using an on-line service or Internet service such as the World Wide Web to select and buy merchandise.
Electronic shopping services in the UK include the UK Shopping Mall on ☞CompuServe and BarclaySquare on the ☞World Wide Web.

Elm mail reader commonly used on on-line systems. It is typically found on older, text-based systems running under ☞UNIX.

Emacs or, more properly, ☞*GNU Emacs* a UNIX ☞text editor. An example of ☞public-domain software, Emacs was created by the US ☞Free Software Foundation.

e-mail abbreviation for ☞*electronic mail*.

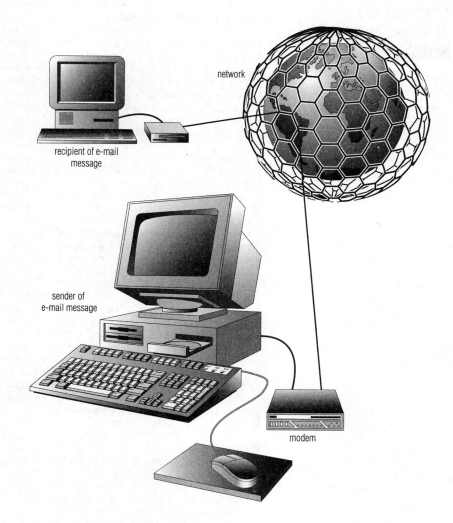

network

recipient of e-mail
message

sender of
e-mail message

modem

electronic mail
The electronic mail system. A message is sent from a computer via a modem to the recipient's 'mail box' provided by the network service. The recipient collects any waiting mail when they dial in, also via a modem, to the network service provider.

emoticon (contraction of *emotion and icon*) symbol composed of punctuation marks designed to express some form of emotion in the form of a human face. Emoticons were invented by ↪e-mail users to overcome the fact that communication using text only cannot convey nonverbal information (body language or vocal intonation) used in ordinary speech.

The following examples should be viewed sideways:

:-) smiling :-O shouting :-(glum 8-) wearing glasses and smiling

EMS abbreviation for ↪*expanded memory specification*.

emulator an item of software or firmware that allows one device to imitate the functioning of another. Emulator software is commonly used to allow one make of computer to run programs written for a different make of computer. This allows a

Electronic and on-line publishing

computerized publishing Most publishing is now 'electronic' in the sense that books, magazines, and newspapers are prepared on computers, and exist as computer files before they are printed on paper. Often there are advantages to giving readers access to the electronic versions of publications as well as – or even instead of – the printed versions.

Today, writers and journalists usually create their texts on computers using word processing programs, but if not, typewritten copy is easily scanned to convert it into electronic form. Many illustrations are also produced on computers using **paint programes**, and the use of digital cameras is becoming increasingly common – though again, images created by more traditional means can easily be scanned. Designers and layout artists then assemble the materials and lay them out on computers running desktop publishing programs, before sending the finished pages to a computer-based photo-typesetter.

Print publications have lots of advantages. Paper is pleasant to handle, easy to read, and very portable: you can read it almost anywhere. On the other hand, print has its drawbacks. Paper is expensive, and articles are often cut to fit the space available. Printing and distributing paper is expensive and takes time. Printed materials are expensive to store and almost impossible to search. Electronic publishing offers solutions to all these problems.

publishing on line Suppose a publisher makes the electronic copy of a newspaper or magazine available online, perhaps on the Internet's World Wide Web. No paper is used and disc space is cheap, so on-line publishing costs very little. Articles don't have to be cut (though there is of course a limit to the amount people are willing to read on line). On-line publishing is fast, and readers can access material as soon as it becomes available:within minutes, instead of the next day, next week or next month. On-line publishing transcends geographical boundaries:the humblest local paper can be read everywhere from New York to London to Delhi to Tokyo. Delivery costs are low because there are no newsagents to pay, and no postal charges:readers pick up the bills for their on-line sessions. Also, computer-based publications are simple to store (on disc) and every word can be searched electronically.

does it pay? But electronic publishing also has its drawbacks. The main problem is getting money for it. People are used to paying for printed publications, and advertisers are used to paying to have their messages included. It is much harder to get people to pay for on-line publications, especially on the Web, where almost everything is free. Few advertisers are convinced by the small banners they are usually offered on Web pages, and may be aware that many users object to the delays and costs involved in downloading them. Anyway, why should companies advertise when they can simply open their own Web sites? Things may change when ***micro-payment*** systems come into widespread use, and readers can be debited a few pennies for accessing a site, but the economics of Internet publishing are far from proven.

At the moment, newspapers and magazines, TV and radio stations, news agencies and book publishers are making content freely available on the Web because they are competing for 'mindshare'. Perhaps they want to find out if they can attract and hold an audience on line, or perhaps they're afraid of missing out because 'everyone else is doing it'. But don't count on things staying that way. Publishers are not in business to lose money.

Jack Schofield

user to select from a wider range of ⌁applications programs, and perhaps to save money by running programs designed for an expensive computer on a cheaper model.

Many printers contain emulator firmware that enables them to imitate ⌁Hewlett Packard and Epson printers, because so much software is written to work with these widely used machines.

encapsulate term used to describe the technique that uses one ⌁protocol as an envelope for another for transmission across a network.

encapsulated PostScript (EPS) computer graphics file format used by the ⌁PostScript page-description language. It is essentially a PostScript file with a special structure designed for use by other applications.

end user the user of a computer program; in particular, someone who uses a program to perform a task (such as accounting or playing a computer game), rather than someone who writes programs (a programmer).

Energy Star US programme requiring all computer equipment to conserve electrical power. Key features of Energy Star-compliant hardware include a built-in function to put the computer and monitor into suspended animation after a specified period of disuse and limits on the amount of power computers and printers can draw.

engine core piece of software around which other features and functions are built. A database ⌁search engine, for example, accepts user input and handles the processing necessary to find matches between the user input and the database records.

In a computer game, the term 'engine' is also used to refer to the core software that allows users to move around the game's levels and pick up weapons and treasure.

EPROM (acronym for *erasable programmable read-only memory*) computer memory device in the form of an ⌁integrated circuit (chip) that can record data and retain it indefinitely. The data can be erased by exposure to ultraviolet light, and new data recorded. Other kinds of computer memory chips are ⌁ROM (read-only memory), ⌁PROM (programmable read-only memory), and ⌁RAM (random-access memory).

EPS abbreviation for ⌁*encapsulated PostScript*.

erasable optical disc in computing, another name for a ⌁*floptical disc*.

ergonomics study of the relationship between people and the furniture, tools, and machinery they use at work. The object is to improve work performance by removing sources of muscular stress and general fatigue: for example, by presenting data and control panels in easy-to-view form, making office furniture comfortable, and creating a generally pleasant environment.

ENERGY STAR

TIP: A list of Energy Star-compliant products is available at http://www.epa.gov.

Good ergonomic design makes computer systems easier to use and minimizes the health hazards and physical stresses of working with computers for many hours a day: it helps data entry workers to avoid conditions like ⌁repetitive strain injury (RSI), eyestrain, and back and muscle aches.

In Europe, many measures intended to protect workers were introduced in the 1992 Ergonomics Directive, which in Britain is enforced by the Health and Safety Executive.

ERIC (abbreviation for *Educational Resources Information Center*) in computing, database of resources for education available on the Internet. Established 1966, ERIC is a federally funded network of educational information. Sixteen clearing houses index educational materials for the database, which is housed at the University of Saskatchewan, Canada. The database is distributed in a variety of formats including printed books, CD-ROM, and microfiche.

error a fault or mistake, either in the software or on the part of the user, that causes a program to stop running (crash) or produce unexpected results. Program errors, or ⌁bugs, are largely eliminated in the course of the programmer's initial testing procedure, but some will remain in most programs. All computer operating systems are designed to produce an ⌁*error message* (on the display screen, or in an error file or printout) whenever an error is detected, reporting that an error has taken place and, wherever possible, diagnosing its cause.

Errors can be categorized into several types:

syntax errors are caused by the incorrect use of the programming language, and include spelling and keying mistakes. These errors are detected when the ⌁compiler or ⌁interpreter fails to translate the program into ⌁machine code (instructions that a computer can understand directly);

logical errors are faults in the program design – for example, in the order of instructions. They may cause a program to respond incorrectly to the user's requests or to crash completely;

execution errors, or *run-time errors*, are caused by combinations of data that the programmer did not anticipate. A typical execution error is caused by attempting to divide a number by zero. This is impossible, and so the program stops running at this point. Execution errors occur only when a program is running, and cannot be detected by a compiler or interpreter.

Computers are designed to deal with a set range of numbers to a given range of accuracy. Many errors are caused by these limitations:

⌁*overflow error* occurs when a number is too large for the computer to deal with; an ⌁*underflow error* occurs when a number is too small;

rounding and *truncation errors* are caused by the need to round off decimal numbers, or to cut them off (truncate them) after the maximum number of decimal places allowed by the computer's level of accuracy.

error detection the techniques that enable a program to detect incorrect data. A common method is to add a check digit to important codes, such as account numbers and product codes. The digit is chosen so that the code conforms to a rule that the program can verify. Another technique involves calculating the sum (called the ↩hash total) of each instance of a particular item of data, and storing it at the end of the data.

error message message produced by a computer to inform the user that an error has occurred.

escape sequence string of characters sent to a ↩modem to switch it from sending data to a state in which it can accept and act upon commands. Most modems use the escape sequence patented by Hayes, which consists of three plus signs (+++) with a brief pause on either side to distinguish the characters from data.

ESPRIT (abbreviation for *European Strategic Programme for Research and Development in Information Technology*) European Union programme that funds technology research at an early stage of development. ESPRIT's goals include encouraging the development of international standards and cooperation between European companies, universities, and research centres in order to develop the infrastructure necessary for Europe to be able to compete with Japan and the USA.

Ethernet a protocol for ↩local area networks. Ethernet was developed principally by the Xerox Corporation, but can now be used on many computers. It allows data transfer at rates up to 10 Mbps.

Eudora popular program for handling and receiving Internet e-mail. Published by the Californian company Qualcomm, Eudora uses ↩POP3, and by the mid-1990s was one of the most commonly used mail programs on the Net.

European Strategic Programme for Research and Development in Information Technology full name for ↩ESPRIT.

Excel ↩spreadsheet program produced by ↩Microsoft 1985. Versions are available for ↩Windows on the IBM PC and for the Apple Macintosh. Excel pioneered many advanced features in the ease of use of spreadsheets, and has displaced ↩Lotus 1–2–3 as the standard spreadsheet program.

executable file a file – always a program of some kind – that can be run by the computer directly. The file will have been generated from a ↩source program by an ↩assembler or ↩compiler. It will therefore not be coded in ↩ASCII and will not be readable as text. On ↩MS-DOS systems executable files have an .EXE or .COM extension.

expanded memory additional memory in an ↩MS-DOS-based computer, usually installed on an expanded-memory board. Expanded memory requires an expanded-memory manager, which gives access to a limited amount of memory at any one time, and is slower to use than ↩extended memory. Software is available under both MS-DOS and ↩Windows to simulate expanded memory for those applications that require it.

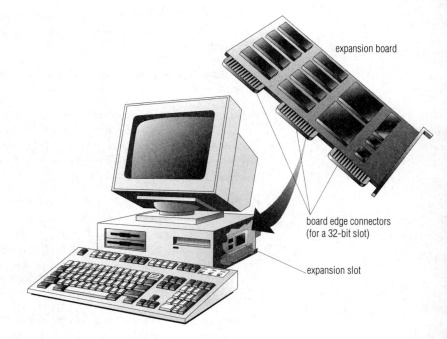

expansion board

board edge connectors
(for a 32-bit slot)

expansion slot

expansion board
An expansion board may
be fitted into any free
expansion slot in a
computer to provide
additional facilities or
functionality.

EXTERNAL MODEM

TIP: Before attaching a
high-speed modem to a
PC, check that it has a
16550 UART; if it does
not, consider getting an
internal modem with one
built in, or install an
expansion card with a
high-speed serial port on
it.

expansion board or *expansion card* printed circuit board that can be inserted
into a computer in order to enhance its capabilities (for example, to increase its
memory) or to add facilities (such as graphics).

expert system computer program for giving advice (such as diagnosing an
illness or interpreting the law) that incorporates knowledge derived from human
expertise. It is a kind of ↪knowledge-based system containing rules that can be
applied to find the solution to a problem. It is a form of ↪artificial intelligence.

expire function for removing old ↪USENET articles from an off-line reader
program. Sometimes also called 'prune' or 'purge', this function is necessary to
make room for new articles.

export file a file stored by the computer in a standard format so that it can be
accessed by other programs, possibly running on different makes of computer.
For example, a word-processing program running on an Apple ↪Macintosh
computer may have a facility to save a file on a floppy disc in a format that can be
read by a word-processing program running on an IBM PC-compatible computer.
When the file is being read by the second program or computer, it is often
referred to as an *↪import file*.

extended memory memory in an ↪MS-DOS-based system that exceeds the 1 Mb
that DOS supports. Extended memory is not accessible to the ↪operating system
and requires an extended memory manager. ↪Windows and Windows
applications require extended memory.

external modem a ↜modem that is a self-contained unit sitting outside a personal computer (PC) and connected to it by a cable. There are two main types of external modems: large desktop modems and smaller pocket modems. External modems have the advantage that they are easy to move from computer to computer as needed. However, high-speed modems outstrip the capabilities of the serial ports on older and cheaper PCs by taking in data too fast for the computer to be able to read it.

extruded shape in computer graphics, a three-dimensional shape created by extending a two-dimensional shape along a third dimension. See illustration.

e-zine (contraction of *electronic magazine*) periodical sent by ↜e-mail. E-zines can be produced very cheaply, as there are no production costs for design and layout, and minimal costs for distribution. Like printed magazines, e-zines typically have multiple contributors and an editor responsible for selecting content. One of the best-known e-zines is the ↜*Computer Underground Digest*, which tracks battles over freedom of speech on-line and issues concerning hacking and computer crime.

F1 on personal computers (PCs), the key to access ⮩on-line help.

FAQ (abbreviation for *frequently asked questions*) file of answers to commonly asked questions on any topic. First used on ⮩USENET, where regular posters to ⮩newsgroups got tired of answering the same questions over and over and wrote these information files to end the repetition. By 1996 FAQ was a common term for any information file, on line or off line.

FAT abbreviation for ⮩*file allocation table*.

favourite places on CompuServe, a listing similar to ⮩bookmarks in a Web browser which enables a user to return quickly to areas of interest on the service.

fax (common name for *facsimile transmission* or *telefax*) the transmission of images over a telecommunications link, usually the telephone network. When placed on a fax machine, the original image is scanned by a transmitting device and converted into coded signals, which travel via the telephone lines to the receiving fax machine, where an image is created that is a copy of the original. Photographs as well as printed text and drawings can be sent. The standard transmission takes place at 4,800 or 9,600 bits of information per second.

fax modem ⮩modem capable of transmitting and receiving data in the form of a fax.

A normal fax machine sends data in binary form down a telephone line, in a similar way to a modem. A modem can therefore act as a fax machine, given suitable software. This means a document does not need to be printed before faxing and an incoming fax can be viewed before printing out on a plain-paper printer. However, the computer must be permanently turned on in order to receive faxes.

A separate ⮩scanner is needed to fax information created outside the computer (such as a picture).

FDDI (abbreviation for *fibre-optic digital device interface*) in computing, a series of network protocols, developed by the ⮩American National Standards Institute, concerned with high-speed networks using ⮩fibre optic cable.

FDDI supports data transmission rates of up to 100 Mb per second and is being introduced in many sites as a replacement for ⮩Ethernet. FDDI not only makes possible transmission of large amounts of data, for example colour pictures, but also allows the transmission of voice and video data. See also ⮩optical fibres.

feedback general principle whereby the results produced in an ongoing reaction become factors in modifying or changing the reaction; it is the principle used in self-regulating control systems, from a simple thermostat and steam-engine governor to automatic computer-controlled machine tools. A fully computerized control system, in which there is no operator intervention, is called a *closed-loop feedback* system. A system that also responds to control signals from an operator is called an *open-loop feedback* system.

fetch-execute cycle or ***processing cycle*** the two-phase cycle used by the computer's central processing unit to process the instructions in a program. During the ***fetch phase***, the next program instruction is transferred from the computer's immediate-access memory to the instruction register (memory location used to hold the instruction while it is being executed). During the ***execute phase***, the instruction is decoded and obeyed. The process is repeated in a continuous loop.

fibre optics branch of physics dealing with the transmission of light and images through glass or plastic fibres known as ➬optical fibres.

Fidonet early network of ➬bulletin board systems (BBSs) which sends mail and news around the world via an arrangement whereby the individual systems call each other to exchange data every night. Such systems are called 'store-and-forward'.

field a specific item of data. A field is usually part of a ***record***, which in turn is part of a ➬file.

field-length check ➬validation check in which the characters in an input field are counted to ensure that the correct number of characters have been entered. For example, a six-figure date field may be checked to ensure that it does contain exactly six digits.

fifth-generation computer anticipated new type of computer based on emerging microelectronic technologies with high computing speeds and ➬parallel processing. The development of very large-scale integration (➬VLSI) technology, which can put many more circuits on to an integrated circuit (chip) than is currently possible, and developments in computer hardware and software design may produce computers far more powerful than those in current use.

file a collection of data or a program stored in a computer's external memory (for example, on ➬disc). It might include anything from information on a company's

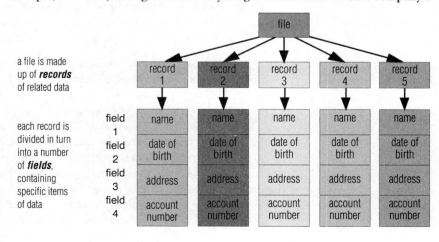

file
The file structure of a simple accounting system which stores the name, date of birth, address, and account number of each client.

employees to a program for an adventure game. *Serial files* hold information as a sequence of characters, so that, to read any particular item of data, the program must read all those that precede it. *Random-access files* allow the required data to be reached directly.

Files usually consist of a set of records, each having a number of *fields* for specific items of data. For example, the file for a class of schoolchildren might have a record for each child, with five fields of data in each record, storing: (1) family name; (2) first name; (3) house name or number; (4) street name; (5) town. To find out, for example, which children live in the same street, one would look in field 4.

file access the way in which the records in a file are stored, retrieved, or updated by computer. There are four main types of file organization, each of which allows a different form of access to the records.

Records in a *serial file* are not stored in any particular order, so a specific record can be accessed only by reading through all the previous records.

Records in a *sequential file* are sorted by reference to a key field (see ⇔sorting) and the computer can use a searching technique, such as a binary search, to access a specific record.

An *indexed sequential file* possesses an index, which records the position of each block of records and is created and updated with that file. By consulting the index, the computer can obtain the address of the block containing the required record, and search just that block rather than the whole file.

A *direct-access* or *random-access file* contains records that can be accessed directly by the computer.

file allocation table (FAT) in computing, a table used by the operating system to record the physical arrangement of files on disc. As a result of ⇔fragmentation, files can be split into many parts sited at different places on the disc.

file extension the last three letters of a file name in DOS or Windows, which indicate the type of data the file contains. Extensions in common use include .TXT for 'text', .GIF for 'graphics interchange format', and .EXE for 'executable'.

In ⇔Windows, the operating system may be configured to associate specific file extensions with specific programs, so that double-clicking on a file name starts the right program and opens the file for editing.

file format specific way data is stored in a file. Most computer programs use proprietary file formats which cannot be read by other programs. As this is inconvenient for users, in recent years software publishers have developed filters which convert older file formats into the ones the program in use can read.

Often ⇔file extensions are used to indicate which program was used to create a particular file. Some formats, such as ⇔GIF (graphics interchange format), have become so popular and widely used that they are supported by many programs.

Before transmitting data over a public network to another user, it is important to check that the receiving user can read the format the data is in. For this purpose, the most commonly readable format is plain ⇔ASCII for text and either GIF or ⇔JPEG (Joint Photographic Experts Group) for graphics.

file generation a specific version of a file. When ↩file updating takes place, a new generation of the file is created, containing accurate, up-to-date information. The old generation of the file will often be stored to provide ↩data security in the event that the new generation of the file is lost or damaged.

file librarian or *media librarian* job classification for ↩computer personnel. A file librarian stores and issues the data files used by the computer department.

file merging combining two or more sequentially ordered files into a single sequentially ordered file.

file searching ↩searching a computer memory (usually ↩backing storage) for a file.

file server computer on a ↩network that handles (and usually stores) the data used by other computers on the network. See also ↩client–server architecture.

file sorting arranging files in sequence; see ↩sorting.

file transfer the transmission of a file (data stored on disc, for example) from one machine to another. Both machines must be physically linked (for example, by a telephone line via a ↩modem or ↩acoustic coupler) and both must be running appropriate communications software.

file updating reviewing and altering the records in a file to ensure that the information they contain is accurate and up-to-date. Three basic processes are involved: adding new records, deleting existing records, and amending existing records.

The updating of a *direct-access file* is a continuous process because records can be accessed individually and changed at any time. This type of updating is typical of large interactive database systems, such as airline ticket-booking systems. Each time a ticket is booked, files are immediately updated so that double booking is impossible.

In large commercial applications, however, millions of customer records may be held in a large sequentially ordered file, called the *master file*. Each time the records in the master file are to be updated (for example, when quarterly bills are being drawn up), a *↩transaction file* must be prepared. This will contain all the additions, deletions, and amendments required to update the master file. The transaction file is sorted into the same order as the master file, and then the computer reads both files and produces a new updated *↩generation* of the master file, which will be stored until the next file updating takes place.

filter a program that transforms data. Filters are often used when data output from one ↩application program is input into a different program, which requires a different data format. For example files transferred between two different word-processing programs are run through either an output filter supplied with the first program or an input filter supplied with the second program.

Filters are also used to expand coding structures, which have been simplified for keyboard input, into the often more verbose form required by such standards as SGML (⮑Standard Generalized Markup Language).

firewall security system built to block access to a particular computer or network while still allowing some types of data to flow in and out onto the ⮑Internet. A firewall allows a company's employees to access sites on the ⮑World Wide Web or exchange e-mail while at the same time preventing hackers from gaining access to the company's data.

firmware computer program held permanently in a computer's ⮑ROM (read-only memory) chips, as opposed to a program that is read in from external memory as it is needed.

First Amendment amendment to the US Constitution that guarantees freedom of religion, of speech, of assembly, and of the press. Adopted 1791, the First Amendment is often quoted on the Net, even by non-US citizens, in arguments over international attempts at censorship.

FIRST VIRTUAL BANK

TIP: First Virtual Bank is at http://www.fv.com.

First Virtual Bank joint project with the bank FirstUSA which allows shoppers on the World Wide Web to open a central account using credit cards. Shoppers use their account numbers to make purchases at any of a number of participating merchants.

fixed font a ⮑font that uses fixed, rather than proportional, spacing. It is a necessary option in off-line reader software and e-mail programs, since some ASCII art and tables do not display correctly without it.

fixed-point notation system in which numbers are represented using a set of digits with the decimal point always in its correct position. For very large and very small numbers this requires a lot of digits. The size of the numbers that can be handled in this way is limited by the capacity of the computer, and so the slower ⮑floating-point notation is often preferred.

flag an indicator that can be set or unset in order to signal whether a particular condition is true – for example, whether the end of a file has been reached, or whether an overflow error has occurred. The indicator usually takes the form of a single binary digit, or bit (either 0 or 1).

flame angry public or private ⮑electronic mail message. Users of the ⮑Internet use flames to express disapproval of breaches of ⮑netiquette or the voicing of an unpopular opinion. An offensive message posted to, for example, a ⮑USENET ⮑newsgroup, will cause those offended to flame the culprit. Such flames maintain a level of discipline among the Internet's users.

flame war heated electronic argument where few good points are made and most of the participants ⮑flame each other repeatedly.

Several flame wars have passed into ⮑USENET legend, including the deliberate 1994 invasion of the rec.pets.cats newsgroup by the alt.tasteless newsgroup.

flash memory type of ⌐EEPROM memory that can be erased and reprogrammed without removal from the computer.

FlashPix a ⌐file format for digital imaging intended as a universal standard for both individual multimedia applications and external communications over on-line services. It was developed collaboratively by Kodak, Hewlett-Packard, Live Picture, and Microsoft 1996.

flash upgrade technique for upgrading firmware by updating the software embedded in it. It is used particularly for modems and ⌐EPROMs.

flat screen type of display suitable for portable computers such as LCD (⌐liquid crystal display) or gas plasma screens (see ⌐plasma display). Flat-screen, or flat-panel, displays are compact and lightweight compared to traditional cathode-ray tube monitors and TV sets.

It is predicted that eventually all TV screens will be made using this type of technology.

flight simulator computer-controlled pilot-training device, consisting of an artificial cockpit mounted on hydraulic legs, that simulates the experience of flying a real aircraft. Inside the cockpit, the trainee pilot views a screen showing a computer-controlled projection of the view from a real aircraft, and makes appropriate adjustments to the controls. The computer monitors these adjustments, changes both the alignment of the cockpit on its hydraulic legs, and the projected view seen by the pilot. In this way a trainee pilot can progress to quite an advanced stage of training without leaving the ground.

flip-flop another name for a ⌐bistable circuit.

floating-point notation system in which numbers are represented by means of a decimal fraction and an exponent. For example, in floating-point notation, 123,000,000,000 would be represented as 0.123×10^{12}, where 0.123 is the fraction, or mantissa, and 12 the exponent. The exponent is the power of 10 by which the fraction must be multiplied in order to obtain the true value of the number.

Floating-point notation enables programs to work with very large and very small numbers using only a few digits; however, it is slower than ⌐fixed-point notation and suffers from small rounding errors.

FLOP (abbreviation for *floating point operations per second*) measure of the speed at which a computer program can be run.

floppy disc a storage device consisting of a light, flexible disc enclosed in a cardboard or plastic jacket. The disc is placed in a disc drive, where it rotates at high speed. Data are recorded magnetically on one or both surfaces.

Floppy discs were invented by ⌐IBM in 1971 as a means of loading programs into the computer. They were originally 20 cm/8 in in diameter and typically held about 240 ⌐kilobytes of data. Present-day floppy discs, widely used on ⌐microcomputers, are usually either 13.13 cm/5.25 in or 8.8 cm/3.5 in in diameter, and generally hold 0.5–2 ⌐megabytes, depending on the disc size, recording method, and whether one or both sides are used.

Floppy discs are inexpensive, and light enough to send through the post, but have slower access speeds and are more fragile than hard discs. (See also ↺disc).

floptical disc or *erasable optical disc* a type of optical disc that can be erased and loaded with new data, just like a magnetic disc. By contrast, most optical discs are read-only. A single optical disc can hold as much as 1,000 megabytes of data, about 800 times more than a typical floppy disc. Floptical discs need a special disc drive, but some such drives are also capable of accepting standard 3.5 inch floppy discs.

flow chart diagram, often used in computing, to show the possible paths that data can take through a system or program.

A *system flow chart*, or *data flow chart*, is used to describe the flow of data through a complete data-processing system. Different graphic symbols represent the clerical operations involved and the different input, storage, and output

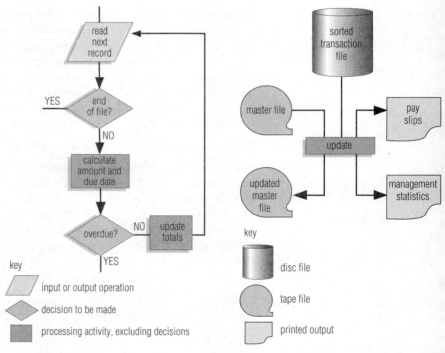

flowchart (program)
A simple program flow chart showing the sequence of data processing operations performed by a program to achieve a task, such as reading customer accounts and calculating the amount due for each customer. After an account has been processed, the program loops back to process the next one.

flowchart (system)
A system flow chart describes the flow of data through a data-processing system. This chart shows the data flow in a basic accounting system.

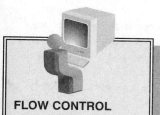

equipment required. Although the flow chart may indicate the specific programs used, no details are given of how the programs process the data.

A *program flow chart* is used to describe the flow of data through a particular computer program, showing the exact sequence of operations performed by that program in order to process the data. Different graphic symbols are used to represent data input and output, decisions, branches, and ☞subroutines.

flow control in data communications, hardware or software signals that control the flow of data to ensure that it is not transmitted too quickly for the receiving computer to handle.

flythrough in ☞virtual reality, animation allowing users to view a model of a proposed or actual site as if they were inside it and moving through it.

For the 1996 Olympics in Atlanta, USA, flythroughs assisted site planners to identify areas in the main stadium where camera positions would be blocked by the audience, allowing solutions to be found in advance of construction.

FM synthesizer (abbreviation for *frequency modulation synthesizer*) method for generating synthetic sounds based on techniques used to transmit FM radio signals.

FMV abbreviation for ☞full-motion video.

folder name for a computer directory in Windows 95 and on the Macintosh operating system.

follow-up post publicly posted reply to a ☞USENET message; unlike a personal e-mail reply, follow-up post can be read by anyone.

Full-featured ☞newsreaders include a facility for setting the names of the newsgroups to which follow-ups should be posted. If, for example, an original message was posted to a number of groups, several of which were inappropriate, the person posting the follow-up might want to restrict further replies to only those groups where the message actually belongs.

font or *fount* complete set of printed or display characters of the same typeface, size, and style (bold, italic, underlined, and so on). In the UK, font sizes are measured in points, a point being approximately 0.3 mm.

This is Courier 10 point
This is Times italic 12 point
This is Script bold 14 point
THIS IS ANNA 15 POINT
This is Univers bold 16 point
This is Kabel ultra 17 point

font
An example of different font typefaces and sizes.

Fonts used in computer setting are of two main types: ⌐bit-mapped and ⌐outline. *Bit-mapped fonts* are stored in the computer memory as the exact arrangement of ⌐pixels or printed dots required to produce the characters in a particular size on a screen or printer. *Outline fonts* are stored in the computer memory as a set of instructions for drawing the circles, straight lines, and curves that make up the outline of each character. They require a powerful computer because each character is separately generated from a set of instructions and this requires considerable computation. Bit-mapped fonts become very ragged in appearance if they are enlarged and so a separate set of bit maps is required for each font size. In contrast, outline fonts can be scaled to any size and still maintain exactly the same appearance.

footprint the area on the desk or floor required by a computer or other peripheral device.

force feedback in ⌐virtual reality, realistic simulation of the physical sense of touch. This is an area of active research, as many applications of virtual reality are useless or impossible without it.

For example, force feedback is essential in medical training systems to teach the students how hard to press with a scalpel in delicate areas of the human body. Even simulated games need force feedback in order to allow objects to respond realistically to falling or being hit.

forgery the art of falsifying either the contents or the origins of a message. On the ⌐Internet, where a person's identity is shaped by his/her words as sent out via e-mail or public conferencing systems such as ⌐USENET, sending out a forged message in another person's name can seriously damage them. Forged messages are, however, used by the ⌐CancelMoose to manage ⌐spamming and keep it from spreading.

formatting short for ⌐disc formatting.

forms on the World Wide Web, facility for accepting structured user input and inserting it into a program such as a database. Most newer graphical Web browsers can handle forms, as can the older, text-based browser Lynx. Forms are needed to manage database queries at sites such as ⌐AltaVista, and to fill out registration forms for those sites that require them.

Web page designers implement forms by using a special set of hypertext markup language (⌐HTML) tags and attaching a ⌐script, which parses the data and feeds it to the program specified in a form the program can use. The results, such as a user name and password or a list of matches, are sent back to the user.

FORTRAN (or *fortran*, acronym for *formula translation*) high-level computer-programming language suited to mathematical and scientific computations. Developed 1956, it is one of the earliest computer languages still in use. A recent version, Fortran 90, is now being used on advanced parallel computers. ⌐BASIC was strongly influenced by FORTRAN and is similar in many ways.

fourth-generation language in computing, a type of programming language designed for the rapid programming of ⌁applications but often lacking the ability to control the individual parts of the computer. Such a language typically provides easy ways of designing screens and reports, and of using databases. Other 'generations' (the term implies a class of language rather than a chronological sequence) are ⌁machine code (first generation); ⌁assembly languages, or low-level languages (second); and conventional ⌁high-level languages such as ⌁BASIC and ⌁PASCAL (third).

fragmentation the breaking up of files into many smaller sections stored on different parts of a disc. The computer ⌁operating system stores files in this way so that maximum use can be made of disc space. Each section contains a pointer to where the next section is stored. The ⌁file allocation table keeps a record of this.

Fragmentation slows down access to files. It is possible to defragment a disc by copying files. In addition, ⌁defragmentation programs, or disc optimizers, allow discs to be defragmented without the need for files to be copied to a second storage device.

frame a single photograph in a sequence representing motion, or movement, on film; in a ⌁network, a unit of data; in word processing or desktop publishing, a marked-out area on a page that can contain text or graphics.

What appears to be motion on a cinema or TV screen is actually a rapid sequence of single shots. Because of limitations in the human eye – known as the Phi phenomenon – those individual shots, if played in sequence at a rate of 24 to 30 frames per second, make the motion thus captured appear continuous.

frame buffer a ⌁buffer used to store a screen image.

frame relay in ⌁wide-area networks, a standard for the transmission of data that is optimized for high speeds up to about 1.5 Mbits/second.

Free-Net free community-based on-line system such as a network of public ⌁bulletin boards and/or municipally owned systems. Free-Net is a registered service mark of the National Public Telecomputing Network. The first Free-Net was set up 1986 in Cleveland, Ohio, USA.

Free Software Foundation (FSF) US organization, based in Boston, which creates and distributes good-quality free software and utilities. FSF is the publisher of the ⌁GNU software, which includes compilers, operating systems, utilities, editors, databases, and PostScript viewers. All the software is free of licensing fees and restrictions.

The FSF was founded 1983 by US artificial intelligence specialist Richard Stallman as a way of bringing back the cooperative spirit of the computing community's early days that had vanished by the early 1980s with the advent of widely sold proprietary software. The project's ultimate goal is to make commercial software obsolete by providing free software to do everything computer users want to do.

FREE SOFTWARE FOUNDATION

TIP: An archive of GNU software is kept at `ftp://prep.ai.mit.edu`; login anonymous; cd pub/gnu.

freeware free software which may or may not be in the public domain (see ↪public-domain software). One of the best-known examples of freeware is the encryption program ↪Pretty Good Privacy (PGP).

frequently asked questions in computing, expansion of the abbreviation ↪FAQ.

front-end processor small computer used to coordinate and control the communications between a large mainframe computer and its input and output devices.

FSF abbreviation for the ↪Free Software Foundation.

FTP (abbreviation for *File Transfer Protocol*) rules for transferring files between computers on the ↪Internet. The use of FTP avoids incompatibility between individual computers. To use FTP over the Internet, a user must have an Internet connection, an FTP client or World Wide Web ↪browser, and an account on the system holding the files.

FTPmail an ↪FTP server that can be operated by e-mail. This service is useful for people with only limited access to the Internet.

full duplex modem setting which means that two-way communication is enabled, so that everything you type is echoed back to the screen. See ↪duplex.

full-motion video (FMV) in computing, video system that can display continuous motion. Some slow-speed CD-ROM drives and low-bandwidth networks are unable to handle the mass of data required for full-motion video, so video playback tends to jerk unevenly.

function a small part of a program that supplies a specific value – for example, the square root of a specified number, or the current date. Most programming languages incorporate a number of built-in functions; some allow programmers to write their own. A function may have one or more arguments (the values on which the function operates). A *function key* on a keyboard is one that, when pressed, performs a designated task, such as ending a program.

functional programming computer programming based largely on the definition of ↪functions. There are very few functional programming languages, HOPE and ML being the most widely used, though many more conventional languages (for example, C) make extensive use of functions.

function key key on a keyboard that, when pressed, performs a designated task, such as ending a computer program.

FurryMUCK popular ↪MUD site where the players take on the imaginary shapes and characters of furry, anthropomorphic animals.

fuzzy logic in mathematics and computing, a form of knowledge representation

FULL DUPLEX

TIP: If the remote system is also echoing your input to your screen, you will see two of every letter you type; in that case, change the modem setting to half duplex. You need not disconnect to do this.

FURRYMUCK

TIP: To try FurryMUCK, follow the instructions at http://furry.org or telnet to furry.org and log in as a guest.

suitable for notions (such as 'hot' or 'loud') that cannot be defined precisely but depend on their context. For example, a jug of water may be described as too hot or too cold, depending on whether it is to be used to wash one's face or to make tea.

The central idea of fuzzy logic is ***probability of set membership***. For instance, referring to someone 175 cm/5 ft 9 in tall, the statement 'this person is tall' (or 'this person is a member of the set of tall people') might be about 70% true if that person is a man, and about 85% true if that person is a woman.

The term 'fuzzy logic' was coined in 1965 by Iranian computer scientist Lofti Zadeh of the University of California at Berkeley, although the core concepts go back to the work of Polish mathematician Jan Lukasiewicz in the 1920s. It has been largely ignored in Europe and the USA, but was taken up by Japanese manufacturers in the mid-1980s and has since been applied to hundreds of electronic goods and industrial machines. For example, a vacuum cleaner launched in 1992 by Matsushita uses fuzzy logic to adjust its sucking power in response to messages from its sensors about the type of dirt on the floor, its distribution, and its depth. Fuzzy logic enables computerized devices to reason more like humans, responding effectively to complex messages from their control panels and sensors.

gain in audio, the volume control.

games console computer capable only of playing games, which are supplied as cartridges that slot directly into the console.
Usually, the price of the console is quite low, while the price of the game cartridges is high. Games consoles are comparatively low in price with higher quality games than those available on similarly cheap microcomputers. Their disadvantages include the narrow range of software and the incompatibility of one console with another. The best known console manufacturer in the late 1970s was Atari; Nintendo and Sega dominated the market 1994.

gate, logic in electronics, see ↝logic gate.

Gates Bill (William) Henry, III 1955– . US businessman and computer scientist. He co-founded ↝Microsoft Corporation 1975 and was responsible for supplying MS-DOS, the operating system that ↝IBM chose to use in the IBM PC. In 1996, Gates' 24% shareholding in Microsoft was nominally worth $20 billion, making him the world's richest individual.

When the IBM deal was struck, Microsoft did not actually have an operating system, but Gates bought one from another company, renamed it MS-DOS, and modified it to suit IBM's new computer. Microsoft also retained the right to sell MS-DOS to other computer manufacturers, and because the IBM PC was not only successful but easily copied by other manufacturers, MS-DOS found its way onto the vast majority of PCs. The revenue from MS-DOS allowed Microsoft to expand into other areas of software, guided by Gates.

To many people, Gates is Microsoft: most of the company's successes have been his ideas (as have the occasional failures). His life revolves around the company and he expects similar dedication from his staff. In 1994, Gates was successful in fending off both US and European investigations into anti-competitive practices which could have seen Microsoft broken up into smaller companies.

In 1994 he invested $10 million into a biotechnology company, Darwin Molecular, with Paul Allen.

gateway the point of contact between two ↝wide-area networks.

geek stereotypical exceptionally bright, obsessive computer user or programmer. See also ↝anorak and ↝nerd.

general MIDI (musical instrument digital interface) or *GM* standard set of 96 instrument and percussion 'voices' that can be used to encode musical tracks which can be reproduced on any GM-compatible synthesizer, or ↝MIDI.

general protection fault computing error message; see ↝GPF.

generation stage of development in computer electronics (see ↝computer generation) or a class of programming language (see ↝fourth-generation language).

geographical information system (GIS) computer software that makes possible the visualization and manipulation of spatial data, and links such data with other information such as customer records.

gesture recognition technique whereby a computer accepts human gestures transmitted via hardware such as a ⮡DataGlove as meaningful input to which it can respond. Gesture recognition is a key technology needed in the development of ⮡virtual reality systems if they are to allow humans to interact fully and naturally with objects in computerized worlds.

GIF (acronym for *Graphics Interchange Format*) popular and economical picture file format developed by ⮡CompuServe. GIF (pronounced with a hard 'g') is one of the two most commonly used file formats for pictures on the World Wide Web (the other is ⮡JPEG) because pictures saved in this format take up a relatively small amount of space. The term is often used simply to mean 'pictures'.

gigabyte a measure of ⮡memory capacity, equal to 1,024 ⮡megabytes. It is also used, less precisely, to mean 1,000 billion ⮡bytes.

GIGO (acronym for *garbage in, garbage out*) expression used in computing to emphasize that inaccurate input data will result in inaccurate output data.

GII abbreviation for the ⮡Global Information Infrastructure.

GIS abbreviation for *⮡geographical information system*.

Global Information Infrastructure (GII) planned worldwide high-bandwidth network. US vice president Al Gore proposed the GII in a 1994 speech to the International Telecommunications Union, saying that it would promote the functioning of democracy, help nations to cooperate with each other, and be the key to economic growth for national and international economies.

Global Network Navigator (GNN) in computing, subscription-based on-line service for the World Wide Web, pioneered by US book publishers O'Reilly & Associates and bought by ⮡America Online 1995. Its Virtual Places software, released 1996, allows users to interact with each other using ⮡avatars and live messages at any Virtual Places-enabled site on the Web. GNN also offers news and resource listings.

GLOBAL NETWORK NAVIGATOR

TIP: Global Network Navigator can be reached at http://gnn.com.

global variable a ⮡variable that can be accessed by any program instruction. See also ⮡local variable.

GM synthesizer synthesizer standard; see ⮡general MIDI.

GNN abbreviation for ⮡Global Network Navigator.

GNS Dialplus data network allowing nationwide dial-up access to on-line services such as CompuServe.

GNU suite of free UNIX software distributed by the ⌐Free Software Foundation. The software includes operating systems, compilers, text editors, and other useful utilities.

Gopher (derived from *go for*; alternatively, named for the mascot of the University of Minnesota, where it was invented) menu-based server on the ⌐indexes resources and retrieves them according to user choice via any one of several built-in methods such as ⌐FTP or ⌐Telnet. Gopher servers can also be accessed via the World Wide Web and searched via special servers called ⌐Veronica.

Gopherspace name for the knowledge base composed of all the documents indexed on all the ⌐Gophers in the world.

Gouraud shading in computer animation, technique for calculating the correct colours and intensity of lighting playing on an on-screen three-dimensional object.
   Developed in 1973, Gouraud shading works by measuring the colour and brightness at the vertices of the polygons that make up the object and mixing these to get values for the areas inside the polygons. Specialized hardware makes this process relatively fast. The technique is named after its inventor, Henri Gouraud.

GPF (abbreviation for *general protection fault*) in Windows 3.1, error message returned by a computer when it crashes. A GPF is the same as a UAE in Windows 3.0.

graphical user interface (GUI) or *WIMP* a type of ⌐user interface in which programs and files appear as icons (small pictures), user options are selected from

GPF

TIP: When you get a GPF, save all data, close all programs, and reboot the computer.

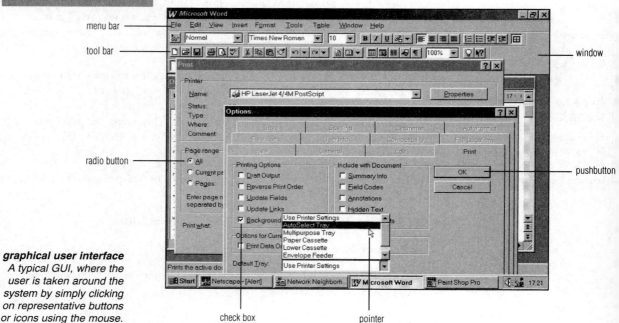

menu bar

tool bar

radio button

window

pushbutton

graphical user interface
A typical GUI, where the user is taken around the system by simply clicking on representative buttons or icons using the mouse.

check box   pointer

Software	Manufacturer	Description
Adobe Illustrator	Adobe	Professional Draw program with PostScript graphics
Adobe Photoshop	Adobe	Professional Paint program offers image creation and manipulation
AutoCAD	AutoDesk	Industry standard and leading CAD software
ClarisDraw	Claris	Paint and Draw with smart tools; strong on presentations
Corel Draw	Corel	Paint and Draw with OCR, animation and presentation
DesignCAD	PMS (Instruments)	Range of programs for CAD and modelling
FreeHand	Macromedia	Established Draw program with built-in effects and colour support
Painter	Fractal Design	Suite of creative artist's tools; provides tutorials and stunning results
Paint Shop Pro	JASC	Popular, easy-to-use image-editing program; with shareware option
Simply 3D	Visual Software	Paint program with full camera animation

Some major graphics and design programs

pull-down menus, and data are displayed in windows (rectangular areas), which the operator can manipulate in various ways. The operator uses a pointing device, typically a ᴄ⁓mouse, to make selections and initiate actions.

The concept of the graphical user interface was developed by the Xerox Corporation in the 1970s, was popularized with the Apple Macintosh computers in the 1980s, and is now available on many types of computer – most notably as Windows, an operating system for IBM PC-compatible microcomputers developed by the software company Microsoft.

graphic file format format in which computer graphics are stored and transmitted. There are two main types: ⁓raster graphics in which the image is stored as a ⁓bit map (arrangement of dots), and ⁓vector graphics, in which the image is stored using geometric formulas. There are many different file formats, some of which are used by specific computers, operating systems or applications. Some formats use file compression, particularly those that are able to handle more than one colour.

graphics used with computers, see ⁓computer graphics.

graphics board another name for ⁓graphics card.

graphics card a ⁓peripheral device that processes and displays graphics.

Graphics Interchange Format in computing, picture file format usually abbreviated to ⁓GIF.

graphics tablet or *bit pad* an input device in which a stylus or cursor is moved, by hand, over a flat surface. The computer can keep track of the position of the

graphics tablet
A graphics tablet enables images drawn freehand to be translated directly to the computer screen.

stylus, so enabling the operator to input drawings or diagrams into the computer.

A graphics tablet is often used with a form overlaid for users to mark boxes in positions that relate to specific registers in the computer, although recent developments in handwriting recognition may increase its future versatility.

graph plotter alternative name for a ⮑plotter.

greeking method used in ⮑desktop publishing and other page make-up systems for showing type below a certain size on screen. Rather than the actual characters being displayed, either a grey bar or graphics symbols are used. Greeking is usually employed when a general impression of the page lay-out is required.

green computing the gradual movement by computer companies toward incorporating energy-saving measures in the design of systems and hardware. The increasing use of energy-saving devices, so that a computer partially shuts down during periods of inactivity, but can reactivate at the touch of a key, could play a significant role in energy conservation.

It is estimated that worldwide electricity consumption by computers amounts to 240 billion kilowatt hours per year, equivalent to the entire annual consumption of Brazil. In the USA, carbon dioxide emissions could be reduced by 20 million tonnes per year – equivalent to the carbon dioxide output of 5 million cars – if all computers incorporated the latest 'sleep technology' (which shuts down most of the power-consuming features of a computer if it is unused for any length of time).

Although it was initially predicted that computers would mean 'paperless offices', in practice the amount of paper consumed continues to rise. Other environmentally costly features of computers include their rapid obsolescence, health problems associated with monitors and keyboards, and the unfavourable economics of component recycling.

GreenNet international computer network used by environmental activists to exchange information and news.

grep UNIX command that allows full-text searching within files. On the Net, grep is sometimes used as an all-purpose synonym for 'search'.

greyscale method of representing continuous tone images on a screen or printer. Each dot in the ⮑bit map is represented by a number of bits and can have a different shade of grey. Compare with ⌐dithering when shades are simulated by altering the density and the pattern of black dots on a white background.

groupware software designed to be used collaboratively by a small group of users, each with his/her own computer and a copy of the software. Examples of groupware are Lotus Notes and Novell GroupWise, both of which provide facilities for sending e-mail and sharing documents.

Standard business applications such as word processors are spoken of as 'groupware-enabled' if they provide facilities for a number of users to make revisions and incorporate them all into a final version.

GUI abbreviation for *⌐graphical user interface*.

guiltware or *nagware* in computing, variety of ⌐shareware software that attempts to make the user register (and pay for) the software by exploiting the user's sense of guilt.

On-screen messages are displayed, usually when the program is started, reminding users that they have an unregistered version of the program that they should pay for if they intend to continue using it. Some programs will also display the message at random intervals while the program is in use.

GZip compression software, properly called ⌐GNU Zip, commonly used on the Internet. Files compressed using GZip can be recognized by the file extension '.GZ'. The software is published by the ⌐Free Software Foundation and was originally developed for ⌐UNIX, although a ⌐DOS version is readily available.

hacking unauthorized access to a computer, either for fun or for malicious or fraudulent purposes. Hackers generally use microcomputers and telephone lines to obtain access. The term is used in a wider sense to mean using software for enjoyment or self-education, not necessarily involving unauthorized access. The most destructive form of hacking is the introduction of a computer ᗌvirus.

Hacking can be divided into four main areas: ᗌviruses, ᗌphreaking, software piracy (stripping away the protective coding that should prevent the software being copied), and accessing operating systems.

A 1996 US survey co-sponsored by the FBI showed 41% of academic, corporate, and government organizations interviewed had had their computer systems hacked into during 1995.

In the UK, hacking is illegal under the ᗌComputer Misuse Act 1990.

A survey 1993–96 of 10,000 organizations in the UK showed that only 3% had been troubled by hackers.

Famous hackers include, in the USA, Kevin ᗌMitnick and, in the UK, Rob Schifreen and Steve Gold, who in 1984 hacked into Prince Philip's mail box on the British Telecom service Prestel.

half duplex a ᗌmodem setting which controls whether or not characters echo to (appear on) the screen. See ᗌfull duplex.

halftone term used in the publishing industry for a black-and-white photograph, indicating the many shades of grey that must be reproduced.

handle term used on ᗌInternet Relay Chat and other live chat services for a nickname.

A given user's handle may or may not be the same as his/her ᗌuser-ID; on many systems users are allowed to pick any name they like to use on chat systems as long as it is not already taken by another user.

Handles are also used on CB and ham radio, and hackers use handles, for cultural reasons as much as to disguise their real identities.

handshake an exchange of signals between two devices that establishes the communications channels and protocols necessary for the devices to send and receive data.

handwriting recognition in computing, ability of a computer to accept handwritten input and turn it into ᗌdigital data that can be processed and displayed or stored as ᗌASCII characters on the computer screen.

Handwriting recognition would free computer users from having to use the keyboard, but it is difficult to implement. A few machines, such as the Apple Newton, have the ability built in, but the technology is still at an early stage of development and such machines typically require users to train the machine by entering a sample alphabet. Technical limitations mean written input has to be printed in small boxes.

hard copy computer output printed on paper.

hard disc a storage device usually consisting of a rigid metal ⚘disc coated with a magnetic material. Data are read from and written to the disc by means of a disc drive. The hard disc may be permanently fixed into the drive or in the form of a disc pack that can be removed and exchanged with a different pack. Hard discs vary from large units with capacities of more than 3,000 megabytes, intended for use with mainframe computers, to small units with capacities as low as 20 megabytes, intended for use with microcomputers. *See illustration on page 75.*

hard-sectored disc floppy disc that is sold already formatted, so that ⚘disc formatting is not necessary. Usually sectors are marked by holes near the hub of the disc. This system is now obsolete.

hardware the mechanical, electrical, and electronic components of a computer system, as opposed to the various programs, which constitute ⚘software.
  Hardware associated with a microcomputer might include the power supply and housing of its processor unit, its circuit boards, VDU (screen), disc drive, keyboard, and printer.

hash function an ⚘algorithm that calculates a value from the content of a message which can then be used to detect alterations to the original message.
  Similar to a ⚘checksum but with greater security, hash functions play an important role in secure cryptographic systems, where authentication is as important as hiding the data from third parties.

hashing the process used to convert a record, usually in a database, into a number that can be used to retrieve the record, or check its validity. The 'hashing algorithm', which may be based on manipulating the ASCII values of letters, will be devised so that different records give a useful range of results. Hashing is faster than storing things alphabetically, for example, where some areas may have lots of very similar records (for example, under c, s, or t) while others are little used (q, x, z).

hash total a ⚘validation check in which an otherwise meaningless control total is calculated by adding together numbers (such as payroll or account numbers) associated with a set of records. The hash total is checked each time data are input, in order to ensure that no entry errors have been made.

HCI abbreviation for ⚘human–computer interaction.

header line or lines of text that appear at the beginning of each e-mail or USENET message sent across the Internet. The header includes important routing and identifying information, such as the sender's name, recipient's name (either a person or a newsgroup), date, time, and machine used when the message was composed, and the path by which the message arrived at its destination.
  In the case of USENET postings, it also indicates if the message is intended for more than one group. The exact material is determined by ⚘RFC (requests for comments) and discussion.

helper application in Web ⌒browsers, an external application that adds the ability to display certain types of files. Common helper applications include ⌒RealAudio, which allows browsers to play live sound tracks such as radio broadcasts or recorded lectures; ⌒Acrobat; and mIRC, which allows access to ⌒Internet Relay Chat via the World Wide Web.

hertz SI unit (symbol Hz) of frequency (the number of repetitions of a regular occurrence in one second). Radio waves are often measured in megahertz (MHz), millions of hertz, and the ⌒clock rate of a computer is usually measured in megahertz. The unit is named after Heinrich Hertz.

Herzog Bertram 1929–   . German-born US computer scientist, one of the pioneers in the use of computer graphics in engineering design.

Herzog was born in Offenburg, near Strasbourg, but emigrated to the USA and studied at the Case Institute of Technology. He has alternated academic posts with working in industry. In 1965 he became professor of industrial engineering at the University of Michigan. Two years later he became professor of electrical engineering and computer science at the University of Colorado.

In 1963, Herzog joined the Ford Motor Company as engineering methods manager, where he extensively applied computers to tasks involved in planning and design. Herzog remained as a consultant to Ford after his return to academic life.

heuristics a process by which a program attempts to improve its performance by learning from its own experience.

Hewlett-Packard (often abbreviated to *HP*) major manufacturer of computer and telecommunications hardware, founded 1939 by William Hewlett and David Packard and based in Palo Alto, California, USA. In 1996 the company was manufacturing more than 24,000 products, including medical equipment, analytical instruments, calculators, PCs, printers, workstations, and palmtops.

HP employs approximately 105,200 people worldwide, and had a net revenue of $31.5 billion in the fiscal year ended 31 Oct 1995.

hexadecimal number system or *hex* number system to the base 16, used in computing. In hex the decimal numbers 0–15 are represented by the characters 0, 1, 2, 3, 4, 5, 6, 7, 8, 9, A, B, C, D, E, F.

Hexadecimal numbers are easy to convert to the computer's internal ⌒binary code and are more compact than binary numbers.

Each place in a number increases in value by a power of 16 going from right to left; for instance, 8F is equal to 15 + (8 × 16) = 143 in decimal. Hexadecimal numbers are often preferred by programmers writing in low-level languages because they are more easily converted to the computer's internal ⌒binary (base-two) code than are decimal numbers, and because they are more compact than binary numbers and therefore more easily keyed, checked, and memorized.

hidden file computer file in an ⌒MS-DOS system that is not normally displayed when the directory listing command is given. Hidden files include certain system files, principally so that there is less chance of modifying or deleting them by accident, but any file can be made hidden if required.

hierarchy on USENET, the structure for naming ⁐newsgroups. All newsgroups on USENET are assigned to a major group. The ⁐Big Seven hierarchies were the first to be set up, and setting up a new newsgroup in these involved following more or less formal procedures. The ⁐alt hierarchy was set up to allow more flexibility. The biz hierarchy was set up 1994, after the first incidence of ⁐spamming, to give advertising its own place.

A number of other hierarchies are available, set up for specific countries (de is Germany, dk is Denmark, uk is Britain); for Internet Service Providers (Demon, CompuServe, and AOL all have their own local groups); or for individual companies.

These newsgroups may be local and reserved for a specific audience, or they may be propagated throughout the world; it is up to the organizations to decide whether to make them available and up to individual Internet Service Providers to take them if they think enough of their users would be interested in the material.

high-definition television (HDTV) television system offering a significantly greater number of scanning lines, and therefore a clearer picture, than that provided by conventional systems. Typically, HDTV has about twice the horizontal and vertical resolution of current 525-line (such as the American standard, NTSC) or 625-line standards (such as the British standard, PAL); a frame rate of at least 24 Hz; and a picture aspect ratio of 9:16 instead of the current 3:4. HDTV systems have been in development since the mid-1970s.

The Japanese HDTV system, or HiVision as it is trade-named in Japan, uses 1,125 scanning lines and an aspect ratio of 16:9 instead of the squarish 4:3 that conventional television uses. A European HDTV system, called HD-MAC, using 1,250 lines, is under development. In the USA, a standard incorporating digital techniques is being discussed.

high-level language a programming language designed to suit the requirements of the programmer; it is independent of the internal machine code of any particular computer. High-level languages are used to solve problems and are often described as *problem-oriented languages* – for example, ⁐BASIC was designed to be easily learnt by first-time programmers; ⁐COBOL is used to write programs solving business problems; and ⁐FORTRAN is used for programs solving scientific and mathematical problems. In contrast, low-level languages, such as ⁐assembly languages, closely reflect the machine codes of specific computers, and are therefore described as *machine-oriented languages*.

Unlike low-level languages, high-level languages are relatively easy to learn because the instructions bear a close resemblance to everyday language, and because the programmer does not require a detailed knowledge of the internal workings of the computer. Each instruction in a high-level language is equivalent to several machine-code instructions. High-level programs are therefore more compact than equivalent low-level programs. However, each high-level instruction must be translated into machine code – by either a ➥compiler or an ➥interpreter program – before it can be executed by a computer. High-level languages are designed to be ***portable*** – programs written in a high-level language can be run on any computer that has a compiler or interpreter for that particular language.

high memory the first 64 kilobytes in the ➥extended memory of an ➥MS-DOS system. The operating system itself is usually installed in this area to allow more conventional memory (below 640 kilobytes) for applications.

High-Sierra format standard format for writing CD-ROM discs; see ➥ISO 9660.

hinting a method of reducing the effects of ➥aliasing in the appearance of ➥outline fonts. Hinting makes use of a series of priorities so that noticeable distortions, such as uneven stem weight, are corrected. ➥PostScript Type 1 and ➥TrueType fonts are hinted.

history a list of sites visited by a Web ➥browser during the current session. The history is usually stored as a list of page titles and is accessed via the browser's menu system. The purpose is to make it easy for users to go back to a recently visited site.

hit request sent to a ➥file server.

Sites on the World Wide Web often measure their popularity in numbers of hits. However, this is misleading, as a single Web page may be made up of many files, each of which counts as a hit when a user downloads the whole page. Counting individual visits is a better indication of a site's success.

Hollerith Herman 1860–1929. US inventor of a mechanical tabulating machine, the first device for data processing. Hollerith's tabulator was widely publicized after being successfully used in the 1890 census. The firm he established, the Tabulating Machine Company, was later one of the founding companies of ➥IBM.

Hollerith was born in Buffalo, New York, and attended the Columbia University School of Mines. From 1884 to 1896 he worked for the US Patent Office.

Working on the 1880 US census, he saw the need for an automated recording process for data, and had the idea of punching holes in cards or rolls of paper. By 1889 he had developed machines for recording, counting, and collating census data. The system was used in 1891 for censuses in several countries, and was soon adapted to the needs of government departments and businesses that handled large quantities of data.

hologram three-dimensional image produced by ➥holography. Small, inexpensive holograms appear on credit cards and software licences to guarantee their authenticity.

holography method of producing three-dimensional (3-D) images, called ➥holograms, by means of laser light. Holography uses a photographic technique (involving the splitting of a laser beam into two beams) to produce a picture, or hologram, that contains 3-D information about the object photographed. Some holograms show meaningless patterns in ordinary light and produce a 3-D image only when laser light is projected through them, but reflection holograms produce images when ordinary light is reflected from them (as found on credit cards).

Although the possibility of holography was suggested as early as 1947 (by Hungarian-born British physicist Dennis Gabor), it could not be demonstrated until a pure coherent light source, the laser, became available 1963. The first laser-recorded holograms were created by Emmett Leith and Juris Upatnieks at the University of Michigan, USA, and Yuri Denisyuk in the Soviet Union. Research into holographic video and other spatial imaging techniques, led by Stephen Benton, is under way at the ⌐MIT Media Lab.

The technique of holography is also applicable to sound, and bats may navigate by ultrasonic holography. Holographic techniques also have applications in storing dental records, detecting stresses and strains in construction and in retail goods, detecting forged paintings and documents, and producing three-dimensional body scans. The technique of detecting strains is of widespread application. It involves making two different holograms of an object on one plate, the object being stressed between exposures. If the object has distorted during stressing, the hologram will be greatly changed, and the distortion readily apparent.

Using holography, digital data can be recorded page by page in a crystal. In 1993 10,000 pages (100 megabytes) of digital data were stored in an iron-doped lithium nobate crystal measuring 1 cm^3.

home page opening page on a particular site on the World Wide Web. The term is also used for the page which loads automatically when a user opens a Web ⌐browser, and for a user's own personal Web pages.

Many Internet Service Providers provide free space to allow all their users to create and maintain their own home pages.

hop on the Internet, an intermediate stage of the journey taken by a message travelling from one site to another.

Internet messages must travel through many machines to get to their destinations. The exact route is recorded in the ⌐bang path.

Hopper Grace 1906–1992. US computer pioneer who created the first compiler and helped invent the computer language ⌐COBOL. She also coined the term 'debug'.

Hopper was educated at Vassar and Yale. She volunteered for duty in World War II with the Naval Ordinance Computation Project. This was the beginning of a long association with the Navy (she was appointed rear admiral 1983). After the war, Hopper joined a firm that eventually would become the Univac division of Sperry-Rand, to manufacture a commercial computer.

In 1945 she was ordered to Harvard University to assist Howard ⌐Aiken in building a computer. One day a breakdown of the machine was found to be due to a moth that had flown into the computer. Aiken came into the laboratory as Hopper was dealing with the insect. 'Why aren't you making numbers, Hopper?' he asked. Hopper replied: 'I am debugging the machine!'

Hopper's main contribution was to create the first computer language, together with the compiler needed to translate the instructions into a form that the computer could work with. In 1959, she was invited to join a Pentagon team attempting to create and standardize a single computer language for commercial use. This led to the development of COBOL, still one of the most widely used languages.

hot key a key stroke (or sequence of key strokes) that triggers a memory-resident program. Such programs are called ⮑terminate and stay resident. Hot keys should be chosen so that they do not conflict with key sequences in commonly used applications.

hotlist stored list of favourite sites which allows users to move quickly to frequently used resources. See also ⮑bookmark.

hot-swapping a technique that allows a user to exchange components without having to shut down the entire system.

The most common example of hot-swapping is ⮑PCMCIA (personal computer memory card interface adapter) components: a user with only one PCMCIA slot can exchange a modem for a network card or hard disc while the machine is running. Special software recognizes the components and allows their immediate use.

HP abbreviation for ⮑Hewlett-Packard.

HPGL (abbreviation for *Hewlett Packard Graphics Language*) file format used in ⮑vector graphics. HPGL is often generated by ⮑CAD systems.

href a tag in ⮑HTML (hypertext markup language) which indicates that the following text is a link either to another portion of the same document or to an external document on the same or a remote site.

HTML (abbreviation for *hypertext markup language*) standard for structuring and describing a document on the ⮑World Wide Web. The HTML standard provides labels for constituent parts of a document (eg. headings and paragraphs) and permits the inclusion of images, sounds, and 'hyperlinks' to other documents. A ⮑browser program is then used to convert this information into a graphical document on-screen.

HTML is a specific example of ⮑SGML (the international standard for text encoding). As such it is not a rigid standard but is constantly being improved to incorporate new features and allow greater freedom of design. In 1995 the specifications for HTML version 3.0 were put forward, including provisions for display of such features as complex tabular information and captioned images.

HTML extension any proprietary addition to the standard specification of ⮑HTML (hypertext markup language).

Both Microsoft and Netscape, publishers of the two leading Web ⮑browsers, have built in such extensions, which are controversial as they clash with the basic ideal that the Net should operate on open standards which allow interoperability. In general, any browser should be able to log on to any site and be able to access most of its information, but the features implemented with proprietary extensions will only display correctly with a browser that supports those extensions.

HTTP (abbreviation for *Hypertext Transfer Protocol*) the ☞protocol used for communications between client (the Web ☞browser) and ☞server on the World Wide Web.

hub central distribution point in a computer ☞network.

human–computer interaction exchange of information between a person and a computer, through the medium of a ☞user interface, studied as a branch of ergonomics.

Hypercard computer application developed for the Apple ☞Macintosh, in which data are stored as if on cards in a card-index system. A group of cards forms a stack. Additional features include the ability to link cards in different ways and, by the use of software buttons (icons that can be clicked or double clicked with a mouse), to access other data. Hypercard is very similar to ☞hypertext, although it does not conform to the rigorous definition of hypertext.

hyperlink link from one document to another or, within the same document, from one place to another. It can be activated by clicking on the link with a ☞mouse. The link is usually highlighted in some way, for example by the inclusion of a small graphic. Documents linked in this way are described as ☞hypertext. Examples of programs that use hypertext and hyperlinks are ☞Windows help files, ☞Acrobat, and ☞Mosaic.

hypermedia system that uses links to lead users to related graphics, audio, animation, or video files in the same way that ☞hypertext systems link related pieces of text. The World Wide Web is an example of a hypermedia system, as is ☞HyperCard.

hypertext system for viewing information (both text and pictures) on a computer screen in such a way that related items of information can easily be reached. For example, the program might display a map of a country; if the user clicks (with a ☞mouse) on a particular city, the program will display information about that city.

Hytelnet (contraction of *hypertext browser for Telnet-accessible sites on the Internet*) program developed in 1990 which indexes Telnet-accessible sites on the Internet so that users can quickly look up the necessary access information.

Versions of Hytelnet exist for PCs, DEC VAXes, and UNIX machines. Hytelnet is distributed as ☞shareware; it is updated via the HYTEL-L electronic mailing list.

IAB abbreviation for ⮐Internet Architecture Board.

IBM (abbreviation for *International Business Machines*) multinational company, the largest manufacturer of computers in the world. The company is a descendant of the Tabulating Machine Company, formed 1896 by US inventor Herman ⮐Hollerith to exploit his punched-card machines. It adopted its present name 1924. By 1991 it had an annual turnover of $64.8 billion and employed about 345,000 people, but in 1992 and 1993 it made considerable losses. The company acquired Lotus Development Corporation June 1995. By 1996 IBM had, under new management, recovered financially, with an annual turnover of more than $70 billion, which means it is still a dominant industry player.

Its aquisition of the Lotus Development Corporation gave IBM access to its wide range of innovative software, including the 1-2-3 spreadsheet and Notes, a market leader in groupware.

history Founded 1924, by former cash register salesman Tom Watson, IBM grew to monopolize the mechanical data processing business, and in the 1950s, thanks mainly to Tom Watson Jr, quickly took over the new electronic (computer-based) data processing business, too. IBM's sales increased from $734 million in 1956 to $51 billion in 1986, when the company dominated most computer markets: mainframes, minicomputers, personal computers and networking. However, the rise of powerful microprocessors and the 'open systems' movement destroyed much of IBM's power; in the early 1990s it lost billions of dollars and shed almost half its 420,000 staff.

IBM became an important patron of modern design in the post-1945 years. Tom Watson Jr hired Eliot Noyes as chief design consultant. Previously an employee of Norman Bel Geddes, Noyes ensured that IBM worked with the best architects – among them Ludwig Mies van der Rohe and Marcel Breuer – and designed many of the company's machines, including the 'Selectric' electric typewriter 1961.

IBM-compatible a clone of an IBM PC; synonymous with PC-compatible.

Although there were successful personal computers before the PC, IBM set the most common standard for these machines when it launched the PC 1981 and created an industry by choosing to license the right to copy its technology to other manufacturers.

icon a small picture on the computer screen, or ⮐VDU, representing an object or function that the user may manipulate or otherwise use. It is a feature of ⮐graphical user interface (GUI) systems. Icons make computers easier to use by allowing the user to point to and click with a ⮐mouse on pictures, rather than type commands.

IDEA (acronym for *International Data Encryption Algorithm*) in computing, an encryption ⮐algorithm, developed 1990 in Zürich, Switzerland. For reasons of speed, it is used in the encryption program ⮐Pretty Good Privacy (PGP) along with ⮐RSA.

id Software computer software company that publishes popular games such as ⮐*Doom* and ⮐*Quake*, based in Texas, USA. An entire subculture has built up around id's games because of its habit of releasing ⮌source code to enable fans to write their own additional game levels using settings of their own choice.

The company's first major product was the 1992 game *Wolfenstein 3-D*, in which players move around a series of complicated mazes retrieving treasure and shooting Nazi troops and guard dogs. *Quake*, released 1996, uses complex, carefully styled 3-D graphics, adds vertical movement and underwater caves, and includes a gruesome collection of fierce aliens. Both *Doom* and *Quake* can be played competitively over networks, including the Internet.

IETF abbreviation for ⮌Internet Engineering Task Force.

IMA abbreviation for ⮌Interactive Multimedia Association.

image compression one of a number of methods used to reduce the amount of information required to represent an image, so that it takes up less computer memory and can be transmitted more rapidly and economically via telecommunications systems. It plays a major role in fax transmission and in videophone and multimedia systems.

image map on the World Wide Web, a large image with multiple hot spots on which users click to navigate around the site.

image processing technique for cleaning up and digitally retouching photographs.

A lot of the fundamental work involved in developing image processing techniques was done at the Jet Propulsion Laboratory in Pasadena, California, USA, which manages unmanned space flight for NASA. Pictures taken in flight of planets have drop-out areas where data is missing due to static or other interference. These pictures are also often taken using parts of the spectrum which the human eye cannot see. Accordingly, computer ⮌algorithms had to be developed to fill in the missing data and compute the correct colours. The images produced in this way are made available publicly and often appear in the media.

immediate access memory in computing, ⮌memory provided in the ⮌central processing unit to store the programs and data in current use.

immersive in ⮌virtual reality, term describing the sense that the user is completely surrounded by and immersed in the virtual world.

impact printer computer printer that creates characters by striking an inked ribbon against the paper beneath. Examples of impact printers are dot-matrix printers, daisywheel printers, and most types of line printer.

Impact printers are noisier and slower than nonimpact printers, such as ink-jet and laser printers, but can be used to produce carbon copies.

import file a file that can be read by a program even though it was produced as an ⮌export file by a different program or make of computer.

incremental backup a ↪backup copy of only those files that have been modified or created since the last incremental or full backup.

indexed sequential file in computing, a type of ↪file access in which an index is used to obtain the address of the ↪block containing the required record.

indexing computerized service on the Internet that automatically scans ↪servers and compiles lists of the information they hold to make it easier for users to find what they are looking for.

Indexing servers for ↪FTP (File Transfer Protocol) are called ↪Archie servers. On the World Wide Web, the best-known indexing service is ↪Yahoo, which organizes sites by categories and subcategories, and also allows free-form searching.

Industrial Light & Magic (ILM) company that creates special effects for films and which has broken new ground in computer animation techniques (see ↪animation, computer). ILM was set up 1975 by US director George Lucas to create special effects for his *Star Wars* films, and is based in San Rafael, California, USA.

The company's best-known computer-generated effects include the sea creature in *The Abyss* 1990, the liquid-metal man in *Terminator 2* 1991, and the dinosaurs in *Jurassic Park* 1993.

infobahn (from German *autobahn* 'motorway') short name for ↪information superhighway.

information service commercial on-line service which offers access to (usually high-priced) periodical databases and other information sources. The two major services are ↪America Online (AOL) and ↪CompuServe.

information superhighway popular collective name for the ↪Internet and other related large-scale computer networks. The term was first used 1993 by US vice president Al Gore in a speech outlining plans to build a high-speed national data communications network.

information technology (IT) collective term for the various technologies involved in processing and transmitting information. They include computing, telecommunications, and microelectronics.

Word processing, databases, and spreadsheets are just some of the computing ↪software packages that have revolutionized work in the office environment. Not only can work be done more quickly than before, but IT has given decisionmakers the opportunity to consider far more data when making decisions.

infotainment (contraction of *information and entertainment*) term applied to software that seeks to inform and entertain simultaneously. Many non-fiction ↪CD-ROM titles are classified as infotainment, such as multimedia encyclopedias or reference discs. Compare ↪edutainment.

infrastructure on the Internet, the underlying structure of telephone links, leased lines, and computer programs that makes communication possible.

ink-jet printer computer printer that creates characters and graphics by spraying very fine jets of quick-drying ink onto paper. Ink-jet printers range in size from small machines designed to work with microcomputers to very large machines designed for high-volume commercial printing.

Because they produce very high-quality printing and are virtually silent, small ink-jet printers (along with ⌐laser printers) are replacing impact printers, such as dot-matrix and daisywheel printers, for use with microcomputers.

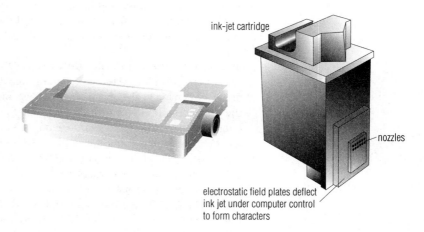

ink-jet cartridge

nozzles

electrostatic field plates deflect
ink jet under computer control
to form characters

ink-jet printer
High-quality print images
are produced by ink-jet
printers by squirting ink
through a series of nozzles.

in-line graphics on the ⌐World Wide Web, images included in Web pages which can be downloaded and viewed on the fly. Web ⌐browsers display these graphics automatically without any action required by the user.

in-line video on the ⌐World Wide Web, video files included in Web pages which can be played back on the fly. Web ⌐browsers typically require a ⌐helper application or ⌐plug-in to be installed to play these files.

input device device for entering information into a computer. Input devices include keyboards, joysticks, mice, light pens, touch-sensitive screens, graphics tablets, speech-recognition devices, and vision systems. Compare ⌐output device.

Input devices that are used commercially – for example, by banks, postal services, and supermarkets – must be able to read and capture large volumes of data very rapidly. Such devices include document readers for magnetic-ink character recognition (MICR), optical character recognition (OCR), and optical mark recognition (OMR); mark-sense readers; bar-code scanners; magnetic-strip readers; and point-of-sale (POS) terminals. Punched-card and paper-tape readers were used in earlier commercial applications but are now obsolete.

instruction register a special memory location used to hold the instruction that the computer is currently processing. It is located in the control unit of the

⌐central processing unit, and receives instructions individually from the immediate-access memory during the fetch phase of the ⌐fetch-execute cycle.

instruction set the complete set of machine-code instructions that a computer's ⌐central processing unit can obey.

integrated circuit (IC), popularly called *silicon chip*, a miniaturized electronic circuit produced on a single crystal, or chip, of a semiconducting material – usually silicon. It may contain many thousands of components and yet measure only 5 mm/0.2 in square and 1 mm/0.04 in thick. The IC is encapsulated within a plastic or ceramic case, and linked via gold wires to metal pins with which it is connected to a ⌐printed circuit board and the other components that make up such electronic devices as computers and calculators.

Integrated Services Digital Network (ISDN) internationally developed telecommunications system for sending signals in ⌐digital format along optical fibres and coaxial cable. It involves converting the 'local loop' – the link between the user's telephone (or private automatic branch exchange) and the digital telephone exchange – from an ⌐analogue system into a digital system, thereby greatly increasing the amount of information that can be carried. The first large-scale use of ISDN began in Japan 1988.

ISDN has advantages in higher voice quality, better quality faxes, and the possibility of data transfer between computers faster than current modems. With ISDN's *Basic Rate Access*, a multiplexer divides one voice telephone line into three channels: two B bands and a D band. Each B band offers 64 kilobits per second and can carry one voice conversation or 50 simultaneous data calls at 1,200 bits per second. The D band is a data-signalling channel operating at 16 kilobits per second. With *Primary Rate Access*, ISDN provides 30 B channels.

British Telecom began offering ISDN to businesses 1991, with some 47,000 ISDN-equipped lines. Its adoption in the UK is expected to stimulate the use of data-communications services such as faxing, teleshopping, and home banking. New services may include computer conferencing, where both voice and computer communications take place simultaneously, and videophones.

Intel manufacturer of the ⌐microprocessors that form the basis of the IBM PC range and its clones. Recent microprocessors are the 80386 and 80486 (the basis of machines referred to as 386 and 486 PCs), and the ⌐Pentium, released in 1993. The Pentium Pro chip is due to be released in early 1996.

In 1994 the company held a 90% share of the the global microprocessor market, and, together with Microsoft, supplied operating systems and computer chips for almost 85% of the world's personal computers.

intellectual property material such as computer software, magazine articles, songs, novels, or recordings which can be described as the expression of ideas fixed in a tangible form.

Generally, intellectual property is protected by copyright law, and distribution, sale, and copying of such material is restricted so that the creators can be paid for their work. On the Internet, intellectual property may include the words, graphics, audio files, and other material which comprise pages on the World Wide Web, as well as the words written by individuals in e-mail or on USENET.

intellectual property rights the right of control over the copying, distribution, and sale of ⌐intellectual property which is codified in the copyright laws.

The future of intellectual property rights is unclear, as the Internet makes mass distribution and copying quick and easy. In the mid-1990s, many schemes were being considered for using encryption to mark computer files or prevent copying in an effort to safeguard these rights.

intelligent agent another name for ⌐agent.

intelligent terminal a ⌐terminal with its own processor which can take some of the processing load away from the main computer.

interactive describing a computer system that will respond directly to data or commands entered by the user. For example, most popular programs, such as word processors and spreadsheet applications, are interactive. Multimedia programs are usually highly interactive, allowing users to decide what type of information to display (text, graphics, video, or audio) and enabling them (by means of ⌐hypertext) to choose an individual route through the information.

interactive computing in computing, a system for processing data in which the operator is in direct communication with the computer, receiving immediate responses to input data. In ⌐batch processing, by contrast, the necessary data and instructions are prepared in advance and processed by the computer with little or no intervention from the operator.

interactive media new technology such as ⌐CD-ROM and on-line systems which allow users to interact with other users or to choose their own path through the material.

The newest attempts to create interactive media are books published on the World Wide Web which allow readers to use ⌐hyperlinks to move around the material at will in the order they choose. Other interactive media include plans for films and other projects which allow viewers to choose how to follow the story, which characters to focus on, or which plot threads to follow.

Interactive Multimedia Association (IMA) organization founded 1987 to promote the growth of the multimedia industry. Based in Anapolis, Maryland, USA, the IMA runs special interest groups, summit meetings, conferences, and trade shows for its member companies.

interactive video (IV) computer-mediated system that enables the user to interact with and control information (including text, recorded speech, or moving images) stored on video disc. IV is most commonly used for training purposes, using analogue video discs, but has wider applications with digital video systems such as CD-I (Compact Disc Interactive, from Philips and Sony) which are based on the CD-ROM format derived from audio compact discs.

Intercast ⇨Intel device that adds TV reception capability to a PC and uses blank lines to deliver data.

A number of leading PC manufacturers expect to bundle Intercast TV tuner boards with new computer systems.

interface the point of contact between two programs or pieces of equipment. The term is most often used for the physical connection between the computer and a ⇨peripheral device, which is used to compensate for differences in such operating characteristics as speed, data coding, voltage, and power consumption. For example, a ***printer interface*** is the cabling and circuitry used to transfer data from a computer to a printer, and to compensate for differences in speed and coding.

Common standard interfaces include the ***Centronics interface***, used to connect parallel devices, and the ***RS232 interface***, used to connect serial devices. For example, in many microcomputer systems, an RS232 interface is used to connect the microcomputer to a modem, and a Centronics device is used to connect it to a printer.

interlacing technique for increasing resolution on computer graphic displays. The electron beam traces alternate lines on each pass, providing twice the number of lines of a non-interlaced screen. However, screen refresh is slower and screen flicker may be increased over that seen on an equivalent non-interlaced screen.

internal modem a ⇨modem that fits into a slot inside a personal computer. On older PCs, an internal modem may prove a better choice for high-speed data communications than an external modem, as it may have built-in features which make up for features missing in older computers. Internal modems are generally also cheaper, except for the small-sized ⇨PCMCIA types.

International Organization for Standardization (ISO) international organization founded 1947 to standardize technical terms, specifications, units, and so on. Its headquarters are in Geneva.

International Telecommunications Union (ITU) international organization, based in Geneva, Switzerland, which manages telecommunications standards such as ⇨modem speeds and ⇨protocols. ITU activities include the coordination, development, regulation, and standardization of telecommunications.

International Traffic in Arms Regulations US laws which prohibit the export of strong encryption by classifying it as a munition. Non-US users of common products such as ⇨Netscape and ⇨Lotus Notes are affected by these laws, as outside the USA American software suppliers must weaken the encryption built in to protect sensitive data.

In the mid-1990s several bills were introduced into the US Congress attempting to change these laws.

Internet global computer network connecting governments, companies, universities, and many other networks and users. ⌐Electronic mail, conferencing, and chat services are all supported across the network, as are the ability to access remote computers and send and retrieve files. By late 1994 it was estimated to have over 40 million users on 11,000 networks in 70 countries, with an estimated one million users joining each month.

The technical underpinnings of the Internet were developed as a project funded by the Advanced Research Project Agency (ARPA) to research how to build a network that would withstand bomb damage. The Internet itself began 1984 with funding from the US National Science Foundation as a means to allow US universities to share the resources of five regional supercomputing centres. The number of users grew quickly, and in the early 1990s access became cheap enough for domestic users to have their own links on home personal computers. As the amount of information available via the Internet grew, indexing and search services such as Gopher, Archie, Veronica, and WAIS were created by Internet users to help both themselves and others. The newer World Wide Web allows seamless browsing across the Internet via ⌐hypertext.

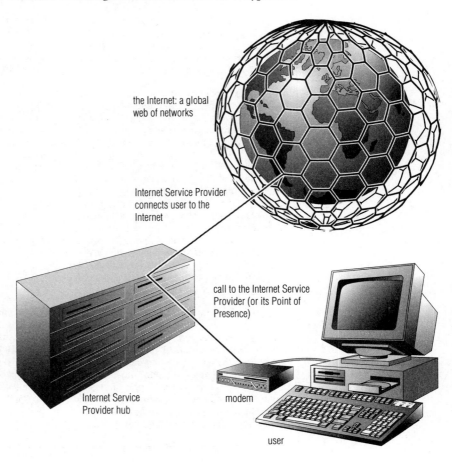

the Internet: a global web of networks

Internet Service Provider connects user to the Internet

call to the Internet Service Provider (or its Point of Presence)

Internet Service Provider hub

modem

user

Internet
The Internet is accessed by users via a modem to the service provider's hub, which handles all connection requests. Once connected, the user can access a whole range of information from many different sources, including the World Wide Web.

Internet: a web of many networks

a web of many networks 1994 was the year that a lot of people heard about the Internet for the first time, even though this network that interconnects other networks has been around since the late 1980s and the technology it depends on was pioneered by the US Defense Department's ARPANET in the mid-1970s. ARPANET was an experiment:the idea was to research building a computer network that could function in the event of partial outages, as if in a bomb attack.

The Internet works along the same lines, which involves routing packets of data from one computer to another in any sequence until the data reaches its destination. But unlike the ARPANET, the Internet grew out of a host of small, independent local area networks owned by companies and other organizations, which could see mutual benefits in being connected to each other. One of the key such networks was NSFnet, named for the USA's National Science Foundation, which needed to ensure that the resources of the five very expensive, regional supercomputing centres it was building could be shared among educational institutions all over the country.

the net spreads wider It didn't take long before institutions in other countries began hooking themselves to the Internet, and by 1994 the net was spreading everywhere, totalling some 25 million users worldwide.

It is estimated that about 25% of all hosts connected to the Internet are located in Europe. In the USA, development is speeding up since the Clinton administration has announced its intention to build a National Information Infrastructure (NII) that will be the data equivalent of the high-speed Interstate road system. As part of this initiative, the White House itself got connected to the Internet in 1993, and uses the Internet to disseminate official government information and to accept electronic mail to the president and vice-president.

Internet for everyone The explosion of interest in the Internet in 1994 was largely fuelled by the advent of affordable Internet access for people outside universities, government organizations, and the big computing companies. Commercial on-line services such as Delphi, America Online, and CompuServe all launched Internet gateways in 1994. Specialist providers of dial-up Internet connections had proved extremely popular in both the USA and the UK over the previous couple of years.

instant information But the point of the Internet is not to deploy technology around the world; the point is to make it possible to share information instantly. Over a dial-up Internet connection, for example, from a desk in London you can view paintings from the Louvre on a computer in Paris; pick up a copy of USA talk show host David Letterman's latest Top Ten list off a computer in the USA; check out player biographies during the World Cup from a computer in Cambridge (UK); and, more practically, browse a database of more than 15,000 publications in Colorado and order specific articles to be sent by fax. Except for the fax part, all of that is free once your Internet connection is paid for.

instant chat A lot of talk goes on as well, both privately by electronic mail (e-mail) and publicly, over USENET. USENET is not actually part of the Internet, although many people confuse the two. USENET is a feed of news, data, and general discussion that is propagated around the world by a number of means, one of which is the Internet. USENET is organized into topics, known as newsgroups. The names generally give a pretty good idea of what the newsgroups are about: `alt.fan. letterman, rec.sport. tennis, news. newusers.questions, alt.sex,` or `uk.misc.`

finding what you want becomes easier The Internet is changing all the time because it has such a large community of technically sophisticated users who write tools they need for their own work and then distribute them.

The file you need is almost certainly out there somewhere, but where? In the early 1990s, therefore, various users started building indexing and search tools that let you scan the net. The first of these, Archie, Veronica, Gopher, and WAIS servers, were all text-based. But a lot of the excitement in 1993 and 1994 was over the World-Wide Web. Developed at CERN, the European particle physics laboratory, the World-Wide Web uses hypertext to let you browse the net in an intuitive manner. Tools like this are what will make the Internet usable by everyone.
Wendy Grossman

INTERNET ARCHITECTURE BOARD

TIP: The chair (1996) is Brian Carpenter, a researcher at CERN. E-mail: brian@dxcoms.cern.ch..

In April 1995 Internet Shopping Network, an interactive shopping facility, went on line. In its first three months 36,000 people subscribed.

Internet Architecture Board (IAB) committee that coordinates the development of Internet ⮑standards. Set up 1983, the IAB is a technical advisory group of the ⮑Internet Society. Its responsibilities include architectural oversight for the ⮑protocols and procedures used by the Internet, standards process oversight and appeal, editorial management and publication of ⮑RFC (request for comments) documents, and advising the Internet Society concerning technical, architectural, procedural, and some policy matters.

Internet-enabled facility that allows desktop applications to exchange information directly across the Internet. The most common Internet facility to build in is e-mail. Also popular is integrated Web access, so that a user can click on a ⮑URL (uniform resource locator) from inside an application such as a word processor or personal information manager and be taken directly to that page on the World Wide Web.

Internet Engineering Task Force (IETF) international group which supervises the development of ⮑RFC (requests for comments), ⮑protocols, and other engineering design for the Internet, reporting to the ⮑Internet Architecture Board. It was formed 1986 and is based in Reston, Virginia, USA.

Internet Explorer Web ⮑browser created by Microsoft 1995 to compete with ⮑Netscape. Internet Explorer is given away free by Microsoft and bundled with the Plus Pack available with its Windows 95 program.

Internet Hunt monthly game played to test contestants' skills at finding information on the Internet.

Internet mail e-mail sent across the Internet. The distinction is primarily made on closed or commercial systems, where Internet mail comes from outside via a ⮑gateway. Systems such as CompuServe used to charge extra for receiving or sending Internet mail, but such charges have been phased out.

Internet phone technology allowing users of the World Wide Web to talk to each other in more or less real time, via microphones and headsets. Network delays mean such connections are not as good quality as traditional telephone connections, but they are much cheaper for long-distance calls since users pay only for their local telephone connection to the Internet.

The earliest products were limited in that they only allowed users to talk to each other if both were logged on to the Vocaltec Web site at the same time. More recent products make it possible for a person using the Internet to dial any telephone in the world.

In mid-1996, a group of US telephone companies asked the Federal Communications Commission to protect their business interests by regulating Internet telephony. The Voice on the Net (VON) coalition opposes this regulation.

Internet Relay Chat (IRC) in computing, service that allows users connected to the Internet to chat with each other over many channels. There are probably hundreds of IRC channels active at any one time, covering a variety of topics. Many abbreviations are used to cut down on typing.

Service	Description
America Online	largest on-line information service, providing access to the Internet integrated into its own software; easy to use
BT Internet	povides browser based on Microsoft Internet Explorer and connection to major UK Internet backbone
CompuServe	second largest on-line information service; provides access to commercial databases
Demon Internet	largest British ISP; provides full Internet connection
IBM Global Network	provides international access {nd} useful for travellers needing to access their mail
UUNET Pipex Dial	good for service and information about the Internet

Some major Internet Service Providers and on-line information services

Internet Service Provider (ISP) in computing, any company that sells dial-up access to the Internet. Several types of company provide Internet access, including on-line information services such as ↪CompuServe and ↪America Online (AOL), electronic conferencing systems such as the ↪WELL and ↪Compulink Information eXchange, and local bulletin board systems (BBSs). Most recently founded ISPs, such as ↪Demon Internet and ↪PIPEX, offer only direct access to the Internet without the burden of running services of their own just for their members.

Such companies typically work out cheaper for their users, as they charge a low, flat rate for unlimited usage. By contrast, commercial on-line services typically charge by the hour or minute.

Country	%
USA and Canada	70
Western Europe	21
Pacific	4
Asia	3
Others	2

World Internet hosts by region, Jan 1995
A host is the computer that provides the services and facilities used by other computers/terminals on the Internet

Internet Society (ISOC) global volunteer group that works to coordinate and develop the Internet and its underlying technology. It was founded 1992 and is based in Reston, Virginia, USA; the president (1996) is Vinton ↪Cerf. Members include individuals, companies, nonprofit-making organizations, and government agencies.

INTERNET TALK RADIO

TIP: Internet makes audio files of its programmes available for download via file transfer protocol (FTP) and also on the World Wide Web.
(http://www.town.hall.org).

INTERNIC

TIP: To access the InterNIC's information server, telnet to internic.net or go to http://www.internic.net on the World Wide Web.

interpreter
The sequence of events when running an interpreter on a high-level language program. Instructions are translated one at a time, making the process a slow one; however, interpreted programs do not need to be compiled and may be executed immediately.

Internet Talk Radio (also known as the *Internet multicasting service*) service that broadcasts radio programmes of interest to the technical community, such as *Geek of the Week*. Based in Washington DC, USA, the service broadcasts via ⬭MBONE.

Internet Worm small experimental program, intended to map the Internet's nodes. It was released 1988 by Robert Morris, Jr, then a student at Cornell University in the USA, and paralysed a large portion of the Net by overloading computer systems throughout the world.

Morris pleaded guilty 1990 and was sentenced to three years' probation and 400 hours of community service, and fined $10,000. The incident inspired a wave of anti-hacking legislation in the USA.

InterNIC service that administers ⬭domain names and maintains a number of Internet user directories. Users interested in registering a particular domain name can use the InterNIC's resources to check if the domain name or a similar one is already in use.

interpolation mathematical technique for using two values to calculate intermediate values. It is used in ⬭computer graphics to create smooth shadings.

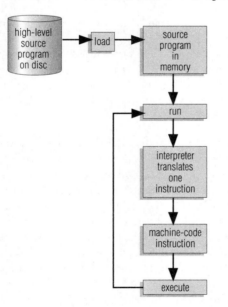

interpreter computer program that translates and executes a program written in a high-level language. Unlike a ⬭compiler, which produces a complete machine-code translation of the high-level program in one operation, an interpreter translates the source program, instruction by instruction, each time that program is run.

Because each instruction must be translated each time the source program is run, interpreted programs run far more slowly than do compiled programs. However, unlike compiled programs, they can be executed immediately without waiting for an intermediate compilation stage.

interrupt a signal received by the computer's central processing unit that causes a temporary halt in the execution of a program while some other task is performed. Interrupts may be generated by the computer's internal electronic clock (clock interrupt), by an input or output device, or by a software routine. After the computer has completed the task to which it was diverted, control returns to the original program.

For example, many computers, while printing a long document, allow the user to carry on with other work. When the printer is ready for more data, it sends an interrupt signal that causes the computer to halt work on the user's program and transmit more data to the printer.

intranet the use of software and other technology developed for the Internet on internal company ↪networks.

Many company networks (and those of other organizations) use the same ↪protocols as the Internet, namely ↪TCP/IP. Therefore the same technology that enables the World Wide Web can be used on an internal network to build an organization-wide web of internal documents that is familiar, easy to use, and comparatively inexpensive.

inverse multiplexing technique for combining individual low-bandwidth channels into a single high-bandwidth channel. It is used to create high-speed telephone links for applications such as ↪videoconferencing which require the transmission of huge quantities of data.

inverse video or *reverse video* a display mode in which images on a display screen are presented as a negative of their normal appearance.

For example, if the computer screen normally displays dark images on a light background, inverse video will change all or part of the screen to a light image on a dark background.

Inverse video is commonly used to highlight parts of a display or to mark out text and pictures that the user wishes the computer to change in some way. For example, the user of a word-processing program might use a pointing device such as a ↪mouse to mark in inverse video a paragraph of text that is to be deleted from the document.

inverted file a file that reorganizes the structure of an existing data file to enable a rapid search to be made for all records having one field falling within set limits.

For example, a file used by an estate agent might store records on each house for sale, using a reference number as the key field for ↪sorting. One field in each record would be the asking price of the house. To speed up the process of drawing up lists of houses falling within certain price ranges, an inverted file might be created in which the records are rearranged according to price. Each record would consist of an asking price, followed by the reference numbers of all the houses offered for sale at this approximate price.

I/O (abbreviation for *input/output*) see ↪input devices and ↪output devices. The term is also used to describe transfer to and from disc – that is, disc I/O.

Iomega leading manufacturer of removable storage and back-up devices, in direct competition with ↪Syquest. Based in Roy, Utah, in the USA, Iomega's two most popular products are the Zip drive, which uses inexpensive 100Mb discs, and the Jaz drive, which uses 1Gb discs.

IP address (abbreviation for *Internet protocol address*) numbered ⇌address assigned to an Internet host. Traditionally, IP addresses are ⇌32-bit, which means that numbered addresses have four sections separated by dots, each a decimal number between 0 and 255.

IRC abbreviation for ⇌Internet Relay Chat.

ISA bus (abbreviation for *industry standard architecture bus*) a data ⇌bus used by IBM PCs based on ⇌Intel 8086 and 80x86 microprocessors.

ISBN (abbreviation for *International Standard Book Number*) code number used for ordering or classifying book titles. Every book printed now has a number on its back cover or jacket, preceded by the letters ISBN. It is a code to the country of origin and the publisher. The number is unique to the book, and will identify it anywhere in the world.

The final digit in each ISBN number is a check digit, which can be used by a computer program to validate the number each time it is input (see ⇌validation).

ISDN abbreviation for *Integrated Services Digital Network*, a telecommunications system.

ISO abbreviation for *International Organization for Standardization*.

ISO 9660 standard file format for ⇌CD-ROM discs, synonymous with High Sierra format. This format is compatible with most systems, so the same disc can contain both Mac and PC versions.

ISOC abbreviation for ⇌Internet Society.

ISP abbreviation for ⇌Internet Service Provider.

iteration a method of solving a problem by performing the same steps repeatedly until a certain condition is satisfied. For example, in one method of ⇌sorting, adjacent items are repeatedly exchanged until the data are in the required sequence.

jack small plug allowing users to connect peripherals to CPUs (◁central processing units).

Hence, in slang, to 'jack in' is to log on to a network or bulletin board, especially in order to participate in a ◁MUD (multi-user dungeon) or other virtual reality game.

Jacquard Joseph-Marie 1752–1834. French textile manufacturer. He invented a punched-card system for programming designs on a carpetmaking loom. In 1801 he constructed looms that used a series of punched cards to control the pattern of longitudinal warp threads depressed before each sideways passage of the shuttle. On later machines the punched cards were joined to form an endless loop that represented the 'program' for the repeating pattern of a carpet. Jacquard-style punched cards were used in the early computers of the 1940s–1960s.

Jacquard was born in Lyon and inherited a small weaving business. He invented the Jacquard loom after becoming bankrupt, and worked on improving it at the Paris Conservatoire des Arts et Métiers from 1804. In Lyon and elsewhere, his machines were smashed by weavers who feared unemployment. By 1812 there were 11,000 Jacquard looms working in France, and they were introduced into many other countries.

Jacquard's attachment for pattern weaving, which was later improved by others, allowed patterns to be woven without the intervention of the weaver. Weavers had always had to plan the pattern before they began their task. This planning now became the essential feature of the weaver's job, and once the pattern had been punched onto cards, it could be used over and over again.

jaggies 'stepped' appearance of curved or diagonal lines in computer graphics caused by ◁aliasing.

JAVA

TIP: If you want to experience the benefits of Java, make sure that your browser is Java-enabled.

Java programming language developed by ◁Sun Microsystems 1995. Java has been adopted as a multipurpose, cross-platform lingua franca for the ◁World Wide Web, and has made many Web sites more dynamic and exciting. When users connect to a Web site that uses Java, they download a small program called an ◁applet onto their computers. The applet then runs on the computer's own processor, perhaps displaying an animation or graph, creating a game or playing a sound.

Jobs Steven Paul 1955– . US computer scientist. He co-founded ◁Apple Computer Inc with Steve Wozniak 1976, and founded ◁NeXT Technology Inc. In 1986 he bought *Pixar* Animation Studios, an established film company specializing in computer animations.

Jobs holds a unique position in the personal computer industry, having been responsible for the creation of three different types of computer. He produced the popular Apple II personal computer, but his greatest success came with the Apple ◁Macintosh 1984, marketed as 'the computer for the rest of us'. A decline in Apple's fortunes led to Jobs' departure and the setting up of NeXT. The NeXT computer met limited commercial success, but its many innovative ideas, particularly in the use of ⏗object-oriented technology, have found their way into mainstream computing.

joystick an input device that signals to a computer the direction and extent of displacement of a hand-held lever. It is similar to the joystick used to control the flight of an aircraft.

Joysticks are sometimes used to control the movement of a cursor (marker) across a display screen, but are much more frequently used to provide fast and direct input for moving the characters and symbols that feature in computer games. Unlike a ⏗mouse, which can move a pointer in any direction, simple games joysticks are often capable only of moving an object in one of eight different directions.

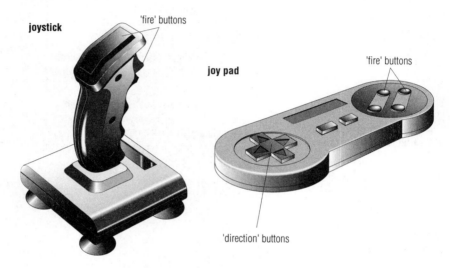

joystick   'fire' buttons

joy pad   'fire' buttons

'direction' buttons

joystick
The directional and other controls on a conventional joystick may be translated to a joy pad, which enables all controls to be activated by buttons.

JPEG (abbreviation for *Joint Photographic Experts Group*) used to describe a compression standard set up by that group and now widely accepted for the storage and transmission of colour images. The JPEG compression standard reduces the size of image files considerably.

Jughead (acronymn for *Jonzy's Universal Gopher Hierarchy Excavation and Display*) in computing, a ⏗search engine enabling users of the Internet server ⏗Gopher to find keywords in ⏗Gopherspace directories.

jump a programming instruction that causes the computer to branch to a different part of a program, rather than execute the next instruction in the program sequence. Unconditional jumps are always executed; conditional jumps are only executed if a particular condition is satisfied.

jumper rectangular plug used to make connections on a circuit board. By pushing a jumper onto a particular set of pins on the board, or removing another, users can adjust the configuration of their computer's circuitry. Most home users, however, prefer to leave the insides of their machines with all the factory settings intact.

justification in word processing, the arrangement of text so that it is aligned with either the left or right margin, or both.

Left-justified text has lines of different length that are perfectly aligned with the left margin but not with the right margin. The left margin is straight but the right margin is uneven, or ragged. *Right-justified text*, normally only used for columns of numbers, has lines of different length that are perfectly aligned with the right margin but not with the left margin. The right margin is straight but the left margin is ragged. *Fully justified text* has lines of the same length that are perfectly aligned with both the left and the right margins. Both margins are even. Many word processors can automatically produce fully justified text by inserting extra spaces between the words in each line, or by adjusting the spacing between the letters (microspacing).

This is an example of text that is left justified. The lines are of unequal length and are aligned with the left margin.

This is an example of text that is right justified. The lines are of unequal length and are aligned with the right margin.

This is an example of text that is fully justified. The lines are of equal length and are aligned with both the left and the right margins.

justification
An example of left, right, and fully justified text.

Kahle Brewster 1960–   . US computing entrepreneur who is best known for inventing the software tool ⌐WAIS system for publishing material on the Internet. Early in his career, Kahle founded Thinking Machines Corporation, a company that designed ⌐supercomputers. He sold his second company, WAIS Inc, to America Online 1995. In 1996 he continued to coordinate WAIS, and set up an Internet archive which aims to keep a copy of every item on the Net.

KA9Q ⌐TCP/IP protocol named after the call sign of Philip Karn, the radio ham who wrote it for ⌐packet radio. The system proved also to be useable on telephone connections, and so was adapted to several other computer platforms. It formed the basis of connections to ⌐Demon Internet for many years.

Kapor Mitchell 1951–   . US entrepreneur and software designer who founded Lotus Development Corporation, a leading business software company, in 1982. Eight years later, he co-founded the Electronic Frontier Foundation, a non-profit-making organization concerned with protecting civil liberties, in particular freedom of speech on the Internet. Kapor is also a professor of media arts and sciences at the Massachussetts Institute of Technology.

Kay Alan US computing expert and a key figure in the development of ⌐graphical users interfaces (later popularized by the Apple Macintosh) and object-oriented languages (Smalltalk) while working at Xerox's Palo Alto Research Centre (Parc) throughout the 1970s. Kay also came up with the inspirational idea of the DynaBook, a sort of computer-based personal digital assistant. Kay spent 1984–96 as an Apple Fellow, working mainly on future-oriented projects with children. In 1996 he joined Walt Disney Imagineering as a Disney Fellow.

Kerberos system of symmetric ⌐key cryptography developed at the Massachussetts Institute of Technology.

kermit a ⌐file-transfer protocol, originally developed at Columbia University and made available without charge. Kermit is available as part of most communications packages and available on most operating systems, but it is now rarely used on the Internet.

key in cryptography, the password needed to both encode and decipher a file. The key performs a sequence of operations on the original data. The recipient of the encoded file will need to apply another key in order to reverse all the operations in the correct order. Current encryption techniques such as ⌐Pretty Good Privacy (PGP) make use of a ⌐public key and a secret one.

keyboard an input device resembling a typewriter keyboard, used to enter instructions and data. There are many variations on the layout and labelling of keys. Extra numeric keys may be added, as may special-purpose function keys, whose effects can be defined by programs in the computer.

key escrow in ⌐public key cryptography, requirement that users store copies of their private keys with the government or other authorities for release to law enforcement officials upon production of the necessary legal documents.

Key escrow was first proposed in the USA, where it was built into the controversial ⮕Clipper chip. In 1996, both the USA and the European Union were considering legislation requiring users of strong encryption to escrow their keys to protect law enforcement interests.

key field a selected field, or portion, of a record that is used to identify that record uniquely; in a file of records it is the field used as the basis for ⮕sorting the file. For example, in a file containing details of a bank's customers, the customer account number would probably be used as the key field.

key frame in animation, a frame which was drawn by the user rather than generated by the computer. Animators feed a sequence of key frames into the computer, allowing the program to draw the intervening stages in a process known as *tweening*.

key-to-disc system or *key-to-tape system* a system that enables large amounts of data to be entered at a keyboard and transferred directly onto computer-readable discs or tapes.

Such systems are used in ⮕batch processing, in which batches of data, prepared in advance, are processed by computer with little or no intervention from the user. The preparation of the data may be controlled by a minicomputer, freeing a larger, mainframe computer for the task of processing.

killer application a program so good or so compelling to certain potential users that they buy the computer that the program runs on for no other reason than to be able to use that program.

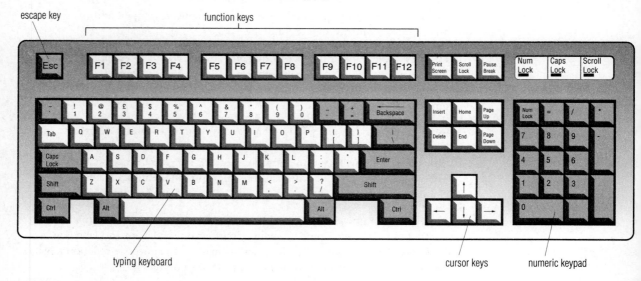

keyboard
A standard 102-key keyboard. As well as providing a QWERTY typing keyboard, the function keys (labelled F1–F12) may be assigned tasks specific to a particular system.

Killer applications are very rare. The most successful was VisiCalc, the first spreadsheet to run on a personal computer (the original Apple microcomputer). VisiCalc succeeded as a killer application because it provided a unique tool for accountants to manipulate numbers easily without the need for programming skills. Another clear example is PageMaker, the first desktop publishing program, which was responsible for selling the Apple ☞Macintosh to the design and publishing community.

The ☞World Wide Web is the killer application for the Internet: by bringing visual excitement and ease of use to the Internet, it inspired people to buy new computers capable of supporting Web ☞browsers.

killfile file specifying material that you do not wish to see when accessing a ☞newsgroup. By entering names, subjects or phrases into a killfile, users can make ☞USENET a more pleasant experience, filtering out tedious threads, offensive subject headings, ☞spamming or contributions from other irritating subscribers.

kilobyte (K or KB) a unit of memory equal to 1,024 ☞bytes. It is sometimes used, less precisely, to mean 1,000 bytes.

In the metric system, the prefix 'kilo-' denotes multiplication by 1,000 (as in kilometre, a unit equal to 1,000 metres). However, computer memory size is based on the ☞binary number system, and the most convenient binary equivalent of 1,000 is 2^{10}, or 1,024.

kilostream link very fast data link.

Kimball tag stock-control device commonly used in clothes shops, consisting of a small ☞punched card attached to each item offered for sale. The tag carries information about the item (such as its serial number, price, colour, and size), both in the form of printed details (which can be read by the customer) and as a pattern of small holes. When the item is sold, the tag (or a part of the tag) is removed and kept as a computer-readable record of sales.

kiosk any computer that has been set up to act as an information centre in a public place. Users navigate the display using keyboards or ☞touch screens, but are never allowed to access the computer's operating system. A kiosk in a museum might show an interactive multimedia display, or one in a library might give readers access to catalogues.

knowbot a program that will search a system or a network, such as the Internet, seeking and retrieving information on behalf of a user and reporting back when it has found it. An example is the Knowbot Information Service, which can process users' queries by e-mail.

knowledge-based system (KBS) computer program that uses an encoding of human knowledge to help solve problems. It was discovered during research into ☞artificial intelligence that adding heuristics (rules of thumb) enabled programs to tackle problems that were otherwise difficult to solve by the usual techniques of computer science.

Chess-playing programs have been strengthened by including knowledge of what makes a good position, or of overall strategies, rather than relying solely on the computer's ability to calculate variations.

LAN abbreviation for ◁*local area network*.

Lanier Jaron. US computing innovator who coined the term ◁virtual reality (VR), and set up a small company, VPL Research Inc, to produce the first VR headsets and data gloves. The headsets enabled wearers to experience graphical worlds created by high-powered computers and to 'meet' in virtual spaces. In 1996 he was chief scientist at New Leaf Systems Inc, and visiting scholar at Columbia University's Department of Computer Science and New York University's Tisch School of the Arts. Lanier is also a musician, a composer and a painter.

Laplink software that allows intelligent transfer of files between computers. Laplink is a key tool for those managing files across more than one computer, such as a mobile executive who has both a desktop computer at his office and a laptop for travelling. It is published by US company Traveling Software.

laptop computer portable microcomputer, small enough to be used on the operator's lap. It consists of a single unit, incorporating a keyboard, ◁floppy disc and ◁hard disc drives, and a screen. The screen often forms a lid that folds back in use. It uses a liquid-crystal or gas-plasma display, rather than the bulkier and heavier cathode-ray tubes found in most display terminals. A typical laptop computer measures about 210 x 297 mm/8.3 x 11.7 in (A4), is 5 cm/2 in depth, and weighs less than 3 kg/6 lb 9 oz.

laser printer computer printer in which the image to be printed is formed by the action of a laser on a light-sensitive drum, then transferred to paper by means of an electrostatic charge. Laser printers are page printers, printing a complete page at a time. The printed image, which can take the form of text or pictures, is made up of tiny dots, or ink particles. The quality of the image generated depends on the fineness of these dots – most laser printers can print up to 120 dots per cm/300 dots per in across the page.

A typical desktop laser printer can print about 4–20 pages per minute. The first low-cost laser printer suitable for office use appeared in 1984.

Laser printers range in size from small black-and-white machines designed to work with microcomputers to very large colour machines designed for high-volume commercial printing. Because they produce very high-quality print and

laser printer
A laser printer works by transferring tiny ink particles contained in a toner cartridge to paper via a rubber belt. The image is produced by laser on a light-sensitive drum within the printer.

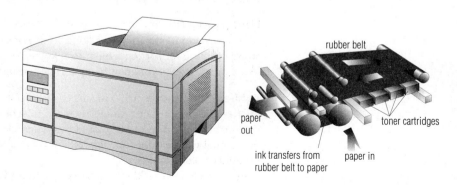

rubber belt

paper out

toner cartridges

ink transfers from rubber belt to paper

paper in

are virtually silent, small laser printers (along with ⌖ink-jet printers) have replaced ⌖dot-matrix and ⌖daisywheel printers as the most popular type of microcomputer printer.

lathe shape in graphics software, a cross-sectional representation of a symmetrical three-dimensional object. The object's shape can be changed by using a mouse-operated tool, much as a piece of wood can be carved on a lathe.

launch to start up a program. Many applications contain embedded programs (such as help screens or formatting options), with the result that users may launch programs without being aware they are doing so.

LCD abbreviation for *liquid-crystal display*.

LDAP (abbreviation for *Lightweight Directory Access Protocol*) Internet standard that enables a client PC or workstation to look up an e-mail address on an LDAP server over a ⌖TCP/IP network. LDAP is a simplified version of the 'heavyweight' X.500 directory access protocol in the ⌖OSI (Open Systems Interconnection) standards suite.

leased line permanent dedicated digital telephone link used for round-the-clock connection within a network or between offices. For example, a bank may use leased lines to carry financial data between branches and head office. The infrastructure of the Internet is a network of leased lines that deliver guaranteed ⌖bandwidth at a fixed cost, regardless of how much traffic they carry. The enormous economies produced by the heavy use of such lines makes the Net a very cheap method of communication.

LED abbreviation for *light-emitting diode*.

legacy application inherited application, usually an old one that runs on a large minicomputer or mainframe, and that may be too important to scrap or too expensive to change. 'Legacy' implies that such applications are valuable and should be looked after. Those who want to be rid of legacy applications use different metaphors, such as 'slum clearance'.

legacy system old system with which new technology must be compatible.

library program one of a collection, or library, of regularly used software routines, held in a computer backing store. For example, a programmer might store a routine for sorting a file into ⌖key field order, and so could incorporate it easily into any new program being developed instead of having to rewrite it.

light-emitting diode (LED) means of displaying symbols in electronic instruments and devices. An LED is made of semiconductor material, such as gallium arsenide phosphide, that glows when electricity is passed through it. The first digital watches and calculators had LED displays, but many later models use ⌖liquid-crystal displays.

In 1993 chemists at the University of Cambridge, England, developed LEDs from the polymer poly(*p*-phenylenevinyl) (PPV) that emit as much light as conventional LEDs and in a variety of colours.

A new generation of LEDs that can produce light in the mid-infrared range (3–10 micrometres) safely and cheaply were developed by British researchers 1995, using thin alternating layers of indium arsenide and indium arsenide antimonide.

light pen a device resembling an ordinary pen, used to indicate locations on a computer screen. With certain computer-aided design (⌐CAD) programs, the light pen can be used to instruct the computer to change the shape, size, position, and colours of sections of a screen image.

The pen has a photoreceptor at its tip that emits signals when light from the screen passes beneath it. From the timing of this signal and a gridlike representation of the screen in the computer memory, a computer program can calculate the position of the light pen.

line input in audio systems, direct input to a tape recorder from a device such as another recorder, rather than a microphone.

line printer computer ⌐printer that prints a complete line of characters at a time. Line printers can achieve very high printing speeds of up to 2,500 lines a minute, but can print in only one typeface, cannot print graphics, and are very noisy. Today, most users prefer ⌐laser printers.

LINK

TIP: To find links when browsing, move the cursor onto highlighted text or an image and watch the pointer change to a hand. Then click the mouse to prompt the browser to move to the new location.

link an image or item of text in a ⌐World Wide Web document that acts as a route to another Web page or file on the Internet. Links are created by using ⌐HTML to combine an on-screen 'anchor' with a hidden Hypertext Reference (HRF), usually the ⌐URL (Web address) of the item in question.

Linux (contraction of *Linus UNIX*) operating system based on an original core program written in ⌐UNIX by Linus Torvalds 1992. Instead of being created by a software house, Linux is a non-proprietary system, made up of freely-available ('open') code created over several years by UNIX enthusiasts all over the world. Each programmer retains the copyright to his or her creation, but makes it freely available on the Internet. Linux retains the flexibility and many of the advanced programming features that make UNIX popular for technically-minded users, but can run on an ordinary PC instead of a UNIX machine.

liquid-crystal display (LCD) display of numbers (for example, in a calculator) or pictures (such as on a pocket television screen) produced by molecules of a substance in a semiliquid state with some crystalline properties, so that clusters of molecules align in parallel formations. The display is a blank until the application of an electric field, which 'twists' the molecules so that they reflect or transmit light falling on them. There two main types of LCD are *passive matrix* and *active matrix*.

LISP (acronym for *list processing*) high-level computer-programming language designed for manipulating lists of data items. It is used primarily in research into ⌐artificial intelligence (AI).

Developed in the late 1950s, and until recently common only in university laboratories, LISP is used more in the USA than in Europe, where the language ⌐PROLOG is often preferred for AI work.

LISTSERV program that receives incoming messages for a mailing list and redistributes them to subscribers.

local area network (LAN) in computing, a ⌐network restricted to a single room or building. Local area networks enable around 500 devices to be connected together.

local bus an extension of the central processing unit (CPU) ⌐bus (electrical pathway), designed to speed up data transfer between the CPU, discs, graphics boards, and other devices. There are two common specifications, **VESA** and ⌐PCI, but PCI is likely to become standard in the late 1990s.

local variable a ⌐variable that can be accessed only by the instructions within a particular ⌐subroutine.

log file file that keeps a record of computer transactions. A log file might track the length and type of connection made to a network, or compile details of faxes sent by computer.

logic gate or **logic circuit** in electronics, one of the basic components used in building ⌐integrated circuits. The five basic types of gate make logical decisions based on the functions NOT, AND, OR, NAND (NOT AND), and NOR (NOT OR). With the exception of the NOT gate, each has two or more inputs.

Information is fed to a gate in the form of binary-coded input signals (logic value 0 stands for 'off' or 'low-voltage pulse', logic 1 for 'on' or 'high-voltage'), and each combination of input signals yields a specific output (logic 0 or 1). An **OR** gate will give a logic 1 output if one or more of its inputs receives a logic 1 signal; however, an **AND** gate will yield a logic 1 output only if it receives a logic 1 signal through both its inputs. The output of a **NOT** or **inverter** gate is the

circuit symbols

| OR gate | AND gate | NOT or inverter gate | NOR gate | NAND gate |

truth tables

logic gate
The circuit symbols for the five basic types of logic gate: OR, AND, NOT, NOR, and NAND. The truth table displays the output results of each possible combination of input signal.

OR gate

inputs		output
0	0	0
0	1	1
1	0	1
1	1	1

AND gate

inputs		output
0	0	0
0	1	0
1	0	0
1	1	1

NOT gate

inputs	output
0	1
1	0

NOR gate

inputs		output
0	0	1
0	1	0
1	0	0
1	1	0

NAND gate

inputs		output
0	0	1
0	1	1
1	0	1
1	1	0

opposite of the signal received through its single input, and a ***NOR*** or ***NAND*** gate produces an output signal that is the opposite of the signal that would have been produced by an OR or AND gate respectively. The properties of a logic gate, or of a combination of gates, may be defined and presented in the form of a diagram called a ***truth table***, which lists the output that will be triggered by each of the possible combinations of input signals. The process has close parallels in computer programming, where it forms the basis of binary logic.

LOGO (Greek *logos* 'word') high-level computer programming language designed to teach mathematical concepts. Developed in about 1970 at the Massachusetts Institute of Technology, it became popular in schools and with home computer users because of its 'turtle graphics' feature. This allows the user to write programs that create line drawings on a computer screen, or drive a small mobile robot (a 'turtle' or 'buggy') around the floor.

LOGO encourages the use of languages in a logical and structured way, leading to 'microworlds', in which problems can be solved by using a few standard solutions.

log off or ***log out*** in computing, the process by which a user identifies himself or herself to a multiuser computer and leaves the system.

log on or ***log in*** in computing, the process by which a user identifies himself or herself to a multiuser computer and enters the system. Logging on usually requires the user to enter a password before access is allowed.

look-and-feel the general appearance of a user interface (usually a ⌐graphical user interface). The concept of look-and-feel was the subject of a court case in the USA, when ⌐Apple sued ⌐Microsoft on the basis that the look-and-feel of Microsoft ⌐Windows infringed their copyright. The case was decided principally in Microsoft's favour.

loop short for ⌐program loop.

loopback any connection that sends an output signal to the same system's input. Loopback adaptors are used in electrical testing.

lossless compression ⌐data compression technique that reduces the number of ⌐bits used to represent data in a file, thereby reducing its size while retaining all the original information. This makes it suitable for computer code and text files. Lossless compression typically achieves space savings of 30%.

lossy compression ⌐data compression technique that dramatically reduces the size of a file by eliminating superfluous data. The lost information is either unnoticeable to the user, or can be recovered during decompression by extrapolation of the existing data. ⌐JPEG and ⌐MPEG are lossy methods that can reduce the size of graphics, audio, and video files by over 90%.

Lotus 1-2-3 ⌐spreadsheet computer program, produced by Lotus Development Corporation. It first appeared in 1982 and its combination of spreadsheet,

LOOPBACK

TIP: On the Internet, certain addresses are loopback addresses; that is, attempting to access that address takes the user back to his or her own system.

graphics display, and data management contributed to the rapid acceptance of the
IBM Personal Computer in businesses.

Lotus Notes business software combining database and message facilities to
help people in an organization to share information and work together. Notes is a
very versatile program that can be customized to suit the needs of the
organization.

low-level language a programming language designed for a particular computer
and reflecting its internal ∽machine code; low-level languages are therefore often
described as *machine-oriented* languages. They cannot easily be converted to
run on a computer with a different central processing unit, and they are relatively
difficult to learn because a detailed knowledge of the internal working of the
computer is required. Since they must be translated into machine code by an
∽assembler program, low-level languages are also called ∽assembly languages.

A mnemonic-based low-level language replaces binary machine-code
instructions, which are very hard to remember, write down, or correct, with short
codes chosen to remind the programmer of the instructions they represent. For
example, the binary-code instruction that means '*sto*re the contents of the
*a*ccumulator' may be represented with the mnemonic STA.

In contrast, ∽high-level languages are designed to solve particular problems
and are therefore described as *problem-oriented languages*.

LSI (abbreviation for *large-scale integration*) the technology that enables
whole electrical circuits to be etched into a piece of semiconducting material just
a few millimetres square.

By the late 1960s a complete computer processor could be integrated on a
single chip, or ∽integrated circuit, and in 1971 the US electronics company Intel
produced the first commercially available ∽microprocessor. Very large-scale
integration (∽VLSI) results in even smaller chips.

lurk to read a ∽USENETnewsgroup without making a contribution. Before
introducing themselves to the group, it is advisable for newcomers to lurk for a
week or two in order to assess its members and their methods. That way, they can
avoid posting an inappropriate message and attracting ∽flames.

Lycos ∽search engine for the ∽World Wide Web. Lycos is a database compiled
by some 700 Web ∽crawlers that comb the Internet for Web, ∽FTP and ∽Gopher
sites, indexing them by title, headings, keywords, and text.

Lycos, named after a particularly voracious hunting spider, started as a research
project at Carnegie Mellon University in Pittsburgh, USA, but became a
commercial venture 1995. By Aug 1996 Lycos had indexed over 60 million
∽URLs.

Lynx text-only Web browser for ∽UNIX computers.

LYCOS

TIP: Lycos can be
reached at
http://www.lycos.com.

machine code a set of instructions that a computer's central processing unit (CPU) can understand and obey directly, without any translation. Each type of CPU has its own machine code. Because machine-code programs consist entirely of binary digits (bits), most programmers write their programs in an easy-to-use ✎high-level language. A high-level program must be translated into machine code – by means of a ✎compiler or ✎interpreter program – before it can be executed by a computer.

Where no suitable high-level language exists or where very efficient machine code is required, programmers may choose to write programs in a low-level, or assembly, language, which is eventually translated into machine code by means of an ✎assembler program.

Microprocessors (CPUs based on a single integrated circuit) may be classified according to the number of machine-code instructions that they are capable of obeying: ✎CISC (complex instruction set computer) microprocessors support up to 200 instructions, whereas ✎RISC (reduced instruction set computer) microprocessors support far fewer instructions but execute programs more rapidly.

machine-readable of data, readable directly by a computer without the need for retyping. The term is usually applied to files on disc or tape, but can also be applied to typed or printed text that can be scanned for ✎optical character recognition or ✎bar codes.

Macintosh range of microcomputers originally produced by Apple Computers. The Apple Macintosh, introduced 1984, was the first popular microcomputer with a ✎graphical user interface. The success of the Macintosh prompted other manufacturers and software companies to create their own graphical user interfaces. Most notable of these are Microsoft Windows, which runs on IBM PC-compatible microcomputers, and OSF/Motif, from the Open Software Foundation, which is used with many UNIX systems.

Apple face major problems 1995: the company's manufacturing side was unable to meet unexpected levels of demand for Macintosh computers, leading to widespread shortages; a massive recall of defective Powerbook laptops damaged the brand's image; and Microsoft's introduction of Windows 95 eroded the competitive advantage of Macintosh's *System 7*.

history In 1977, Apple's founders were Steve ✎Jobs and Steve Wozniak. They received backing from a rich venture capitalist, Mike Markkula, who backed the production of the Apple II. Apple's early market lead in personal computing was destroyed by the entry of the computer industry's behemoth, ✎IBM 1981. Unfortunately Apple's imaginative response – the Macintosh, launched 1984 – was a proprietary design and was never able to gain enough market share to compete with thousands of firms making computers compatible with IBM's PCs. In 1994 Apple licensed the Macintosh for the first time, thus enabling other manufacturers to make cheaper machines, the first appearing 1996, but too late to avoid financial problems, and its long-term future is not assured. However, the Macintosh still has a very strong following in the creative world, particularly in the publishing and the multimedia industries, thanks to its ease of use and the availability of the most popular software for these applications.

macro in computer programming, a new command created by combining a number of existing ones. For example, a word processing macro might create a letterhead or fax cover sheet, inserting words, fonts, and logos with a single keystroke or mouse click. Macros are also useful to automate computer communications – for example, users can write a macro to ask their computer to dial an *Internet Service Provider* (ISP), retrieve e-mail and ⌐USENET articles, and then disconnect. A *macro key* on the keyboard combines the effects of pressing several individual keys.

magnetic-ink character recognition (MICR) a technique that enables special characters printed in magnetic ink to be read and input rapidly to a computer. MICR is used extensively in banking because magnetic-ink characters are difficult to forge and are therefore ideal for marking and identifying cheques.

magnetic-ink character recognition
An example of one of the uses of magnetic ink in automatic character recognition. Because of the difficulties in forging magnetic-ink characters, and the speed with which they can be read by computer systems, MICR is used extensively in banking.

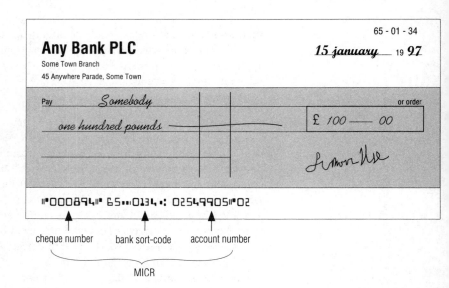

magnetic strip or *magnetic stripe* thin strip of magnetic material attached to a plastic card (such as a credit card) and used for recording data.

magnetic tape narrow plastic ribbon coated with an easily magnetizable material on which data can be recorded. It is used in sound recording, audiovisual systems (videotape), and computing. For mass storage on commercial mainframe computers, large reel-to-reel tapes are still used, but cartridges are coming in. Various types of cartridge are now standard on minis and PCs, while audio cassettes are sometimes used with home computers.

Magnetic tape was first used in *sound recording* 1947, and made overdubbing possible, unlike the direct-to-disc system it replaced. Two-track tape was introduced in the 1950s and four-track in the early 1960s; today, studios use 16-, 24-, or 32-track tape, from which the tracks are mixed down to a stereo master tape.

magnetic tape was first used to record data and programs in 1951 as part of the UNIVAC 1 system. It was very popular as a storage medium for external memory in the 1950s and 1960s. Since then it has been largely replaced by magnetic ⌐discs as a working medium, although tape is still used to make backup copies of important data. Information is recorded on the tape in binary form, with two different strengths of signal representing 1 and 0.

mail-bombing or *dumping* sending large amounts of ⌐e-mail to an individual or organization, usually in retaliation for a breach of ⌐netiquette. The aim is to completely fill the recipient's ⌐hard disc with immense, useless files, causing at best irritation, and at worst total computer failure. While mail-bombing often achieves its aim of annoying the individual concerned, it also inconveniences systems administrators and other users.

mailbox folder in which electronic mail is stored, typically divided into 'in' and 'out' trays. Users usually have two mailboxes: one on their PC, and another at their mail ⌐server at the ⌐Internet Service Provider (ISP), where incoming messages await collection.

mailbox name in an e-mail address, the name to the left of the @ sign, signifying the individual's mailbox for handling mail. All e-mail addresses appear in the form *mailbox name@ ⌐domain name*.

mail-enabled a piece of software that can generate ⌐e-mail without launching a separate electronic mail program.

mailing list list of people who receive a given piece of ⌐e-mail. Mailing lists are an easy way for people to share professional and technical information: hackers (see ⌐hacking) often set up ad hoc mailing lists so that they can collaborate on a single piece of programming. It is also possible to join mailing lists devoted to special topics, social and leisure interests.

mail merge a feature offered by some word-processing packages that enables a list of personal details, such as names and addresses, to be combined with a general document outline to produce individualized documents.

For example, a club secretary might create a file containing a mailing list of the names and addresses of the club members. Whenever a letter is to be sent to all club members, a general letter outline is prepared with indications as to where individual names and addresses need to be added. The mail-merge feature then combines the file of names and addresses with the letter outline to produce and print individual letters addressed to each club member.

mail reflector an ⌐e-mail address that acts as an ⌐alias, redistributing all mail received to another address or to a ⌐mailing list. Individuals use mail reflectors to hide their true identities or to forward messages following a change of e-mail address.

The same method can be used to address a particular group of people – for example, Bloggs College might create mail reflectors for all staff (staff@bloggs.ac.uk), for students (students@bloggs.ac.uk), former students (alumni@bloggs.ac.uk), and so on.

mail server software in client/server computing (see ⌐client–server architecture), software that stores e-mail and distributes it only to the authorized recipient.

mainframe large computer used for commercial data processing and other large-scale operations. Because of the general increase in computing power, the differences between the mainframe, ⌐supercomputer, ⌐minicomputer, and ⌐microcomputer (personal computer) are becoming less marked.

Mainframe manufacturers include IBM, Amdahl, Fujitsu, and Hitachi. Typical mainframes have from 32 to 256 MB of memory and tens of gigabytes of disc storage.

Majordomo ⌐freeware mailing list processor for ⌐UNIX systems.

mark sensing a technique that enables pencil marks made in predetermined positions on specially prepared forms to be rapidly read and input to a computer. The technique makes use of the fact that pencil marks contain graphite and therefore conduct electricity. A *mark sense reader* scans the form by passing small metal brushes over the paper surface. Whenever a brush touches a pencil mark a circuit is completed and the mark is detected.

mask restriction placed on the type of character that can be entered in a given field of a database or spreadsheet. For example, a 'dd-mm-yy' mask will only allow operators to enter a date in the field, and a field operating under a text mask will accept only letters, not numbers. See also ⌐validation.

Mauchly John William 1907–1980. US physicist and engineer who, in 1946, constructed the first general-purpose computer, the ENIAC, in collaboration with John ⌐Eckert. Their company was bought by Remington Rand 1950, and they built the UNIVAC 1 computer 1951 for the US census.

The work on ENIAC was carried out by the two during World War II, and was commissioned to automate the calculation of artillery firing tables for the US Army. In 1949 Mauchly and Eckert designed a small-scale binary computer, BINAC, which was faster and cheaper to use. Punched cards were replaced with magnetic tape, and the computer stored programs internally.

Mauchly was born in Cincinnati, Ohio, and studied at Johns Hopkins University, becoming professor of physics at Ursinus College in Collegeville, Pennsylvania. In 1941 he moved to the Moore School of Electrical Engineering of the University of Pennsylvania, and became principal consultant on the ENIAC project. A dispute over patent policy with the Moore School caused Mauchly and Eckert to leave and set up a partnership 1948. Mauchly was a consultant to Remington Rand (later Sperry Rand) during 1950–59 and again from 1973, after setting up his own consulting company 1959.

MBONE (contraction of *multicast backbone*) layer of the Internet designed to deliver ⚲packets of multimedia data, enabling video and audio communication. It can be used for telephony and video-conferencing – however, it can only deliver a maximum of only five video frames per second, as opposed to television's 30. Large rock concerts are occasionally broadcast on the MBONE.

MCI US-based long distance telecommunications company, active in Net communications since the 1980s, when it ran the backbone for the National Science Foundation's ⚲NSFnet. In 1996 MCI announced Concert Internet Plus, a joint venture with British Telecom aiming to provide a single network spanning the globe.

media (singular *medium*) the collective name for materials on which data can be recorded. For example, paper is a medium that can be used to record printed data; a floppy disc is a medium for recording magnetic data.

megabyte (MB) a unit of memory equal to 1,024 ⚲kilobytes. It is sometimes used, less precisely, to mean 1 million bytes.

memory the part of a system used to store data and programs either permanently or temporarily. There are two main types: immediate access memory and backing storage. Memory capacity is measured in ⚲bytes or, more conveniently, in kilobytes (units of 1,024 bytes) or megabytes (units of 1,024 kilobytes).
   Immediate access memory, or *internal memory*, describes the memory locations that can be addressed directly and individually by the central processing unit. It is either read-only (stored in ⚲ROM, ⚲PROM, and ⚲EPROM chips) or read/write (stored in ⚲RAM chips). Read-only memory stores information that must be constantly available and is unlikely to be changed. It is nonvolatile – that is, it is not lost when the computer is switched off. Read/write memory is volatile – it stores programs and data only while the computer is switched on.
   Backing storage, or *external memory*, is nonvolatile memory, located outside the central processing unit, used to store programs and data that are not in current use. Backing storage is provided by such devices as magnetic ⚲discs (floppy and hard discs), ⚲magnetic tape (tape streamers and cassettes), optical discs (such as ⚲CD-ROM), and ⚲bubble memory. By rapidly switching blocks of information between the backing storage and the immediate-access memory, the limited size of the immediate-access memory may be increased artificially. When this technique is used to give the appearance of a larger internal memory than physically exists, the additional capacity is referred to as ⚲virtual memory.

memory address number specifying the location of a particular item in a computer's ⚲RAM.

memory resident present in the main (⚲RAM) memory of the computer. For an application to be run, it has to be memory resident. Some applications are kept in memory (see ⚲terminate and stay resident), while most are deleted from the memory when their task is complete. However, the memory is usually not large enough to hold all applications and ➷swapping in and out of memory is necessary. This slows down the application.

menu a list of options, displayed on screen, from which the user may make a choice – for example, the choice of services offered to the customer by a bank cash dispenser: withdrawal, deposit, balance, or statement. Menus are used extensively in ➷graphical user interface (GUI) systems, where the menu options are often selected using a pointing device called a ➷mouse.

message-ID special number given to every item of ➷e-mail as it travels across the Internet. Message-IDs are especially important for controlling traffic in ➷USENET. Articles are initially offered across the network by their message-IDs, enabling ➷news servers to check whether they have already received them and either take the rest of the message or move on to the next message-ID.

MICR abbreviation for ➷magnetic-ink character recognition.

microbilling technique of charging for software by usage. Instead of being sold to users in a box over the counter, programs are divided into small segments which can be quickly downloaded over a network on demand. Each time the program is used, the customer's account is debited by a small amount.

microchip popular name for the silicon chip, or ➷integrated circuit.

microcomputer or *micro* or ***personal computer*** small desktop or portable computer, typically designed to be used by one person at a time, although individual computers can be linked in a network so that users can share data and programs.

Its central processing unit is a ➷microprocessor, contained on a single integrated circuit.

Microcomputers are the smallest of the four classes of computer (the others are ➷supercomputer, ➷mainframe, and ➷minicomputer). Since the appearance in 1975 of the first commercially available microcomputer, the Altair 8800, micros have become ubiquitous in commerce, industry, and education.

microfiche sheet of film on which printed text is photographically reduced. See ➷microform.

microform generic name for media on which text or images are photographically reduced. The main examples are *microfilm* (similar to the film in an ordinary camera) and *microfiche* (flat sheets of film, generally 105 mm/4 in x 148 mm/ 6 in, holding the equivalent of 420 standard pages). Microform has the advantage of low reproduction and storage costs, but it requires special devices for reading the text. It is widely used for archiving and for storing large volumes of text, such as library catalogues.

Computer data may be output directly and quickly in microform by means of COM (computer output on microfilm/microfiche) techniques.

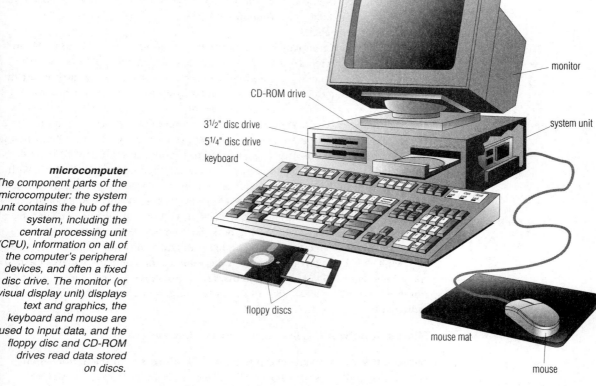

CD-ROM drive

3¹/₂" disc drive
5¹/₄" disc drive
keyboard

monitor

system unit

floppy discs

mouse mat

mouse

microcomputer
The component parts of the microcomputer: the system unit contains the hub of the system, including the central processing unit (CPU), information on all of the computer's peripheral devices, and often a fixed disc drive. The monitor (or visual display unit) displays text and graphics, the keyboard and mouse are used to input data, and the floppy disc and CD-ROM drives read data stored on discs.

microprocessor complete computer ⌐central processing unit contained on a single ⌐integrated circuit, or chip. The appearance of the first microprocessor 1971 designed by ⌐Intel for a pocket calculator manufacturer heralded the introduction of the microcomputer. The microprocessor has led to a dramatic fall in the size and cost of computers, and ⌐dedicated computers can now be found in washing machines, cars, and so on. Examples of microprocessors are the Intel Pentium family and the IBM/Apple Power PC.

Microsoft US software corporation, now the world's largest supplier. Microsoft's first major product was ⌐MS-DOS, written for IBM, but it has increased its hold on the personal computer market with the release of ⌐Windows and related applications. Microsoft was founded by Bill ⌐Gates and Paul Allen 1975.

Together with ⌐Intel, the company supplied operating systems and computer chips for almost 85% of the world's personal computers 1994, while 70% carried Microsoft's own MS-DOS operating system. This virtual monopoly was relatively unchallenged by the IBM, Apple, and Motorola launch of a joint venture to develop a universal PC model 1994.

A US federal probe into charges that Microsoft was engaging in anticompetitive behaviour was carried out in 1990–93, from which date the US Justice Department launched its own investigations. Under a settlement reached 1994, Microsoft agreed to end the uncompetitive practice of demanding a licensing fee from computer makers on certain models of processor irrespective of the software to be installed.

In Aug 1995 the company launched a new operating system, Windows 95, and its own on-line service, *Microsoft Network* (to which users of Windows 95 automatically gain access). 1996 saw the company develop new strategies for the Internet, including giving away its *Internet Explorer* browser free and turning its ActiveX web programming architecture into an open standard to rival ⌐Java.

history Microsoft's first program was a version of the ⌐BASIC computer language written for the MITS Altair, the first personal computer. In 1980, when it had a staff of 40, Microsoft was contracted to produce a BASIC and DOS (Disk Operating System) for IBM's first mass market microcomputer, the IBM PC. With the success of the IBM PC, Microsoft grew rapidly to 6,000 staff and a turnover of $1 billion in 1990, when it launched Windows 3, a hugely successful graphical user interface for DOS. With ancilliary sales of Windows applications (Word, Excel, Microsoft Office) and CD-ROM programs (for example *Encarta*, *Cinemania*), Microsoft then grew to more than 20,000 staff and a turnover of almost $9 billion in 1996. The accompanying growth in the value of the company's shares created three billionaires (Gates, Allen, and marketing executive Steve Ballmer) while hundreds, perhaps thousands, of Microsoft's programmers have become millionaires.

Microsoft Network on-line service operated by ⌐Microsoft.

Microsoft Word versatile and powerful word processing program for ⌐IBM-compatible and ⌐Macintosh PCs. The program began its life as an ⌐MS-DOS program in 1983, and a year later it was released as one of the first programs for the Macintosh. The advanced features and ease of use of Version 6.0, released 1994, established Word as the market leader in its field.

MIDI (acronym for *musical instrument digital interface*) manufacturer's standard allowing different pieces of digital music equipment used in composing and recording to be freely connected.

The information-sending device (any electronic instrument) is called a controller, and the reading device (such as a computer) the sequencer. Pitch, dynamics, decay rate, and stereo position can all be transmitted via the interface. A computer with a MIDI interface can input and store the sounds produced by the connected instruments, and can then manipulate these sounds in many different ways. For example, a single keystroke may change the key of an entire composition. Even a full written score for the composition may be automatically produced.

MIME (acronymn for *Multipurpose Internet Mail Extensions*) standard for transferring multimedia ⌐e-mail messages and ⌐World Wide Web ⌐hypertext documents over the Internet. Under MIME, binary files (any file not in plain text, such as graphics and audio) are translated into a form of ⌐ASCII before transmission, and then turned back into binary form by the recipient. See also ⌐Uuencode.

minicomputer multiuser computer with a size and processing power between those of a ⌐mainframe and a ⌐microcomputer. Nowadays almost all minicomputers are based on ⌐microprocessors.

Minicomputers are often used in medium-sized businesses and in university departments handling ⌐database or other commercial programs and running scientific or graphical applications.

Minitel the dedicated terminal attached to France's teletext system, Teletel, which was launched in 1981 and has millions of users. Many Minitels – most of which have small black and white screens – were installed on free loan by France Telecom to subscribers who opted not to have telephone directories, and the on-line directory is still the most widely-used Minitel service. Erotic 'chat lines' have also proved very popular. Today in France, many PC users access Teletel using software that emulates a Minitel terminal.

mips (acronym for *million instructions per second*) a measure of the speed of a processor. It does not equal the computer power in all cases.

The original IBM PC had a speed of one-quarter mips, but now 50 mips PCs and 100 mips workstations are available.

mirror site archive site which keeps a copy of another site's files for downloading by ⌐FTP. Software archives such as those of the University of Michigan, and the many companies that distribute software by FTP, have several mirror sites around the world, so that users can choose the nearest site.

MIT media lab one of several important computer research centres at the Massachussetts Institute of Technology in Cambridge, Massachussetts, USA. The MIT media lab is at the forefront of multimedia technology.

Mitnick Kevin 1963–   . US computer criminal known as 'the world's most wanted hacker' (see ⌐hacking) during the three years he spent on the run before being caught 1994. Mitnick was a compulsive hacker who specialized in penetrating communications systems including ⌐MCI, Pacific Bell, the Manhattan telephone system and a Pentagon defence computer.

Mitnick was sentenced to jail 1988 for stealing program code from ⌐DEC, but was released 1990 on condition that he never used a computer or modem again. Within two years, however, he had resumed his activities and was wanted once again by the FBI. He kept in touch with fellow hacks on ⌐Internet Relay Chat (IRC) and via ⌐bulletin boards. In an act of bravura, Mitnick broke into the computer of Tsutomu Shimomura, one of the world's leading computer-security experts. Shimomura spent eight weeks on his trail before finally tracking him down in North Carolina.

mixer in sound recording, equipment that allows an engineer to set a different volume level for each individual sound track so that solos can be highlighted and loud instruments can be kept from dominating softer ones. Multimedia systems that allow recording generally include similar, though not as sophisticated, functions through software. This is useful in applications such as adding background music to a scene where two people are talking and it is important to hear the voices clearly over the music.

MMX latest ⌐Pentium chip designed for improved ⌐multimedia capabilities. The chip, scheduled for release 1997, has special features which enable it to process swiftly the repetitive operations demanded by programs with sophisticated graphics, such as computer games.

mnemonic a short sequence of letters used in low-level programming languages (see ⌐low-level language) to represent a ⌐machine code instruction.

mobile phone cordless telephone linked to a digital cellular radio network. Mobile phones can connect to the Internet via a datacard, which converts computer data into a form that can be passed over the network and vice versa. Users can connect them to a ⌐laptop computer and others incorporate a full pocket organizer. A trend for greater integration of phone and computer emerged 1996.

model set of assumptions and criteria based on actual phenomena, used to conduct a computer simulation. Models are used to predict the behaviour of a system such as the movement of a hurricane or the flow of goods from a store. In industry, they are an important tool for testing new products: engineers subject ⌐virtual prototypes of aircraft or bridges to various scenarios to find out what adjustments are necessary to the design. However, a model is only as good as the assumptions that underlie it.

modem (acronym for *modulator/demodulator*) device for transmitting computer data over telephone lines. Such a device is necessary because the ⌐digital signals produced by computers cannot, at present, be transmitted directly over the telephone network, which uses analogue signals. The modem converts the digital signals to analogue, and back again. Modems are used for linking remote terminals to central computers and enable computers to communicate with each other anywhere in the world. The fastest modems transmit at a maximum rate of about 28,000 bps (bits per second) (1996).

modem tax urban legend that surfaces regularly on Internet bulletin boards. It says that the US government's Federal Communications Commission (FCC) is planning to introduce a telecommunications surcharge for using a modem on the public telephone network, and urges readers to write to the FCC to complain. The FCC, however, has no such plans.

moderator person or group of people that screens submissions to certain ⌐newsgroups and ⌐mailing lists before passing them on for wider circulation.

The aim of moderation is not to censor, but to ensure that the quality of debate is maintained by filtering out ✎spamming, irrelevant ('off-topic'), or gratuitously offensive postings.

monitor or *screen* output device on which a computer displays information for the benefit of the operator user – usually in the form of a ✎graphical user interface such as ✎Windows. The commonest type is the cathode-ray tube (CRT), which is similar to a television screen. Portable computers often use ✎liquid crystal display (LCD) screens. These are harder to read than CRTs, but require less power, making them suitable for battery operation.

MOO (abbreviation for *MUD, object-oriented*) a ✎MUD (multi-user dungeon) that uses ✎object-oriented programming, enabling participants to create their own personalized characters – which may well be specially equipped to attack the characters created by other players.

Moog Robert 1934–   . US engineer who developed the first synthesizers widely used in popular music. Moog is also known for building theremins, an electronic instrument which musicians play by moving their hands between two antennas. In 1996 his company, Big Briar, based in Asheville, North Carolina, announced a ✎MIDI interface for theremins.

external modem　　　　　　　　　**external modem for a notebook computer**

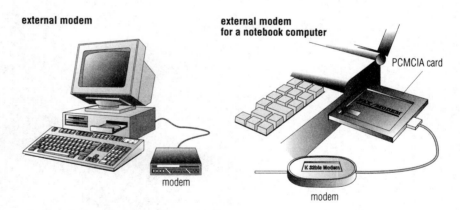

PCMCIA card

modem　　　　　　　　　　　　　　　　modem

modem
Modems are available in various forms: microcomputers may use an external device connected through a communications port, or an internal device, which takes the form of an expansion board inside the computer. Notebook computers use an external modem connected via a special interface card.

internal modem

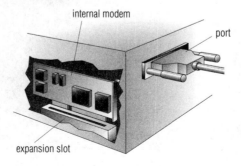

internal modem

port

expansion slot

Moore Gordon 1928– . US co-founder, with the late Robert Noyce, of microchip manufacturers ⌁Intel in 1968. In the 1960s Moore formulated what has since been named *Moore's Law*: the power and complexity of silicon chips would double, and their price halve, every 18 months. His prediction has more or less come true (the processing technology of 1996, for example, was some 8 million times more powerful than that of 1966), due in no small measure to his own achievements.

Mosaic ⌁browser program used for searching the ⌁World Wide Web. It was distributed for free on the Internet as NCSA Mosaic, and made a significant contribution to the huge growth in the Internet's popularity.

Mosaic was developed at the National Center for Supercomputing Applications at the University of Illinois 1993, and the team behind it went on to create ⌁Netscape Navigator, which quickly became a ⌁killer application for browsing the Web.

motherboard ⌁printed circuit board that contains the main components of a microcomputer. The power, memory capacity, and capability of the microcomputer may be enhanced by adding expansion boards to the motherboard.

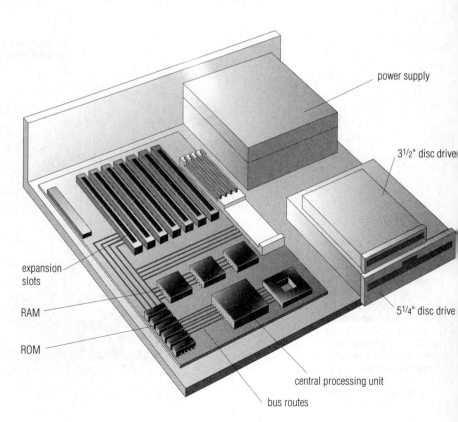

power supply

3¹/₂" disc drive

5¹/₄" disc drive

expansion slots

RAM

ROM

central processing unit

bus routes

motherboard
The position of a motherboard within a computer's system unit. The motherboard contains the central processing unit, random-access memory (RAM) chips, read-only memory (ROM), and a number of expansion slots.

Motorola US semiconductor and electronics company. In computing Motorola is best known for the 680x0 series of microprocessors used for many years by the Apple ⌐Macintosh range and other computers. Its main microprocessor 1996 is the ⌐PowerPC chip.

mouse an input device used to control a pointer on a computer screen. It is a feature of ⌐graphical user interface (GUI) systems. The mouse is about the size of a pack of playing cards, is connected to the computer by a wire, and incorporates one or more buttons that can be pressed. Moving the mouse across a flat surface causes a corresponding movement of the pointer. In this way, the operator can manipulate objects on the screen and make menu selections.

The mouse was invented 1963 at the Stanford Research Institute, USA, by Douglas Engelbart, and developed by the Xerox Corporation in the 1970s. The first was made of wood; the Microsoft mouse was introduced 1983, and the Apple Macintosh mouse 1984. Mice work either mechanically (with electrical contacts to sense the movement in two planes of a ball on a level surface), or optically (photocells detecting movement by recording light reflected from a grid on which the mouse is moved).

MPC (abbreviation for *Multimedia PC*) standard defining the minimum specification for developing and running CD-ROM software. The current MPC specification, MPC II, includes 8 MB of RAM, a VGA monitor, and a CD-ROM disc drive.

MPEG (pronounced 'empeg'; acronym for *Moving Picture Experts Group*) in computing, committee of the International Standards Organization, formed 1988, that sets standards for digital audio and video compression: hence, any file that has been compressed using those standards. The *MPEG-1* is the standard for the digital coding of video pictures for CD recording; *MPEG-2* is a common standard for broadcast-quality video; and *MPEG-4* for Internet telephony. (There is no MPEG-3 as it was absorbed into MPEG-2.)

MPR-II (Mat och ProvRad) in computing, Swedish standard that limits the amount of possibly harmful electromagnetic radiation that may be produced by visual display units (VDUs). A monitor tested for MPR-II compliance should have low emission rates.

MSCDEX.EXE (*Microsoft Compact Disc Extensions*) device driver used by Microsoft MS-DOS and Windows 3 to provide access to files on CD-ROM drives as though they were on a hard drive or floppy disc.

MS-DOS (abbreviation for *Microsoft Disc Operating System*) computer ⌐operating system produced by Microsoft Corporation, widely used on ⌐microcomputers with Intel x 86 and Pentium family microprocessors. A version called PC-DOS is sold by IBM specifically for its personal computers. MS-DOS and PC-DOS are usually referred to as DOS. MS-DOS first appeared 1981, and was similar to an earlier system from Digital Research called CP/M.

MTBF abbreviation for *mean time between failures*, the statistically average time a component can be used before it goes wrong. The MTBF of a computer hard disc, for example, is around 150,000 hours.

MUD (acronym for *multi-user dungeon* or *multi-user domain*) interactive multi-player game, played via the Internet or modem connection to one of the participating computers. MUD players typically have to solve puzzles, avoid traps, fight other participants and carry out various tasks to achieve their goals.

multicasting sending a simultaneous message across a ⌐network to two or more workstations.

multimedia computerized method of presenting information by combining audio and video components using text, sound, and graphics (still, animated, and video sequences). For example, a multimedia database of musical instruments may allow a user not only to search and retrieve text about a particular instrument but also to see pictures of it and hear it play a piece of music. Multimedia applications emphasize interactivity between the computer and the user.

As graphics, video, and audio are extremely demanding of storage space, multimedia PCs are usually fitted with ⌐CD-ROM drives because of the high storage capacity of CD-ROM discs.

In the mid-1990s developments in compression techniques and software made it possible to incorporate multimedia elements into Internet Web sites.

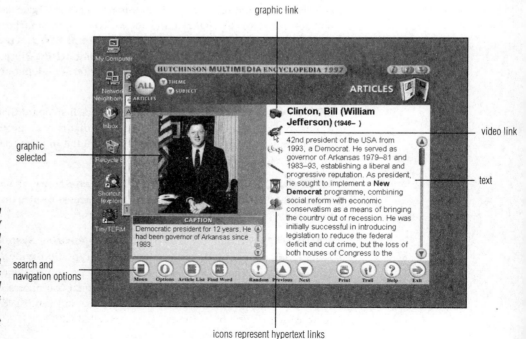

graphic link

graphic selected

video link

text

multimedia
An example of how various elements can be combined to create a multimedia presentation. Text is combined with still images, and icons signify related video, audio, and hypertext links.

search and navigation options

icons represent hypertext links

Recent multimedia developments

multimedia: the video game grows up

Buying a computer has never been simpler. Almost every customer, large or small, wants an IBM PC-compatible with an Intel 486 processor, four megabytes of RAM, Super VGA colour screen and Microsoft Windows 3.1 software. There are variations – faster processors, bigger hard discs and screens, more memory – but the market has a working standard:one that has made Microsoft and Intel very rich; one that is being extended, and challenged.

beyond the desktop

Microsoft, Intel, and numerous PC manufacturers want to expand beyond the desktop. Firms like Grid and NCR are selling battery-powered, portable 'pen-driven' computers for people who do not need a keyboard – van drivers making deliveries, or field service engineers. They can use PCs with power-saving processors and Microsoft's Windows for Pen Computing. Home users can have interactive CD players with infrared controllers and Microsoft's Modular Windows. Corporate users can have multiprocessor 'servers' using Windows NT (New Technology) to replace minicomputers and small mainframes. RAID (redundant arrays of inexpensive discs) storage systems use multiple PC hard drives instead of large, expensive, mainframe discs.

Modular systems comprising PC processors and drives appeal to a market where large computers have been expensive and incompatible. Since PCs sell in large volumes, intense competition and economies of scale have driven down prices, and propagated a huge range of software. But some suppliers offer faster processors than Intel, and operating systems designed for specific tasks, without the inevitable compromises of standardization.

the market

Many firms have produced reduced instruction set computer (RISC) processors – simpler and faster than traditional designs like Intel's x86 line. Examples include AT&T's Hobbit, DEC's Alpha, the ARM (Acorn Risc Machine), Hewlett-Packard's Precision Architecture, Mips' R4000, and Sun's Sparc (scalable processor architecture). The Sparc chip is the most popular, but the market is confusing and confused. There is a plethora of alternative operating systems exploiting these various chips. One is Go's PenPoint, which AT&T, IBM, and others are adopting for pen-driven computers and personal communicators. On minis and workstations, UNIX is becoming dominant but, instead of backing the industry-standard UNIX System V Release 4, several firms have developed variants, confusing the market and introducing unnecessary incompatibilities. The resulting 'UNIX wars' over the last five years have provided Microsoft's NT with its opportunity. Paradoxically, the challenges to Intel and Microsoft have reinforced the PC's appeal. The slogan is:'evolution not revolution'. When fast PCs are so cheap, why take a risk?

CD-ROM

The biggest development is CD-ROM (compact disc, read-only memory). One disc can store more than 600 megabytes of data, equivalent to 450 standard floppies or 150 million words of text. Prices are low, because the industry benefits from the R&D investment and high-volume production facilities for audio CD, with which CD-ROM is compatible.

A large operating system or suite of programs, occupying from 25 to 80 or more floppy discs, can be packed onto a single CD. 'Multimedia' programs can be produced, with digital data, sound, still and moving images on the same disc. Typical discs include dictionaries which have pictures and can say the words you look up, atlases including national anthems, and encyclopedias with moving diagrams. Computer games are also appearing on CD-ROM.

the CD-ROM market

Suppliers have started 'format wars' that make the VHS–Betamax video battle look trivial. Most CD-ROMs are designed for a specific system; there are products for PCs and Apple Macintoshes, Sun workstations, Commodore Amigas (the CDTV system), Fujitsu's FM-Towns, and Sega Megadrive and NEC games consoles. There are other consumer offerings, including CD-I (compact disc–interactive) from Philips and Sony, Photo CD from Philips and Kodak, the Video Information System from Tandy and Zenith, and Sony's Electronic Book. There is also a recordable format, CD-R.

Millions of CD-ROM drives will be sold for Sega, Nintendo, and NEC games consoles, but the emerging standards are CD-I (incorporating Photo CD) and MPC, the Microsoft-backed Multimedia Personal Computer specification based on Windows 3. CD-I systems look like high-end CD players:they plug into a TV set, and can be used for audio CDs as well as multimedia programs. MPC systems are usually 386SX-based PCs upgraded with CD-ROM drive, sound card and, usually, two small stereo loudspeakers. The CD-ROM drive should be able to play 'multi-session' discs (enabling it to handle Photo CD discs, holding more than one set of pictures) and have XA (extended architecture) capabilities, to interleave sound with graphics.

computers for all The original PC was expensive, and its handling of colour graphics and sound primitive, limiting its appeal to the business market. The MPC is becoming affordable and suitable for use in homes and schools, ushering in a new age of electronic books in which people can speak, cows can moo, cartoons can be animated, and you can display the text any size you like. CDs of plays, operas, and musicals can have moving video clips plus the libretto and score. Viewers will become interactive participants, making 'director's cuts' of films, steering plot-lines, or choosing their own endings. Offered such power, will anyone want to resist?

Jack Schofield

multiplexer in telecommunications, a device that allows a transmission medium to carry a number of separate signals at the same time – enabling, for example, several telephone conversations to be carried by one telephone line, and radio signals to be transmitted in stereo.

In *frequency-division multiplexing*, signals of different frequency, each carrying a different message, are transmitted.

Electrical frequency filters separate the message at the receiving station. In *time-division multiplexing*, the messages are broken into sections and the sections of several messages interleaved during transmission. Pulse-code modulation allows hundreds of messages to be sent simultaneously over a single link.

multisession the ability of a compact disc or other ↝WORM ('write once, read many times') medium, to record information at different times. Multisession technology allows archives to be built up gradually, as in the ↝PhotoCD system, where users can progressively fill up a CD as they take pictures.

multitasking or *multiprogramming* a system in which one processor appears to run several different programs (or different parts of the same program) at the same time. All the programs are held in memory together and each is allowed to run for a certain period.

For example, one program may run while other programs are waiting for a ↝peripheral device to work or for input from an operator.

The ability to multitask depends on the ↝operating system rather than the type of computer. ↝UNIX is one of the commonest.

multi-threading executing two or more ↝threads, or sections, of a program at a time. Multi-threading is much faster than ↝multitasking because it switches very quickly between instructions.

multi-user dungeon interactive game usually abbreviated to ⮑MUD.

multi-user shared hallucination in computing, interactive game usually abbreviated to ⮑MUSH.

multi-user system or ***multi-access system*** an operating system that enables several users to access centrally-stored data and programs simultaneously over a network. Each user has a terminal, which may be local (connected directly to the computer) or remote (connected to the computer via a modem and a telephone line).

Multi-access is usually achieved by ⮑*time-sharing*: the computer switches very rapidly between terminals and programs so that each user has sole use of the computer for only a fraction of a second but can work as if he or she had continuous access.

Multi-user systems are becoming increasingly common in the workplace, and have many advantages – such as enabling employees to refer to and update a shared corporate database.

MUSE (abbreviation for ***multi-user shared environment***) type of ⮑MUD.

MUSH (acronym for ***multi-user shared hallucination***) a ⮑MUD (multi-user dungeon) that can be altered by the players. Participants in a MUSH construct new environments or 'rooms' and devise new obstacles to challenge other players.

nagware another name for ➥guiltware.

name server (abbreviated from ***domain name server***) on the Internet, a type of ➥server which matches an Internet Protocol address to a ➥domain name and vice versa.

Humans remember names, but computers work with numbers. Domain name servers translate between the two, so that a human can type an e-mail address such as janedoe@anywhere.com and the computer can route the message correctly.

NAND gate type of ➥logic gate.

National Computing Centre (NCC) UK centre set up 1966 to offer advice and technical assistance to businesses on every aspect of information technology. The NCC is also the world's largest provider of escrow services for source code, a service necessary for businesses using custom-built software from a single supplier. It is based in Manchester.

National Education and Research Network communications backbone usually abbreviated to ➥NERN.

National Information Infrastructure (NII) US network, often referred to as the ***information superhighway***, that embraces every component of the Internet – from the satellites that carry the data to the PCs and telephone links that Americans use to access the Net. The NII was a 1995 US government initiative, the implementation of which was left to the private sector. Still under construction in 1996, the project aims to give all Americans access to the country's information and computing resources.

National Institute of Standards and Technology (NIST) US body that plays an important role in setting computing and communications standards. NIST's Advanced Technology Program, which gives financial assistance to companies developing technologically advanced products during the research and development period, has played a considerable role in nurturing the US computer industry.

National Security Agency (NSA) US communications intelligence agency set up secretly in 1952 by President Harry S Truman and instrumental in defining US policy on encryption.

Little was known about the NSA until 1982, when journalist James Bamford published *The Puzzle Palace*, a detailed report on its operations.

navigate to find your way around hyperspace or a ➥hypertext document, especially when using a ➥browser.

navigation map specialized tool to help users find their way around a Web site. Colourful graphics overlay a hidden grid, like that on a conventional map, containing ➥hypertext links. Users navigate by placing their cursor on an image and clicking the mouse, sending a 'map reference' back to the Web site which activates a link. Navigation maps give the designer more control over how the page will appear on the screen, and are more attractive than conventional links.

Negroponte Nicholas. US founder and the director of the ⮎MIT Media Lab and columnist for ⮎*Wired* magazine.

In 1996 he published *Being Digital*, in which he makes an analogy between that bits of data ('the DNA of information') and atoms of matter. Negroponte also predicted that mass media such as newspapers and television will give way to consumer-led electronic media in which people will take only the information they need.

Nelson Ted (Theodore) 1937– . US computer scientist who coined the term ⮎hypertext 1965 to propose a type of literature that used links embedded in text to connect readers to sources of further information. He went on to develop a global electronic publishing project called Xanadu, and was appointed professor of environmental information at Keio University, Japan, 1996.

nerd slang term for someone who seems to spend more time interacting with computers than with human beings. The term was originally an abusive one, applied to weedy, diffident but studious US high school students by their more sporty and outgoing colleagues.

NERN (abbreviation for *National Education and Research Network*) in computing, communications backbone capable of transferring data at the rate of one gigabit per second. It was designed for computer research, and is not accessible to the public.

Net abuse action that upsets participants in ⮎USENET. Common forms include ⮎spamming (advertising), crossposting (sending the same message to several groups), scams (financial frauds), and attempts to rig or prevent discussions. In theory, ⮎Internet Service Providers (ISPs) can punish Net abuse by blocking access to the Net, but in practice this sanction is very rarely invoked as the offender merely finds a new ISP.

Netcom major US-based Internet Service Provider (ISP), founded 1988 to provide college students with off-campus access to university computer facilities. In 1996 the company claimed to be the world's largest ISP, with some 500,000 subscribers.

Netfind ⮎search engine designed to locate personal ⮎e-mail addresses. Users supply an individual's name and a possible ⮎domain name, and Netfind searches a database of domain names, offering users a series of choices to help narrow down the range of options.

netiquette (derived from *Internet etiquette*) behaviour guidelines evolved by users of the ⮎Internet. The rules of netiquette include: no messages typed in upper case (considered to be the equivalent of shouting); new users, or new members of a ↝newsgroup, should read the frequently asked questions (FAQ) file before asking a question; no advertising via ↝USENET newsgroups.

Users who contravene netiquette can expect to receive ↝electronic mail flames (angry messages) pointing out the error of their ways. The Internet community is fiercely protective of netiquette.

net police (or *net cops*) ↝USENET readers who monitor and 'punish' postings which they find offensive or believe to be in breach of ↝netiquette. Many unmoderated (see ↝moderator) newsgroups are policed by these self-appointed guardians, whose attempts to enforce their vision of the group sometimes make them a target for 'punishment' themselves.

Netscape ↝browser program used for searching the ↝World Wide Web. Developed in 1994 by the Netscape Communications Corporation in the USA, it has become an extremely popular browser with an estimated 40 million copies in use1996.

During 1996, Netscape worked closely with finance companies and other software houses on *SET (Secure Electronic Transactions)*, an encryption method designed to facilitate secure bank card transactions over the Web. The company also unveiled Netscape ONE (Open Network Environment), designed to help developers to create new on-line applications. Navigator version 3.0, released 1996, features integrated video, audio, 3-D, and Internet telephone communications capabilities.

Net, the abbreviation for the ↝Internet. The term is often used to denote the entire community of people with computer access to the Internet.

Netware leading ↝local area network operating system, supplied by Novell.

network a method of connecting computers so that they can share data and ↝peripheral devices, such as printers. The main types are classified by the pattern

network
Some examples of local area networks (LANs): ring networks have all devices (including the file server, printers, and so on) connected to a central ring; star networks have the file server as the hub of the network, with all devices connected to it; bus networks consist of a line of cable (typically Ethernet), with all devices connected to that line.

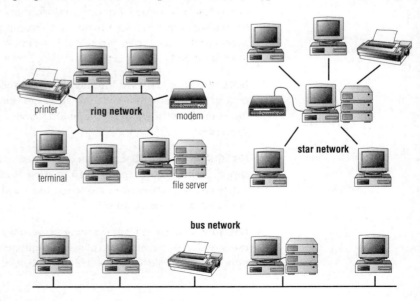

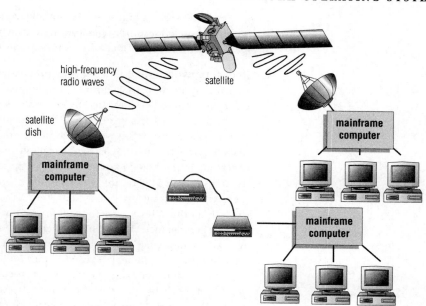

network
A wide area network (WAN). WANs enable remote systems to connect via telephone lines or satellite links.

of the connections – star or ring network, for example – or by the degree of geographical spread allowed; for example, *local area networks* (LANs) for communication within a room or building, and *wide area networks* (WANs) for more remote systems. Internet is the computer network that connects major English-speaking institutions throughout the world, with around 12 million users. Janet (joint academic network), a variant of Internet, is used in Britain. SuperJanet, launched 1992, is an extension of this that can carry 1,000 million bits of information per second.

One of the most common networking systems is Ethernet, developed in the 1970s (released 1980) at Xerox's Palo Alto Research Center, California, by Rich Seifert, Bob Printis, and Dave Redell.

network computer (NC) simple computer consisting essentially of a microprocessor, a ⌐RAM chip and a monitor. NCs are designed to function as part of a network, connected to a central ⌐server via the Internet or an ⌐intranet, downloading software (especially ⌐object oriented programs) as required. The absence of internal storage makes them much cheaper to buy and maintain than PCs, and they are easier to manage and upgrade, as all the software is stored in one place. Some commentators believe that the NC will eventually replace the networked PC as the standard computer setup for business.

network interface card (NIC) in computing, item of computer hardware that allows computers to be connected to a computer network.

network operating system (NOS) in computing, software designed to enable a ⌐LAN or other network to operate. The main task of every NOS is to tell both the central ⌐file server and the ⌐workstations connected to it how to communicate with each other. Network operating systems may also include security and backup features, remote access facilities, and a centralized database.

neural network artificial network of processors that attempts to mimic the structure of nerve cells (neurons) in the human brain. Neural networks may be electronic, optical, or simulated by computer software.

A basic network has three layers of processors: an input layer, an output layer, and a 'hidden' layer in between. Each processor is connected to every other in the network by a system of 'synapses'; every processor in the top layer connects to every one in the hidden layer, and each of these connects to every processor in the output layer. This means that each nerve cell in the middle and bottom layers receives input from several different sources; only when the amount of input exceeds a critical level does the cell fire an output signal.

The chief characteristic of neural networks is their ability to sum up large amounts of imprecise data and decide whether they match a pattern or not. Networks of this type may be used in developing robot vision, matching fingerprints, and analysing fluctuations in stock-market prices. However, it is thought unlikely by scientists that such networks will ever be able accurately to imitate the human brain, which is very much more complicated; it contains around 10 billion nerve cells, whereas current artificial networks contain only a few hundred processors.

Neural networks

computer brains Neural networks – strictly 'artificial' neural networks – represent a radically different approach to computing. They are called 'neural' networks because they are loosely modelled on the networks of neurons – nerve cells – that make up brains. Neural networks are characterized by their ability to 'learn', and can be described as 'trainable pattern recognizers'. The study and use of neural networks is sometimes called **neurocomputing**.

brain power Brains perform remarkable computational feats: recognizing music from just a few seconds of a recording, or faces seen only once before – accomplishments that defeat even the most modern computers. Yet brains stumble with arithmetic and make errors with simple logic. The reason for these anomalies might be found in the differences between brain and computer architecture – their internal structure and operating mechanisms.

the difference between brain and computer Conventional computers possess distinct processing and memory units, controlled by programs, but animal nervous systems and neural networks are instead made up of highly interconnected webs of simple processing units. They have no specific memory locations, information instead being stored as patterns of interconnections between the processing units. Neural networks are not programmed, but are trained by example. They can, therefore, learn things that cannot easily be stated in programs, making them attractive in a wide range of application areas.

Although neural networks are a form of parallel processing, the essence of the approach can be simulated on ordinary computers. Indeed, many packages are now available to enable personal computers to function as neuro-computers. Dedicated neural computing hardware, however, runs far faster.

artificial intelligence Neurocomputing can be considered a branch of artificial intelligence. Artificial intelligence has two principal motivations: technology and psychology. The first concerns the use of computers to mimic biological intelligence and perform technologically useful tasks. The second is about understanding human perception and understanding. Neural networks have had dramatic effects on both – indeed, a distinct approach to psychology called **connectionism**, or **parallel distributed processing**, has grown up around them.

high hopes and disappointments
Although neurocomputing might seem a recent development, research started at around the same time as the early work on digital computers. In the 1940s McCulloch and Pitts devised simple electrical networks, crudely modelling neural circuits, which could perform simple logical computations.

More sophisticated networks, called **perceptrons**, followed in the 1950s – the ancestors of modern neural networks. Simple networks of amplifiers, perceptrons could learn to recognize patterns. This generated tremendous excitement, but significant limits to their abilities were discovered. For example, they were unable to learn the exclusive-OR relation (a logical relationship, 'A *or* B but *not* A and B together').

Marvin Minsky and Seymour Papert of the Massachusetts Institute of Technology proved that certain problems could never be solved by the perceptrons. They published their results in an important book – *Perceptrons* – and research into neural networks effectively ceased for over a decade. At around the end of the 1970s, however, theoretical breakthroughs made it possible for more complex neural networks to be developed, which overcame these problems, and the flurry of excitement began again.

the way ahead Neural networks are of interest to computer technologists because they have the potential to offer solutions to a range of problems that have proved difficult to solve using conventional computing approaches. These problems include pattern recognition, machine learning, time series forecasting, machine vision, and robot control. Underpinning all this is their ability to 'learn'.

In a famous example, a neural network was trained to recognize speech – with eerily realistic results. The network, called NET-talk, was developed by T J Sejnowski and C R Rosenberg at Johns Hopkins University in the USA. It was linked to a computer that could produce synthetic speech, so its progress could be heard. After producing formless noise for a few hours, it started babbling like a baby. Overnight training improved its performance still further so that it could read text with 95% accuracy. No conventionally programmed computer could do this.

how learning takes place Although humans often have to be taught, a great deal of important learning takes place unsupervised. We are not 'taught' to speak our first language, we acquire it from experience. Neural networks cannot learn entire languages, but an important area of neurocomputing research is concerned with 'unsupervised learning'. One of the most important approaches, discovered by David Willshaw of Edinburgh University, enables the neural network automatically to find patterns in batches of data. This has been applied by Finnish researcher Teuvo Kohonen to produce a phonetic typewriter, which converts speech to text.

Some people think that traditional approaches to artificial intelligence, such as expert systems, have been superseded by neurocomputing. This is wrong. Neural networks are less suitable for some problems than expert systems, and vice versa. There are other concerns about neural systems, such as the time required to train the network, and the difficulties of having a network explain the decision it has reached. The future of artificial intelligence rests with combined techniques, producing 'hybrid systems' that exploit techniques best suited to the task in hand.

Peter Lafferty

newbie insulting term for a new user of a ⌐USENET newsgroup, whose naive or off-topic comments irritate established members of the group. A classic newbie *faux pas* is to post a question that is answered in the group's ⌐FAQ (file of frequently asked questions).

new media general term for ⌐CD-ROM, the ⌐World Wide Web, and other electronic media, including ⌐multimedia.

Most publishing companies now have a 'new media' division which manages a Web site and studies how best to compete and exploit the company's assets in the electronic future.

newsgroup discussion group on the ⌐Internet's ⌐USENET. Newsgroups are organized in seven broad categories: *comp.* – computers and programming; *news.* – newsgroups themselves; *rec.* – sports and hobbies; *sci.* – scientific research and ideas; *talk.* – discussion groups; and *misc.* – everything else. In addition, there are alternative hierarchies such as the wide-ranging and anarchic *alt.* (alternative). Within these categories there is a hierarchy of subdivisions.

Newsgroups exist for almost any subject one might care to think of, whether serious or frivolous. Because USENET cannot be censored at source, some of the newsgroups are inevitably tasteless and offensive to many users. Some newsgroups are moderated, however, so that all postings are assessed in order to maintain the standards of debate.

newsreader program that gives access to ⌐USENET newsgroups, interpreting the standard commands understood by ⌐news servers in a simple, user-friendly interface. Popular newsreaders include rn for ⌐UNIX, Turnpike and Agent for PCs and NewsReader for Macintosh. It is also possible to access USENET with a ⌐browser such as ⌐Netscape Navigator.

news server computer that stores ⌐USENET messages for access by users. Most ⌐Internet Service Providers (ISPs) offer a news server as part of the service.

Newton small portable computer, also called a ⌐personal digital assistant (PDA), produced by ⌐Apple. The Newton combines many functions, including address book, diary, word processor, fax terminal, and e-mailing and Internet browsing facilities, in a pocket-sized unit. Its keyboardless interface and handwriting recognition software allow users to enter data in their own handwriting using a stylus and a touch screen. Apple planned to make the Newton more Internet-capable in 1996.

NeXTStep ⌐operating system and development environment, originally created for the ⌐NeXT computer, but now available for other computers, including the IBM PC. NeXTStep is based on ⌐UNIX but contains a high level of ⌐object orientation. Many of the ideas incorporated in NeXTStep have found their way into mainstream operating systems.

NeXT Technology Inc US computer manufacturer founded by Steve Jobs. NeXT's first product was an advanced computer (called NeXT) based on the ⌐Motorola 680X0 series of ⌐microprocessors.

NeXT had limited commercial success, and has been discontinued, but its operating system and development environment, ⌐NeXTStep, has been made available to other computers.

nickname an alternative ⌐user-id, as used by participants in ⌐MUDs, ⌐Internet Relay Chat and other interactive setups.

NII abbreviation for ⌐National Information Infrastructure.

Nintendo Japanese ⌐games console and software manufacturer. In 1996, the company introduced the N64 – the first 64-bit games console. Nintendo's most successful game is *Super Mario Brothers*.

NIST abbreviation for ⌐National Institute of Standards and Technology.

NNTP (abbreviation for *Network News Transfer Protocol*) set of standard procedures by which ⌐USENET news is distributed across the Internet. NNTP governs both the way e-mailed messages travel between news servers and the way ⌐newsreaders retrieve news from servers.

NO CARRIER error message returned by a modem when the telephone line drops unexpectedly because of line noise or other interruptions.

node any device connected to a network, such as a ⌐router, a ⌐bridge, a ⌐hub, and a ⌐server.

nondisclosure agreement (NDA) in computing, agreement signed with suppliers by manufacturers, programmers, journalists, and so, in exchange for detailed information or copies of new products in advance of their public launch. For example, a manufacturer might sign an NDA to get a copy of a new operating system in order to have compatible hardware ready for the program's launch. NDAs are often required in order to participate in beta (pre-launch) tests of important pieces of software.

nonlinear video editing in computing, video editing method that processes compressed video data stored on a hard disc. This makes it much easier for editors to find their way around the material, and enables them to commence editing at any point in the tape – hence the name. Editors use a computer to rearrange the material and produce an Edit Decision List (EDL) bearing all information on cuts, fades, and other effects. The EDL can then be used to create an automated final edit using the original tapes. The main video editing programs are Avid VideoShop for the Macintosh and Lightworks for PCs.

nonvolatile memory ⌐memory that does not lose its contents when the power supply to the computer is disconnected.

NOR gate in electronics, a type of ⌐logic gate.

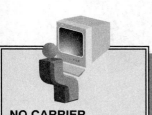

NO CARRIER

TIP: Users generally shouldn't have to worry about port addresses, as applications like Telnet and the World Wide Web mostly use standard addresses (for Telnet, port 23) and the client software will fill these in automatically.

Occasionally, a non-standard address will specify a different port, and in these cases the user must add the non-standard port number to the end of the address.

notebook computer small ⌐laptop computer. Notebook computers became available in the early 1990s and, even complete with screen and hard-disc drive, are no larger than a standard notebook.

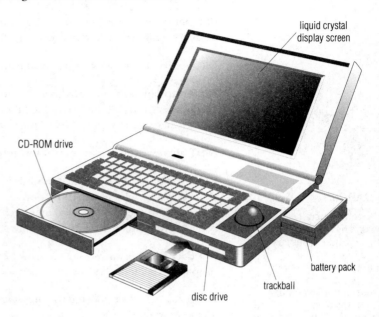

liquid crystal
display screen

CD-ROM drive

battery pack

trackball

disc drive

notebook computer
The component parts of a
notebook computer.
Although as powerful as a
microcomputer, the battery
pack enables the notebook
to be used away from any
source of power.

NOT gate or *inverter gate* in electronics, a type of ⌐logic gate.

Novell US ⌐network operating system specialist. Novell's ⌐NetWare operating system for IBM-compatible PCs dominates the market for ⌐local area networks and is used as an industry standard.

Noyce Robert Norton 1927–1990. US scientist and inventor, with Jack Kilby, of the ⌐integrated circuit (chip), which revolutionized the computer and electronics industries in the 1970s and 1980s. In 1968 he and six colleagues founded the Intel Corporation, which became one of the USA's leading semiconductor manufacturers.

Noyce was awarded a patent for the integrated circuit 1959. In 1961 he founded his first company, Fairchild Camera and Instruments Corporation, around which Silicon Valley was to grow. The company was the first in the world to understand and exploit the commercial potential of the integrated circuit. It quickly became the basis for such products as the personal computer, the pocket calculator, and the programmable microwave oven. At the time of his death, he was president of Sematech Incorporated, a government–industry research consortium created to help US firms regain a lead in semiconductor technology that they had lost to Japanese manufacturers.

NSFnet (shorthand for *National Science Foundation Network*) in computing, network funded by the US National Science Foundation, and an important part of the Internet backbone. In 1993 the National Science Foundation started building a very high speed Backbone Network Service (vBNS) to connect five government supercomputing centres at speeds of up to 2.5 gigabits per second - fast enough to transmit the entire contents of several public libraries every second.

NTSC (abbreviation for *National Television Standards Committee*) in computing, the US television standard signal format. Sometimes believed to stand for 'Never Twice the Same Colour'. Compare ⬦PAL.

null character character with the ⬦ASCII value 0. A null character is used by some programming languages, most notably C, to mark the end of a character string.

null-modem special cable that is used to connect the ⬦serial interfaces of two computers, so as to allow them to exchange data.

null string a string, usually denoted by '-', containing nothing or a ⬦null character. A null string is used in some programming languages to denote the last of a series of values.

object linking and embedding (OLE) enhancement to ⌐dynamic data exchange, which makes it possible not only to include live data from one application in another application, but also to edit the data in the original application without leaving the application in which the data has been included.

object-oriented programming (OOP) computer programming based on 'objects', in which data are closely linked to the procedures that operate on them. For example, a circle on the screen might be an object: it has data, such as a centre point and a radius, as well as procedures for moving it, erasing it, changing its size, and so on.

The technique originated with the Simula and Smalltalk languages in the 1960s and early 1970s, but it has now been incorporated into many general-purpose programming languages, including ⌐Java.

object program the ⌐machine code translation of a program written in a ⌐source language.

OCR abbreviation for ⌐*optical character recognition*.

octal number system number system to the base eight, used in computing. The highest digit that can appear in the octal system is seven. Whereas normal decimal, or base-ten, numbers may be considered to be written under column headings based on the number ten, octal, or base-eight, numbers can be thought of as written under column headings based on the number eight. The octal number 567 is therefore equivalent to the decimal number 375, since $(5 \times 64) + (6 \times 8) + (7 \times 1) = 375$.

The octal number system is sometimes used by computer programmers as an alternative to the ⌐hexadecimal number system.

office automation introduction of computers and other electronic equipment, such as fax machines, to support an office routine. Increasingly, computers are used to support administrative tasks such as document processing, filing, mail, and schedule management; project planning and management accounting have also been computerized.

office suite set of bundled programs designed especially for business use. An office suite will typically contain a ⌐spreadsheet, scheduling and presentation

Package	Manufacturer	Content (word processing; spreadsheet; presentation and other software)
CorelOffice	Corel	with WordPerfect, Quattro Pro, Presentations, and a personal information manager and document packaging tool
Microsoft Office	Microsoft	with Word, Excel, Presentation, Mail, Office Assistant, and (Professional version) Access database; allows Web-site hyperlinks
SmartSuite	Lotus	with Word Pro, 1-2-3, Freelance, Approach (database), time management system and screen action recorder

office suite
Some major office suites

software, a ⌐word processor, a database, and e-mail facilities. The programs are set up to work individually and in concert, so that the user can (for example) create a report with charts created from a spreadsheet, and then e-mail the document to a list of clients selected from the database. Popular office suites include Lotus SmartSuite and Microsoft Office.

off line not connected, so that data cannot be transferred, for example, to a printer. The opposite of ⌐on line.

off-line browser in computing, program that downloads and copies Web pages onto a computer so that they can be viewed without being connected to the Internet. By taking advantage of off-peak hours, when telephone charges are low and the network responds faster, off-line browsers are a thrifty way of using the ⌐World Wide Web.

off-line editing in video and film, process of editing a scratch copy of the footage rather than the expensively created footage itself. Once the edit has been finalized, the real footage is edited by a machine.

off-line reader in computing, program that downloads information from ⌐newsgroups, ⌐FTP servers or other Internet resources, storing it locally on a hard disc so that it can be read without running up a large telephone bill.

OMR abbreviation for ⌐*optical mark recognition*.

on line connected, so that data can be transferred, for example, to a printer or from a network. The opposite of ⌐off line.

on-line help in computing, guidance and assistance in using a program which is given by the software itself, instead of a manual or a customer services representative over the telephone.

on-line service in computing, commercial service like ⌐America Online (AOL), ⌐Compulink Information eXchange (CIX), or ⌐CompuServe, which offers proprietary conferencing and other services to subscribers on top of access to the Internet.

on-line system in computing, originally a system that allows the computer to work interactively with its users, responding to each instruction as it is given and prompting users for information when necessary. Since almost all the computers used now work this way the, 'on-line system' is now used to refer to large database, electronic mail, and conferencing systems accessed via a dial-up modem. These often have tens or hundreds of users from different places – sometimes from different countries – 'on line' at the same time.

Under 1996 US legislation, the transmission of 'indecent material' over on-line computer services that are accessible to minors became a crime punishable by up to two years in prison and a fine of $100,000.

on-site warranty in computing, after-sales service offered free by many hardware manufacturers for a limited period after purchase – usually one year. An on-site warranty entitles purchasers to a visit from an peripatatic engineer in case of problems.

Open Software Foundation (OSF) in computing, organization created by several major industry players (including Bull, DEC, Hewlett-Packard, IBM and Philips) to engineer a standard operating system and user interface for the ⊃UNIX platform.

opensystems systems that conform to ⊃Open Systems Interconnection or ⊃POSIX standards. ⊃UNIX was the original basis of open systems and most non-proprietary open systems still use this ⊃operating system.

The term is also used more loosely to describe any system that can communicate with other systems and to describe other standards, such as ⊃MS-DOS and ⊃Windows. Open systems were developed partly to make better communication possible, but also to reduce users' dependence on (and lock-in to) suppliers of proprietary systems.

Open Systems Interconnection (OSI) ⊃International Standards Organization standard, defining seven layers of communication protocols. Although OSI is an international standard, existing protocols, such as ⊃TCP/IP and IBM's ⊃System Network Architecture are more commonly used in commercial systems.

operating system (OS) in computing, a program that controls the basic operation of a computer. A typical OS controls the ⊃peripheral devices, organizes the filing system, provides a means of communicating with the operator, and runs other programs.

Some operating systems were written for specific computers, but some are accepted standards. These include CP/M (by Digital Research) and MS-DOS (by Microsoft) for microcomputers. UNIX (developed at AT&T's Bell Laboratories) is the standard on workstations, minicomputers, and supercomputers; it is also used on desktop PCs and mainframes.

Operating system	Developer	Interface	Use	Features
DOS	Microsoft and IBM 1981	command line	IBM-compatible PCs	most widely used system
OS/2	IBM and Microsoft late 1980s	GUI	IBM-compatible computers	multitasking
Mac Operating System	Apple 1984	pioneered GUI	Macintosh	allows plug and play peripherals
UNIX	AT&T late 1960s	complex commands	from mainframes to PCs	multiuser, multitasking
Windows	Microsoft	GUI	dominates the PC market	support for peripheral devices
Windows 95	Microsoft 1995	GUI	Intel-based PCs	multitasking and multimedia

Major operating systems (OS)

optical character recognition (OCR) a technique for inputting text to a computer by means of a document reader. First, a ⌐scanner produces a digital image of the text; then character-recognition software makes use of stored knowledge about the shapes of individual characters to convert the digital image to a set of internal codes that can be stored and processed by computer.

OCR originally required specially designed characters but current devices can recognize most standard typefaces and even handwriting. OCR is used, for example, by gas and electricity companies to input data collected on meter-reading cards, and by ⌐personal digital assistants to recognize users' handwriting.

optical computer computer in which both light and electrical signals are used in the ⌐central processing unit. The technology is still not fully developed, but such a computer promises to be faster and less vulnerable to outside electrical interference than one that relies solely on electricity.

optical disc a storage medium in which laser technology is used to record and read large volumes of digital data. Types include ⌐CD-ROM, ⌐WORM, and erasable optical disc.

optical fibre very fine, optically pure glass fibre through which light can be reflected to transmit images or data from one end to the other. Although expensive to produce and install, optical fibres can carry more data than traditional cables, and are less susceptible to interference.

Optical fibres are increasingly being used to replace metal communications cables, the messages being encoded as digital pulses of light rather than as fluctuating electric current. Current research is investigating how optical fibres could replace wiring inside computers.

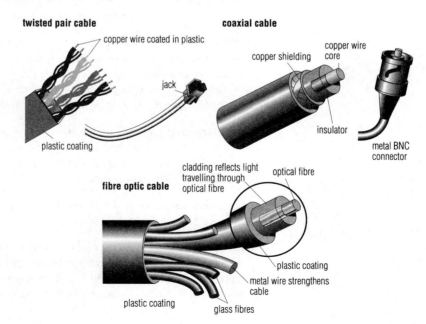

optical fibre
The major differences in construction between twisted pair (telephone), coaxial (Ethernet), and fibre optic cable.

Bundles of optical fibres are also used in endoscopes to inspect otherwise inaccessible parts of machines or of the living body.

optical mark recognition (OMR) in computing, a technique that enables marks made in predetermined positions on computer-input forms to be detected optically and input to a computer. An *optical mark reader* shines a light beam onto the input document and is able to detect the marks because less light is reflected back from them than from the paler, unmarked paper.

OR gate in electronics, a type of ⌐logic gate.

original equipment manufacturer in computing, company that actually makes computers and other items of ⌐hardware, as opposed to one that assembles components to make a marketable product.

OSI abbreviation for *⌐Open Systems Interconnection*.

OS/2 single-user computer ⌐operating system produced jointly by Microsoft Corporation and IBM for use on large microcomputers. Its main features are ⌐multitasking and the ability to access large amounts of internal ⌐memory.

OS/2 was announced 1987. Microsoft abandoned it 1992 to concentrate on ⌐DOS, but it continues to be marketed by IBM. *OS/2 Warp* is a variation optimized to run Windows programs.

outline font ⌐font in which the outline of each character is defined by a mathematical formula, making the font scalable to any size. Outline fonts can be output using the resolution of the output device, unlike ⌐bit map fonts, which can be output only at one size and one resolution. The most common forms of outline fonts are ⌐PostScript and ⌐TrueType.

output device any device for displaying, in a form intelligible to the user, the results of processing carried out by a computer.

The most common output devices are the ⌐VDU (visual display unit, or screen) and the printer. Other output devices include graph plotters, speech synthesizers, and COM (computer output on microfilm/microfiche).

OverDrive chip a plug-in replacement for an Intel microprocessor, designed to speed up the PC in which it is used. Intel OverDrive chips are expensive but are cheaper than buying a new PC and offer a simpler upgrade path than replacing the computer's ⌐motherboard.

overflow error an ⌐error that occurs if a number is outside the computer's range and is too large to deal with.

overlay set of specialized data for use with a larger database. A database of a particular country's geography, for example, that includes roads, towns, and natural features such as rivers and lakes might come with overlays that can be displayed or turned off at the user's command, such as the distribution of speed cameras.

packet unit of data sent across a network. As well as the actual substance of the message, every packet carries error-control information and details of its origin and its final target, enabling a ➥router to send it on to the intended recipient. This means that packets belonging to the same file can travel via different routes over the network, to be automatically reassembled in the correct sequence when they arrive at their destination. All traffic on the Internet consists of packets. See also ➥TCP/IP and ➥X.25.

packet radio the use of amateur (ham) radio, instead of telephones, to communicate between computers. A terminal node controller (TNC) replaces the modem, a radio transceiver takes the place of the telephone, and the phone system is replaced by radio waves. Packet radio, which works on several different frequencies, has a complete network of its own, complete with satellite links and terrestrial relays. It cannot be used to access the Internet, but it can be connected through the Internet.

packet switching a method of transmitting data between computers connected in a ➥network. A complete packet consists of the data being transmitted and information about which a computer is to receive the data. The packet travels around the network until it reaches the correct destination.

page-description language in computing, a control language used to describe the contents and layout of a complete printed page. Page-description languages are frequently used to control the operation of ➥laser printers. The most popular page-description languages are Adobe Postscript and Hewlett-Packard Printer Control Language.

page printer computer ➥printer that prints a complete page of text and graphics at a time. Page printers use electrostatic techniques, very similar to those used by photocopiers, to form images of pages, and range in size from small ➥laser printers designed to work with microcomputers to very large machines designed for high-volume commercial printing.

paging method of increasing a computer's apparent memory capacity. See ➥virtual memory.

paint program in computing, program that enables users to 'paint' a picture on their computer screens, using a variety of brushes, spray-guns, and colours.

Paintshop Pro in computing, popular graphics or 'paint' program for Microsoft Windows created by US software house JASC Inc. It is distributed as ➥shareware.

PAL (abbreviation for *Phase Alternation by Line*) British and Chinese video standard, with a higher definition and different screen format from the US NTSC standard. Running a program written for PAL on an NTSC system can result in the bottom of the screen image being cut off.

Pantone Matching System trade name for a standard set of colours used in graphics and printing, precisely graded and numbered using a universal system.

Colours shown on monitors and computer printers are not reliable enough for most designers, so print graphics programs usually include the facility to specify the desired Pantone colours.

parallax in ↩virtual reality, the distance between the viewer's left and right eyes in the virtual world.

This difference is what creates the impression of depth. Right and left images of distant objects look the same; but left and right images of nearby objects look markedly different owing to the difference of perspective. Manipulating this variable in a virtual world helps make objects look large or small.

parallel device a device that communicates binary data by sending the bits that represent each character simultaneously along a set of separate data lines, unlike a ↩serial device.

parallel processing emerging computer technology that allows more than one computation at the same time. Although in the 1980s this technology enabled only a small number of computer processor units to work in parallel, in theory thousands or millions of processors could be used at the same time.

Parallel processing, which involves breaking down computations into small parts and performing thousands of them simultaneously, rather than in a linear sequence, offers the prospect of a vast improvement in working speed for certain repetitive applications.

parallel running a method of implementing a new computer system in which the new system and the old system are run together for a short while. The old system is therefore available to take over from its replacement should any faults arise. An alternative method is ↩pilot running.

parameter variable factor or characteristic. For example, length is one parameter of a rectangle; its height is another. It is frequently useful to describe a program or object with a set of variable parameters rather than fixed values.

For example, if a programmer writes a routine for drawing a rectangle using general parameters for the length, height, line thickness, and so on, any rectangle can be drawn by this routine by giving different values to the parameters.

Similarly, in a word-processing application that stores parameters for font, page layout, type of ↩justification, and so on, these can be changed by the user.

parity of a number, the state of being either even or odd. The term refers to the number of 1s in the binary codes used to represent data. A binary representation has *even parity* if it contains an even number of 1s and *odd parity* if it contains an odd number of 1s.

For example, the binary code 1000001, commonly used to represent the character 'A', has even parity because it contains two 1s, and the binary code 1000011, commonly used to represent the character 'C', has odd parity because it contains three 1s. A *parity bit* (0 or 1) is sometimes added to each binary representation to give all the same parity so that a ↩validation check can be carried out each time data are transferred from one part of the computer to

Character	Binary code	Parity	Base-ten representation
A	1000001	even	65
B	1000010	even	66
C	1000011	odd	67
D	1000100	even	68

parity

another. So, for example, the codes 1000001 and 1000011 could have parity bits added and become *0*1000001 and *1*1000011, both with even parity. If any bit in these codes should be altered in the course of processing, the parity would change and the error would be quickly detected.

parity check a form of ⌒validation of data.

parse software facility for breaking down a data stream into individual pieces of information that can be acted upon. On the World Wide Web, for example, data entered by a user can be sent to a database program for storage and later analysis; the ability to do this depends on being able to feed the right bit of data into the right record field.

PASCAL (French acronym for *program appliqué à la sélection et la compilation automatique de la littérature*) a high-level computer-programming language. Designed by Niklaus Wirth (1934–   ) in the 1960s as an aid to teaching programming, it is still widely used as such in universities, and as a good general-purpose programming language. Most professional programmers, however, now use ⌒C or ⌒C++. Pascal was named after 17th-century French mathematician Blaise Pascal.

passive matrix display or *passive matrix LCD* ⌒liquid crystal display (LCD) produced by passing a current between an array of electrodes set between glass plates. Passive matrix screens lack the transistors that enhance the performance of ⌒active matrix LCDs, which makes them relatively inexpensive, but lacking in contrast and slow to react.

password secret combination of characters used in computing to ensure ⌒data security.

patch modification or update made to a program, consisting of a short segment of additional code. Developers often correct bugs or fine-tune software by releasing a patch which rewrites existing codes and adds new material.

PC card standard for 'credit card' memory and device cards used in ⌒portable computers. As well as providing ⌒flash memory, PC cards can provide either additional disc storage, or modem or fax functionality.

PCI (abbreviation for *peripheral component interconnect*) form of ⌒local bus connection between external devices and the main ⌒central processing unit.

Developed (but not owned) by ⌒Intel, it was 32-bit 1993, but is now available as 64-bit.

PCL ⌒page description language, developed by Hewlett Packard for use on Laserjet laser printers. Versions PCL 1 to PCL 4 used ⌒raster graphics fonts; PCL 5 uses ⌒outline fonts.

PCMCIA (abbreviation for *Personal Computer Memory Card International Association*) another name for a *PC card*.

PCX bitmapped ⌒graphics file format, originally developed by Z-Soft for use with PC-Paintbrush, but now used and generated by many applications and hardware such as scanners.

PDF (abbreviation for *portable document format*) file format created by Adobe's ⌒Acrobat system that retains the entire content of an electronic document (including layouts, graphics, styled text, and navigation features) regardless of the computer system on which it is viewed. Because they are platform-independent, PDF files are a good way to send documents over the Internet.

PeaceNet computer network dedicated to the cause of world peace and social justice. PeaceNet carries specialist news and information services which are used by many human rights and disarmament organizations. Compare ⌒GreenNet.

peer-to-peer networking in computing, method of file-sharing in which computers are linked to each other as opposed to being linked to a central file server.

pen-based computer computer (usually portable), for which input is by means of a pen or stylus, rather than a keyboard. It incorporates handwriting recognition software, although prior to the release of the Apple ⌒Newton and similar models, this had effectively meant using separate characters rather than 'joined-up' writing.

Pentium microchip produced by ⌒Intel 1993. The Pentium was designed to take advantage of the ⌒PCI ⌒local bus architecture, which increases the bandwidth available between devices. It was the first 64-bit microprocessor (see ⌒bit). The *Pentium Pro* was launched Nov 1995. It is a 64-bit microprocessor containing 5.5 million transistors compared with Pentium's 3.1 million, and can execute 166 million instructions per second, with a clock speed of up to 200 MHz (megahertz).

An error in the 5 million Pentium chips manufactured 1993–Dec 1994 cost Intel at least $30 million to replace the chips.

peripheral device in computing, any item connected to a computer's ⌒central processing unit (CPU). Typical peripherals include keyboard, mouse, monitor and printer. Users who enjoy playing games might add a ⌒joystick or a ⌒trackball; others might connect a ⌒modem, ⌒scanner, or ⌒integrated services digital network (ISDN) terminal to their machines.

personal computer (PC) another name for ⌐microcomputer. The term is also used, more specifically, to mean the IBM Personal Computer and computers compatible with it.

The first IBM PC was introduced in 1981; it had 64 kilobytes of random access memory (RAM) and one floppy-disc drive. It was followed in 1983 by the XT (with a hard-disc drive) and in 1984 by the AT (based on a more powerful ⌐microprocessor). Many manufacturers have copied the basic design, which is now regarded as a standard for business microcomputers. Computers designed to function like an IBM PC are ***IBM-compatible computers***.

personal digital assistant (PDA) handheld computer designed to store names, addresses, and diary information, and to send and receive faxes and e-mail. They aim to provide a more flexible and powerful alternative to the filofax or diary, but have met limited success.

Some PDAs (such as Apple's ⌐Newton) can recognize the user's handwriting and store it as digital text (with variable accuracy). Less ambitious PDAs, such as the Psion Series 3, have achieved modest success.

personal identification device (PID) device, such as a magnetic card, carrying machine readable identification, which provides authorization for access to a computer system. PIDs are often used in conjunction with a ⌐PIN.

printer

*trackball
(alternative to mouse)*

computer projector

*microphone
and speaker
(if computer has
soundcard)*

mouse

scanner

modem

peripheral device
*Some of the types of
peripheral device that may
be connected to a
computer include printers,
scanners, and modems.*

personal productivity software in computing, work-oriented software such as ⌐word processors, ⌐spreadsheets, or ⌐databases.

PGP abbreviation for the encryption program ⌐Pretty Good Privacy.

phong shading type of shading used in animation and 3-D graphics, based on a computerized model of how light is reflected from surfaces.

PhotoCD picture storage and viewing system developed by Kodak and Philips. The aim of Kodak's PhotoCD is to allow the user to put up to 100 photos onto compact disc: images are transferred from film to a PhotoCD disc and can then be viewed by means of Kodak's own PhotoCD player, which plugs into a television set, or by using suitable software on a multimedia PC.

PhotoCD is based on **multisession** ⌐WORM (write-once read many times) technology. The images can be written to the disc in multiple recording sessions. Later versions of the PhotoCD format will allow the user to add graphics and sound.

phreaking using computer technology to make free long-distance phone calls, charge them to another account, or otherwise illegally access the telephone network. In the 1980s, phreaking was semi-respectable among hackers (see ⌐hacking, but it is now less reputable – and thanks to improved security in the phone network, much more difficult. The case of Kevin ⌐Mitnick did much to bring phreaking to public attention.

PICS (abbreviation for *platform for Internet oontent selection*) in computing, method of classifying data according to its content. Under PICS, the creator and the reader of a file can add descriptive electronic labels to it, making it possible for users to sort documents according to keywords on the label. The system, introduced 1996, aims to help parents to control what their children can see on the Internet, for example by blocking access to pornographic or violent material; it also enables people to highlight subjects in which they are especially interested.

PICT object-oriented file format used on the ⌐Macintosh computer. The format uses ⌐Quickdraw and is supported by almost all graphics applications on the Macintosh.

pilot running a method of implementing a new computer system in which the work is gradually transferred from the old system to the new system over a period of time. This ensures that any faults in the new system are resolved before the old system is withdrawn. An alternative method is ⌐parallel running.

PIN (acronym for *personal identification number*) in banking, a unique number used as a password to establish the identity of a customer using an automatic cash dispenser. The PIN is normally encoded into the magnetic strip of the customer's bank card and is known only to the customer and to the bank's computer. Before a cash dispenser will issue money or information, the customer must insert the card into a slot in the machine (so that the PIN can be read from the magnetic strip) and enter the PIN correctly at a keyboard. This helps to prevent stolen cards from being used to obtain money from cash dispensers.

Pine (acronym for *program for Internet news and e-mail*) electronic mail program for ⮑UNIX and ⮑MS-DOS. Pine grew out of ⮑Elm, an older UNIX e-mailer, and includes on-line help and a user-friendly text editor called Pico.

PING (contraction of *Packet Internet Groper*) short message sent over a network by one computer to check whether another is correctly connected to it. By extension, one can 'ping' other people – for example, checking addresses on a ⮑mailing list by sending an ⮑e-mail to all members requesting an acknowledgement.

PIPEX (contraction of *public Internet protocol exchange*) UK-based Internet provider which started operations 1992, specializing in serving the commercial sector. The company became one of the UK's major ⮑backbone providers and was acquired by ⮑UUNET 1996.

Pixar Hollywood animation company bought by Steve ⮑Jobs in 1986. In 1995 Pixar, together with Walt Disney, released *Toy Story*, the first ever feature-length computer-animated cartoon film.

pixel (derived from *picture element*) single dot on a computer screen. All screen images are made up of a collection of pixels, with each pixel being either off (dark) or on (illuminated, possibly in colour). The number of pixels available determines the screen's resolution. Typical resolutions of microcomputer screens vary from 320 x 200 pixels to 640 x 480 pixels, but screens with 1,024 x 768 pixels are now common for high-quality graphic (pictorial) displays.

The number of bits (binary digits) used to represent each pixel determines how many colours it can display: a two-bit pixel can have four colours; an eight-bit (one-byte) pixel can have 256 colours. The higher the resolution of a screen and the more colours it is capable of displaying, the more memory will be needed in order to store that screen's contents.

PKZIP widely-used shareware file compression utility. Files created with PKZIP (often posted to ⮑newsgroups and ⮑bulletin boards) bear the suffix .zip and are said to be 'zipped'. A purported update of the program, called PKZIP3, appeared in 1995, carrying a Trojan horse which attempted to reformat the user's hard disc on installation.

plaintext another name for ⮑cleartext.

.plan file publicly accessible on ⮑UNIX systems that holds whatever information users wish to make public about themselves.

On other services such records may be called a resumé, bio, or directory entry. The purpose is generally the same, to allow users of the same system to find out a little more about the real-world identity of the people with whom they are interacting.

plasma display type of flat display, which uses an ionized gas between two panels containing grids of wires. When current flows through the wires a ⮜pixel is charged, causing it to light up.

platform the ⮜operating system, together with the ⮜hardware on which it runs.

Platform for Internet Content Selection method of classifying data, usually abbreviated to ⮜PICS.

Playstation ⮜games console made by ⮜Sony.

plotter or *graph plotter* device that draws pictures or diagrams under computer control.

Plotters are often used for producing business charts, architectural plans, and engineering drawings. *Flatbed plotters* move a pen up and down across a flat drawing surface, whereas *roller plotters* roll the drawing paper past the pen as it moves from side to side.

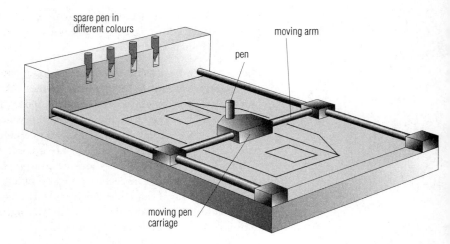

plotter
A flatbed plotter, which may be used to produce plans, graphs, and other drawings. The moving arm, holding a pen of the appropriate colour, travels over the surface of the paper.

plug and play item of hardware or software that configures itself and the user's system automatically when first installed. Having been thus 'plugged' in, it can be used ('played' with) immediately.

plug-and-play in computing, manufacturer's promise that hardware and software components will work together without complicated configuring.

plug-in small add-on file which enhances the operation of an application program, often by enabling it to launch, display or interpret a file created using another one. The first plug-ins were made for graphics programs in the 1980s, but the practice became very popular in the mid-1990s, when a range of plug-ins became available to enhance the multimedia capabilites of ⮜Netscape's Navigator ⮜browser. Plug-ins are often created and distributed by independent developers rather than the manufacturer of the program they extend.

Plug-in	Web address	Description
CoolFusion	wwwr.iterated.com	streaming AVI player for movie clips
CoolTalk	www.insoft.com	integrated into Netscape 3.0; allows talking in real time with sound card and microphone
Crescendo 2.0	www.liveupdate.com	compact MIDI player for audio
Quicktime	quicktime.apple.com	Apple's digitized video format
RealAudio	www.realaudio.com	standard audio plug in; streaming sound and music player
Shockwave	www.macromedia.com	allows appreciation of effects used in hundreds of Web sites
WIRL	www.vream.com	supports VRML standard; allows 3D interaction with objects

Some popular plug-ins

point and click in computing, basic method of navigating a ⮑Web page or a multimedia CD-ROM. The user points at an object using a cursor and a mouse, and clicks to activate it.

point of sale (POS) in business premises, the point where a sale is transacted, for example, a POS terminal such as a supermarket checkout. In conjunction with electronic funds transfer, point of sale is part of the terminology of 'cashless shopping', enabling buyers to transfer funds directly from their bank accounts to the shop's.

point-of-sale terminal (POS terminal) computer terminal used in shops to input and output data at the point where a sale is transacted; for example, at a supermarket checkout. The POS terminal inputs information about the identity of each item sold, retrieves the price and other details from a central computer, and prints out a fully itemized receipt for the customer. It may also input sales data for the shop's computerized stock-control system.

A POS terminal typically has all the facilities of a normal till, including a cash drawer and a sales register, plus facilities for the direct capture of sales information – commonly, a laser scanner for reading bar codes. It may also be equipped with a device to read customers' bank cards, so that payment can be transferred electronically from the customers' bank accounts to the shop's (see ⮑EFTPOS).

Point-to-Point Protocol in computing, methods of connecting a computer to the Internet; usually abbreviated to ⮑PPP.

polling a technique for transferring data from a terminal to the central computer of a ⮑multi-user system. The computer automatically makes a connection with each terminal in turn, interrogates it to check whether it is holding data for transmission, and, if it is, collects the data.

polyphony ability of a synthesizer to play more than one note at a time. If the synthesizer can produce more than one type of sound – for example, a flute and a guitar – simultaneously, it is ***multi-timbral***.

PoP (acronym for *point of presence*) place where users can access a network via a telephone connection. A PoP is a collection of modems and other equipment which are permanently connected to the network. Compare ⌐vPoP.

POP3 (abbreviation for *Post Office Protocol*) on the Internet, one of the two most common mail ⌐protocols.

Internet Service Providers (ISPs) offer ⌐SMTP, POP3, or both. The primary difference to most users is the choice of software available. SMTP is older and more flexible, but POP3 is generally simpler for those accessing the Internet via a dial-up account.

Commercial services such as CompuServe generally have their own proprietary mail software which uses proprietary protocols for internal mail and accesses Internet mail via a gateway.

pop-up menu a menu that appears in a (new) window when an option is selected with a mouse or key-stroke sequence in a ⌐graphical user interface (GUI), such as Windows 95. Compare with ⌐pull-down menu.

pornography, Internet material of an explicitly sexual nature, whether it be text, photographs, graphics, audio, or video available on the Internet.

The amount of pornography and the ease of finding it has been exaggerated by both politicians and mass media. Nonetheless, there is material available on the Internet to offend almost everyone, and most governments are either attempting or considering some means of ⌐censorship.

port a socket that enables a computer processor to communicate with an external device. It may be an *input port* (such as a joystick port), or an *output port* (such as a printer port), or both (an *i/o port*).

Microcomputers may provide ports for cartridges, televisions and/or monitors, printers, and modems, and sometimes for hard discs and musical instruments (MIDI, the musical-instrument digital interface). Ports may be serial or parallel.

port
The two types of communications port in a microcomputer. The parallel port enables upto eight bits of data to travel through it at any one time; the serial port enables only one.

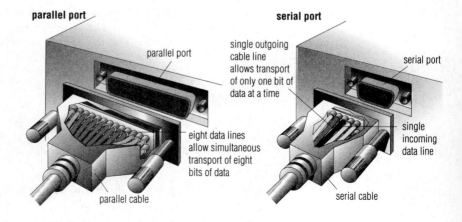

parallel port

parallel port

single outgoing cable line allows transport of only one bit of data at a time

serial port

serial port

eight data lines allow simultaneous transport of eight bits of data

single incoming data line

parallel cable

serial cable

portability the characteristic of certain programs that enables them to run on different types of computer with minimum modification. Programs written in a ⇔high-level language can usually be run on any computer that has a compiler or interpreter for that particular language.

portable computer computer that can be carried from place to place. The term embraces a number of very different computers – from those that would be carried only with some reluctance to those, such as ⇔laptop computers and ⇔notebook computers, that can be comfortably carried and used in transit.

port address on the Internet, a way for a host system to specify which ⇔server a particular application will use.

Users generally should not have to worry about port addresses, as applications like Telnet and the World Wide Web mostly use standard addresses (for Telnet, port 23) and the client software will fill these in automatically. Occasionally, a non-standard address will specify a different port, and in these cases the user must add the non-standard port number to the end of the address.

POSIX (acronym for *portable operating system interface for computers – developed from UNIX*) ⇔ANSI standard, developed to describe how the programming interfaces and other features of ⇔UNIX worked, in order to remove control from the developers, AT&T Bell Laboratories. Subsequently many other (proprietary) ⇔operating systems were modified in order to become POSIX-compliant, that is, they provide an ⇔open systems interface, so that they can communicate with other POSIX-compliant systems, even though the operating systems themselves are internally quite different. See also ⇔open systems interconnection.

post to send a message to a ⇔newsgroup or ⇔bulletin board for others to read.

POS terminal acronym for ⇔point of sale terminal, a cash register linked to a computer.

posting another word for ⇔article.

postmaster in computing, ⇔systems administrator in charge of a mail server. The term is especially used for people who manage the electronic mail system in a ⇔local area network (LAN) or other local network.

PostScript a page-description language developed by Adobe that has become a standard. PostScript is primarily a language for printing documents on laser printers, but it can be adapted to produce images on other types of devices.

PostScript is an object-oriented language, meaning that it treats images, including fonts, as collections of geometrical objects rather than as ⇔bit maps. PostScript fonts are ⇔outline fonts stored in the computer memory as a set of instructions for drawing the circles, straight lines and curves that make up the outline of each character. This means they are also scalable. Given a single typeface definition, a PostScript printer can thus produce a multitude of fonts.

The principal advantage of ↝vector graphics over bit-mapped graphics is that object-oriented images take advantage of high-resolution output devices whereas bit-mapped images do not. A PostScript drawing looks much better when printed on a 600 ↝dpi printer than on a 300 dpi printer. Object-oriented images also generally require less memory than bit-mapped images.

PowerPC ↝microprocessor produced by ↝Motorola as the successor to its 680X0 series of microprocessors. It uses ↝RISC technology to provide great processing speed. The PowerPC chip was introduced in Apple's PowerMacintosh 1994.

PowerPoint in computing, ↝presentation graphics program made by ↝Microsoft.

PPP (abbreviation for *Point-to-Point Protocol*) one of two standard methods for connecting a computer to the Internet via a modem and line. PPP is faster and more versatile than its counterpart, ↝SLIP, and performs its own error correction.

presentation graphics in computing, program that helps users to create presentations such as visual aids, handouts, and overhead slides. Presentation graphics programs process artwork, graphics, and text to produce a series of 'slides' – images which help speakers to get their message across. Leading programs include Microsoft ↝PowerPoint and (for ↝multimedia presentations, incorporating moving pictures and sounds) Macromedia Director.

Software	Manufacturer	Description
Adobe Persuasion	Adobe	with outlines, speaker's notes
ASAP WordPower	SPC	few features but extremely simple to use
Astound	Gold Disk	easy-to-use business presentation package with multimedia features
Freelance	Lotus	full of features; very effective outline view
PowerPoint	Microsoft	allows incorporating spreadsheet and wp elements into presentations
Presentation	Corel	formerly WordPerfect Presentation
Also: Fanfare! (Softkey), Harvard Graphics (SPC)		

Some major presentation software programs

Prestel the ↝viewdata service provided by British Telecom (BT), which provides information on the television screen via the telephone network. BT pioneered the service 1975.

Pretty Good Privacy (PGP) in computing, strong encryption program that runs on personal computers and is distributed on the Net free of charge. It was written by Phil ↝Zimmermann and released to the Net in 1991 amid growing fears that the USA would pass a law requiring all secure communications systems to incorporate a 'back door' to make it easy for law enforcement officials to read encrypted messages.

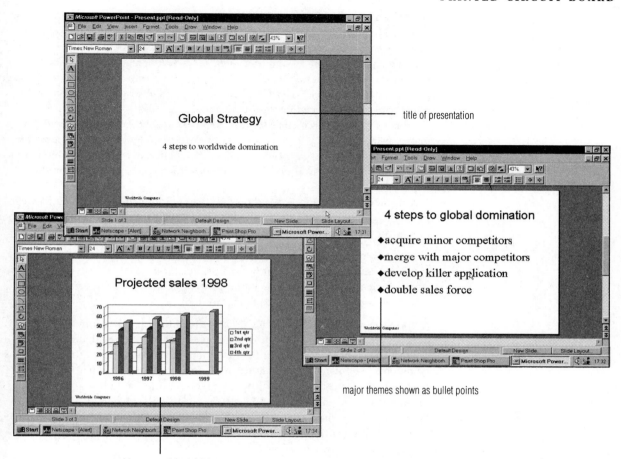

title of presentation

major themes shown as bullet points

graphic representaion of data

presentation graphics
An example of how a presentation may be created on computer using an appropriate software package. The presentation is built up in stages, and may include graphical images as well as text.

PGP is based on the ⟳RSA ⟳algorithm and uses ⟳public-key cryptography; its source code has been released to the cryptographic community for study and testing. Since version 1.0, its development has proceeded in multiple locations around the world to avoid conflicts with the US laws banning the export of strong encryption. A companion product, PGPfone, released 1996, runs across the Internet to give users the equivalent of a military grade secure telephone.

print to transfer data to a ⟳printer, to a screen or to another file.

printed circuit board (PCB) electrical circuit created by laying (printing) 'tracks' of a conductor such as copper on one or both sides of an insulating board. The PCB was invented in 1936 by Austrian scientist Paul Eisler, and was first used on a large scale in 1948.

Components such as integrated circuits (chips), resistors and capacitors can be soldered to the surface of the board (surface-mounted) or, more commonly, attached by inserting their connecting pins or wires into holes drilled in the board. PCBs include ⟳motherboards, ⟳expansion boards, and adaptors.

printer an output device for producing printed copies of text or graphics. Types include the ⌐*daisywheel printer*, which produces good-quality text but no graphics; the ⌐*dot matrix printer*, which produces text and graphics by printing a pattern of small dots; the ⌐*ink-jet printer*, which creates text and graphics by spraying a fine jet of quick-drying ink onto the paper; and the ⌐*laser printer*, which uses electrostatic technology very similar to that used by a photocopier to produce high-quality text and graphics.

Printers may be classified as ***impact printers*** (such as daisywheel and dot-matrix printers), which form characters by striking an inked ribbon against the paper, and ***nonimpact printers*** (such as ink-jet and laser printers), which use a variety of techniques to produce characters without physical impact on the paper.

A further classification is based on the basic unit of printing, and categorizes printers as character printers, line printers, or page printers, according to whether they print one character, one line, or a complete page at a time.

print spooler in computing, ⌐utility program that stores information in a temporary file before sending it on to a printer. Print spoolers help computers to work efficiently, allowing the ⌐central processing unit (CPU) to carry on with other work while a document is being printed.

privacy on the Internet, generally used to mean the right to control who has access to the personal information generated by interaction with computers.

The right to privacy is one of the most hotly debated issues on the Internet, as commercial suppliers seek to gather more and more information about their customers. The most common approaches to securing the right to privacy are technological, via encryption, and legislative, via laws such as Britain's Data Protection Act. A third approach is to use services such as ⌐anonymous remailers to strip identifying information from individual messages when posting contentious or sensitive material.

privacy enhanced mail (PEM) in computing, Internet protocol that gives a degree of confidentiality to ⌐e-mail, using various ⌐public-key cryptography methods.

procedural programming programming in which programs are written as lists of instructions for the computer to obey in sequence. It closely matches the computer's own sequential operation.

procedure a small part of a computer program that performs a specific task, such as clearing the screen or sorting a file. A ***procedural language***, such as ⌐BASIC, is one in which the programmer describes a task in terms of how it is to be done, as opposed to a ***declarative language***, such as ⌐PROLOG, in which it is described in terms of the required result. See ⌐programming.

Careful use of procedures is an element of ⌐structured programming. In some programming languages there is an overlap between procedures, ⌐functions, and ⌐subroutines.

process control automatic computerized control of a manufacturing process, such as glassmaking. The computer receives ⌐feedback information from sensors about the performance of the machines involved, and compares this with ideal performance data stored in its control program. It then outputs instructions to adjust automatically the machines' settings.

Because the computer can monitor and reset each machine hundreds of times each minute, performance can be maintained at levels that are very close to the ideal.

processing cycle the sequence of steps performed repeatedly by a computer in the execution of a program. The computer's CPU (central processing unit) continuously works through a loop, involving fetching a program instruction from memory, fetching any data it needs, operating on the data, and storing the result in the memory, before fetching another program instruction.

processor another name for the ↝central processing unit or ↝microprocessor of a computer.

Prodigy on-line service launched 1988 by a partnership of ↝IBM and leading US retailer Sears Roebuck; bought 1996 by the global communications company International Wireless, which relaunched it as an Internet service.

Even though Prodigy has been lavishly funded, throughout its history it has lagged behind ↝CompuServe and ↝America Online (AOL). By 1996, it had 1.4 million subscribers, but had never marketed itself outside North America. In late 1996, Prodigy announced it would launch a Spanish-language service in Mexico.

program a set of instructions that controls the operation of a computer. There are two main kinds: ↝applications programs, which carry out tasks for the benefit of the user – for example, word processing; and ↝systems programs, which control the internal workings of the computer. A ↝utility program is a systems program that carries out specific tasks for the user. Programs can be written in any of a number of ↝programming languages but are always translated into machine code before they can be executed by the computer.

program counter an alternative name for ↝sequence-control register.

program documentation ↝documentation that provides a complete technical description of a program, built up as the software is written, and is intended to support any later maintenance or development of the program.

program files files which contain the code used by a computer program.

program flow chart type of ↝flow chart used to describe the flow of data through a particular computer program.

program loop part of a computer program that is repeated several times. The loop may be repeated a fixed number of times (***counter-controlled loop***) or until a certain condition is satisfied (***condition-controlled loop***). For example, a counter-controlled loop might be used to repeat an input routine until exactly ten numbers have been input; a condition-controlled loop might be used to repeat an input routine until the ↝data terminator 'XXX' is entered.

Program Manager the main screen, or 'front end', of the software product Microsoft Windows. All Windows operations can be accessed from Program Manager.

programmer job classification for ⌒computer personnel. Programmers write the software needed for any new computer system or application.

programming writing instructions in a programming language for the control of a computer. ***Applications programming*** is for end-user programs, such as accounts programs or word-processing packages. ***Systems programming*** is for operating systems and the like, which are concerned more with the internal workings of the computer.

There are several programming styles:

procedural programming, in which programs are written as lists of instructions for the computer to obey in sequence, is by far the most popular. It is the 'natural' style, closely matching the computer's own sequential operation; ***declarative programming***, as used in the programming language ⌒PROLOG, does not describe how to solve a problem, but rather describes the logical structure of the problem. Running such a program is more like proving an assertion than following a procedure; ***functional programming*** is a style based largely on the definition of functions. There are very few functional programming languages, HOPE and ML being the most widely used, though many more conventional languages (for example ⌒C) make extensive use of functions; ***object-oriented programming***, the most recently developed style, involves viewing a program as a collection of objects that behave in certain ways when they are passed certain 'messages'. For example, an object might be defined to represent a table of figures, which will be displayed on screen when a 'display' message is received.

programming language in computing, a special notation in which instructions for controlling a computer are written. Programming languages are designed to be easy for people to write and read, but must be capable of being mechanically translated (by a ⌒compiler or an ⌒interpreter) into the ⌒machine code that the computer can execute. Programming languages may be classified as ⌒high-level languages or ⌒low-level languages. See also ⌒source language.

program trading in finance, buying and selling a group of shares using a computer program to generate orders automatically whenever there is an appreciable movement in prices.

One form in use in the USA in 1989 was ***index arbitrage***, in which a program traded automatically whenever there was a difference between New York and Chicago prices of an equivalent number of shares. Program trading comprised some 14% of daily trading on the New York Stock Exchange by volume in Sept 1989, but was widely criticized for lessening market stability. It has been blamed, among other factors, for the Stock Market crashes of 1987 and 1989.

Project Gutenberg an electronic 'library' containing hundreds of 'etexts' – books made freely accessible via the ⌒World Wide Web and downloadable via ⌒FTP. The

Language	Main uses	Description
Ada	defence applications	high level
assembler languages	jobs needing detailed control of the hardware, fast execution, and small program size	fast and efficient but require considerable effort and skill
BASIC (**b**eginners' **a**ll-purpose **s**ymbolic **i**nstruction **c**ode)	mainly in education, business, and the home, and among nonprofessional programmers, such as engineers	easy to learn; early versions lacked the features of other languages
C	systems programming; general programming	fast and efficient; widely used as a general-purpose language; especially popular among professional programmers
C++	systems and general programming; commercial software development	developed from C, adding the advantages of object-oriented programming
COBOL (**co**mmon **b**usiness-**o**riented **l**anguage)	business programming	strongly oriented towards commercial work; easy to learn but very verbose; widely used on mainframes
FORTH	control applications	reverse Polish notation language
FORTRAN (**for**mula **tran**slation)	scientific and computational work	based on mathematical formulae; popular among engineers, scientists, and mathematicians
Java	developed for consumer electronics; used for many interactive Web sites	multipurpose cross-platform object-oriented language with similar features to C and C++ but simpler
LISP (**lis**t **p**rocessing)	artificial intelligence	symbolic language with a reputation for being hard to learn; popular in the academic and research communities
Modula-2	systems and real-time programming; general programming highly structured	intended to replace Pascal for 'real-world' applications
OBERON	general programming	small, compact language incorporating many of the features of PASCAL and Modula-2
PASCAL (**p**rogram **a**ppliqué à la **s**élection et la **c**ompilation **a**utomatique de la **l**ittérature)	general-purpose language	highly structured; widely used for teaching programming in universities
Perl (**p**athological **e**clectic **r**ubbish **l**ister)	systems programming and Web development	easy manipulation of text, files, and processes, especially in UNIX environment
PROLOG (**pro**gramming in **log**ic)	artificial intelligence	symbolic-logic programming system, originally intended for theorem solving but now used more generally in artificial intelligence

programming languages

project started in 1971 at the University of Illinois. For copyright reasons, most of the books available are classics dating from before the 20th century, but there are also some current reference books – including the current *CIA factbook*.

PROLOG (acronym for *programming in logic*) high-level computer-programming language based on logic. Invented in 1971 at the University of Marseille, France, it did not achieve widespread use until more than ten years later. It is used mainly for ∾artificial intelligence programming.

PROM (acronym for *programmable read-only memory*) a memory device in the form of an integrated circuit (chip) that can be programmed after manufacture to hold information permanently. PROM chips are empty of information when manufactured, unlike ROM (read-only memory) chips, which have information built into them. Other memory devices are ∾EPROM (erasable programmable read-only memory) and ∾RAM (random-access memory).

prompt symbol displayed on a screen indicating that the computer is ready for input. The symbol used will vary from system to system and application to application. The current cursor position is normally next to the prompt. Generally prompts only appear in command line interfaces.

proportional font font in which individual letters of the alphabet take up different amounts of space according to their shape.

Computer *fixed fonts* are designed so that each letter has the same width and takes up the same amount of space on a line. A letter 'l', however, logically is thinner than a letter 'o'. Proportional fonts allow spacing according to these differences, and are therefore easier to read. Until the advent of personal computers and font software such as Adobe ∾PostScript, proportional spacing was the province of professional typography, used in books, newspapers, magazines, and other commercial publishing.

protected mode operating mode of ∾Intel microprocessors (80286 and above), which allows multitasking and provides other features such as ∾extended memory and ∾virtual memory (above 1 Gbyte). Protected mode operation also improves ∾data security.

protocol an agreed set of *standards* for the transfer of data between different devices. They cover transmission speed, format of data, and the signals required to synchronize the transfer. See also ∾interface.

proxy server on the ∾World Wide Web, a server which 'stands in' for another server, storing and forwarding files on behalf of a computer which might be slower or too busy to deal with the request itself. Many ∾URLs (Web addresses) redirect the enquirer to a proxy server which then supplies the requested page.

In 1996, the authorities in Singapore imposed a legal requirement on local Internet providers to filter all traffic via a government-run proxy server that can block access to various sites – the first serious government attempt to censor the Internet.

pseudonym name adopted by someone on the Internet, especially to participate in ⌐USENET or discussions using IRC (⌐Internet Relay Chat). Pseudonyms are often jokey or witty, and are sometimes used to conceal the user's gender or identity.

PSTN (abbreviation for *Public Switched Telephone Network*) telephone network used by the general public, and sometimes used as the medium to link ⌐LANs. PSTNs are minor roads which lead to the ⌐information superhighway.

public-domain software any computer program that is not under copyright and can therefore be used freely without charge. Much of this software has been written in US universities, under government contract. Public-domain software should not be confused with ⌐shareware, which is under copyright.

public key in ⌐public-key cryptography, a string of ⌐bits that is associated with a particular person and that may be used to decrypt messages from that person or to encrypt messages to him/her.

public-key cryptography system that allows remote users to exchange encrypted data without the need to transmit a secret key in advance. Under this system, first proposed by Whitfield Diffie and Martin Hellman in a widely read and influential paper *New Directions in Cryptography* 1976, each party has a personal pair of keys, one private and one public. The private key is kept secret and not given out to anyone. The public key, however, is distributed widely, to friends, business partners, and even to public key servers – computers which store many users' public keys so that anyone can obtain a copy. Each user asks as many people as possible to sign his/her public key, to verify that it is actually his/hers.

    The two keys are complementary. The sender of a message – usually known as Bob – encrypts his message with his private key and sends it to the recipient, usually called Alice. She decrypts it with her public key and by doing so verifies that the message came from him. If Bob wants the message to be unreadable by anyone but Alice, he encrypts it with her public key so it can only be decrypted with her private key, which she is keeping secret. Using both sets of keys authenticates the message and ensures its privacy.

    Several ⌐algorithms in common use apply public-key cryptography, including the ⌐RSA algorithm, published 1977 in *Scientific American* and named after its inventors, Ronald Rivest, Adi Shamir, and Leonard Adleman, and the Skipjack algorithm used in the ⌐Clipper chip. The disadvantage is that it is extremely slow, so it is common on the Net to see ⌐Pretty Good Privacy (PGP), which uses RSA, being used only to encrypt a digest of the message generated using a ⌐hash function. This is appended to the end of the message along with a listing of the user's public key.

public news server in computing, site, often provided by an institution, which provides free access to ⌐USENET. Public news servers offer an alternative to taking a news feed from an ⌐Internet Service Provider (ISP).

pull-down menu a list of options provided as part of a ⌐graphical user interface. The presence of pull-down menus is normally indicated by a row of single words at the top of the screen. When the user points at a word with a ⌐mouse, a full menu appears (is pulled down) and the user can then select the required option. Compare with ⌐pop-up menu.

In some graphical user interfaces the menus appear from the bottom of the screen and in others they may appear at any point on the screen when a special menu button is pressed on the mouse.

punched card an early form of data storage and input, now almost obsolete. The 80-column card widely used in the 1960s and 1970s was a thin card, measuring 190 mm x 84 mm/7.5 in x 3.33 in, holding up to 80 characters of data encoded as small rectangular holes.

The punched card was invented by French textile manufacturer Joseph-Marie Jacquard (1752–1834) in about 1801 to control weaving looms. The first data-processing machine using punched cards was developed by US inventor Herman ⌐Hollerith in the 1880s for the US census.

push-button in a ⌐dialog box or ⌐toolbar, a square, oval, or oblong button which presents the user with an option. By clicking on the button, the user opts to initiate an action such as centering text or saving a file. Most programs offer keyboard ⌐shortcuts as an alternative to using a pushbutton, for example one can often hit the return key instead of clicking the 'OK' button in a dialogue box. Compare ⌐radio button.

quad speed a ⮐CD-ROM drive that transfers data at 600 ⮐kilobytes per second – four times as fast as the first CD-ROM drives on the market. Because ⮐access time remains a key factor in the movement of data, the extra speed does not necessarily translate into a fourfold improvement in performance.

Quake computer game released 1996 as a successor to ⮐*Doom* and produced by ⮐id Software. It is a strategy game using ⮐3-D graphics.

Players navigate their way around 32 levels of mazes, uncovering secrets and combatting alien enemies. A command line console system allows players to enter ⮐source code to enhance play.

? wild card character standing for any single character in most operating systems. It allows a user to specify a group of files whose names differ by only one character for mass handling. Typing 'dir part?.doc' in a DOS directory would display a list of files such as part1.doc, party.doc, and so on. The letter 'x' is often used to mean the same thing.

queue backup of ⮐packets of data awaiting processing, or of ⮐e-mail waiting to be read.

Quickdraw object-based graphics display system used by the Apple ⮐Macintosh range of microcomputers. The use of Quickdraw gives most Macintosh applications the same ⮐look-and-feel.

Quicktime multimedia utility developed by Apple, initially for the ⮐Macintosh, but now also available for ⮐Windows. Allows multimedia, such as sound and video, to be embedded in other documents, including Web pages.

quoting common practice in electronic communications. When replying to an e-mail, or adding to a ⮐newsgroup ⮐thread, users quote all or part of the original message in their response. The usual method of doing this is by preceding each quoted line with the symbol >.

QWERTY standard arrangement of keys on a UK or US typewriter or computer keyboard. Q, W, E, R, T, and Y are the first six keys on the top alphabetic line. The arrangement was made to slow typists down in the days of mechanical keyboards in order that the keys would not jam together. Other European countries use different arrangements, such as AZERTY and QWERTZ, which are more appropriate to the language of the country.

radio button in a ↝dialog box, a round button denoting an option. Users are offered a choice of radio buttons, and can choose only one.

Raid (acronym for *redundant array of independent* (or *inexpensive*) *discs*) arrays of discs, each connected to a bus, that can be configured in different ways, depending on the application. Raid 1 is, for example, disc mirroring, while Raid 5 spreads every character between discs. Raid is intended to improve performance and data security.

RAM (acronym for *random-access memory*) a memory device in the form of a collection of ↝integrated circuits (chips), frequently used in microcomputers. Unlike ↝ROM (read-only memory) chips, RAM chips can be both read from and written to by the computer, but their contents are lost when the power is switched off. Many modern commercial programs require a great deal of RAM to work efficiently. The 8 megabytes (MB) of RAM with which most computers are sold with may not be enough: 16 MB is a minimum recommendation, and 32 MB, if you can afford it, will be ample for many years.

RAMdisc ↝RAM that has been configured to appear to the operating system as a disc. It is much faster to access than an actual hard disc and therefore can be used for applications that need frequent read-and-write operations. However, as the data is stored in RAM, it will be lost when the computer is turned off.

random access an alternative term for ↝direct access.

random number one of a series of numbers having no detectable pattern. Random numbers are used in ↝computer simulation and ↝computer games. It is impossible for an ordinary computer to generate true random numbers, but various techniques are available for obtaining pseudo-random numbers – close enough to true randomness for most purposes.

range check a ↝validation check applied to a numerical data item to ensure that its value falls in a sensible range.

RARE (abbreviation for *Réseaux Associés pour la Recherche Européenne*) association of national and international European computer networks and their users.

raster graphics computer graphics that are stored in the computer memory by using a map to record data (such as colour and intensity) for every ↝pixel that makes up the image. When transformed (enlarged, rotated, stretched, and so on), raster graphics become ragged and suffer loss of picture resolution, unlike ↝vector graphics. Raster graphics are typically used for painting applications, which allow the user to create artwork on a computer screen much as if they were painting on paper or canvas.

raster image processor full name for printer program ↝RIP.

ray-tracing in computer graphics, method of rendering sharp, detailed images. Designers specify the size, shape, colour, and texture of objects and the type and location of light sources, and use a program to devise a mathematical model tracing how light rays would bounce off the surfaces. The results, complete with shading, shadows, and reflections, depict 'virtual worlds' with near-photographic clarity.

read-only storage a permanent means of storing data so that it can be read any number of times but cannot be modified. CD-ROM is a read-only storage medium; CD-ROMs come with the data already encoded on them.

RealAudio software system for broadcasting sound over the Internet in real time. Broadcasters use an encoder and a special server to provide content, and members of the 'audience' can listen to live radio or create a customized news broadcast which they can download whenever they wish. RealAudio is also used to help ⮌multicasting live events such as rock concerts.

real-time system a program that responds to events in the world as they happen. For example, an automatic-pilot program in an aircraft must respond instantly in order to correct deviations from its course. Process control, robotics, games, and many military applications are examples of real-time systems.

record a collection of related data items or *fields*. A record usually forms part of a ⮌file.

recursion in computing and mathematics, a technique whereby a function or ⮌procedure calls itself into use in order to enable a complex problem to be broken down into simpler steps. For example, a function that finds the factorial of a number n (calculates the product of all the whole numbers between 1 and n) would obtain its result by multiplying n by the factorial of $n - 1$.

redundancy duplication of information. Redundancy is often used as a check, when an additional check digit or bit is included. See also ⮌validation.

refresh to redraw the image on a ⮌VDU. All such images are a series of frames created by a device – in the case of a cathode ray tube, an electron beam – which 'paints' the image on the screen, ⮌pixel by pixel. This process is too rapid for the human eye to detect, although a high *refresh rate* (number of times a screen is redrawn per second) is said to reduce eye strain.

register a memory location that can be accessed rapidly; it is often built into the computer's central processing unit.

Some registers are reserved for special tasks – for example, an *instruction register* is used to hold the machine-code command that the computer is currently executing, while a *sequence-control register* keeps track of the next command to be executed. Other registers are used for holding frequently used data and for storing intermediate results.

registration informing a manufacturer that you have bought their product. For computer hardware, registration brings the consumer benefits such as on-site service and access to a free telephone helpline. Software houses also give registered customers telephone support and may supply them with upgrades and new product information.

For ⇨shareware, registration is virtually synonymous with payment. Programs are supplied save-disabled, incomplete, or with frequent, annoying built-in reminders to register. Only by sending the small fee requested can the user obtain a code to release the program's full potential, as well as the legal right to continue using it.

relational database ⇨database in which data are viewed as a collection of linked tables. It is the most popular of the three basic database models, the others being *network* and *hierarchical*.

relative in computing (of a value), variable and calculated from a base value. For example, a *relative address* is a memory location that is found by adding a variable to a base (fixed) address, and a *relative cell reference* locates a cell in a spreadsheet by its position relative to a base cell – perhaps directly to the left of the base cell or three columns to the right of the base cell. The opposite of relative is ⇨absolute.

reload command which asks a ⇨browser to reopen a currently-displayed ⇨URL. Reloading may 'unstall' a partially-loaded page or bring a faster download from a busy server.

remote imaging photographing the Earth's surface with orbiting satellites. With a simple aerial, receiver and software it is possible to download images straight on to a personal computer – helping amateur meteorologists, for example, to make weather forecasts.

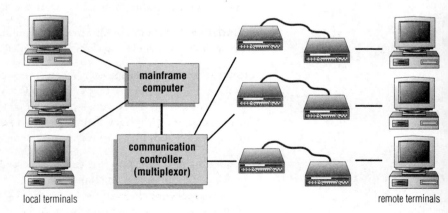

remote terminal
Remote terminals are able to communicate with the central mainframe via modems and telephone lines. The multiplexor allows more than one terminal to use the same communications link at the same time (multiplexing).

local terminals   remote terminals

remote terminal a terminal that communicates with a computer via a modem (or acoustic coupler) and a telephone line.

rendering using a computer to draw an image on a computer screen. In graphics this often means using ⇨ray-tracing, ⇨phong shading, or a similar program to turn an outline sketch into a detailed image of a solid object.

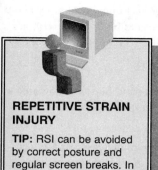

REPETITIVE STRAIN INJURY

TIP: RSI can be avoided by correct posture and regular screen breaks. In particular, keyboard users should ensure that their wrists are as straight as possible when inputting.

repetitive strain injury (RSI) inflammation of tendon sheaths, mainly in the hands and wrists, which may be disabling. It is found predominantly in factory workers involved in constant repetitive movements, and in those who work with computer keyboards. The symptoms include aching muscles, weak wrists, tingling fingers and in severe cases, pain and paralysis. Some victims have successfully sued their employers for damages.

The Trades Union Congress estimates that around 100,000 people a year visit their doctors because of upper limb injuries caused by RSI.

request for comments the expansion of the abbreviation ⬦RFC.

reserved word word that has a meaning special to a programming language. For example, 'if' and 'for' are reserved words in most high-level languages.

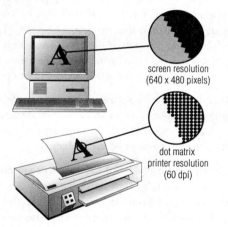

screen resolution
(640 x 480 pixels)

dot matrix
printer resolution
(60 dpi)

resolution
An example of typical resolutions of screens and printers. The resolution of a screen image when printed can only be as high as the resolution supported by the printer itself.

resolution the number of dots per unit length in which an image can be reproduced on a screen or printer. A typical screen resolution for colour monitors is 75 dpi (dots per inch). A ⬦laser printer will typically have a printing resolution of 300 dpi, and ⬦dot matrix printers typically have resolutions from 60 dpi to 180 dpi. Photographs in books and magazines have a resolution of 1,200 dpi or 2,400 dpi.

resolver see ⬦name server.

response time the delay between entering a command and seeing its effect.

return-to-base warranty in computing, a warranty on a piece of hardware that requires the owner to return it to the retailer or the factory for service. Compare ⬦on-site warranty.

reverse engineering analysing an existing piece of computer hardware or software by finding out what it does and then working out how it does it. Companies perform this process on their own products in order to iron out faults, and on their competitors' products in order to find out how they work. For example, the microchips in the first IBM PCs were reverse engineered by other computer firms to make compatible machines without infringing IBM's copyright.

reverse video alternative term for ⬦*inverse video*.

RFC (abbreviation for ***request for comments***) discussion document on the subject of standards for the Internet. RFCs start as technical proposals lodged with the Internet Architecture Board by computer engineers. The proposals are published on the Internet, where they are subject to general review. After any necessary amendments are made, RFCs become agreed procedures across the network.

RGB (abbreviation of *red–green–blue*) method of connecting a colour screen to a computer, involving three separate signals: red, green, and blue. All the colours displayed by the screen can be made up from these three component colours.

rich text format file format usually abbreviated to ☞RTF.

right click on IBM-compatible PCs, a click on the right-hand button of the mouse that brings up a context-sensitive menu presenting a range of options relevant to the user's current activity.

RIP (abbreviation for *raster image processor*) program in a laser printer (or other high-resolution printer) that converts the stream of printing instructions from a computer into the pattern of dots that make up the printed page. A separate program is required for each type of printer and for each page description language (such as ☞PostScript or ☞PCL).

RIPs are very demanding programs because of the complexity of a typical printed page. It is not unusual for RIPs to run on extremely fast and powerful ☞RISC ☞microprocessors, which are sometimes more powerful than the processor in the computer attached to the printer.

RiPEM (contraction of *Riordan's Internet Privacy Enhanced Mail*) in computing, ☞public domain software for sending and receiving e-mail using ☞Pretty Good Privacy (PGP) for improved security. The name refers to Mark Riordan, who wrote most of the program.

RISC (acronym for *reduced instruction-set computer*) a microprocessor (processor on a single chip) that carries out fewer instructions than other (☞CISC) microprocessors in common use in the 1990s. Because of the low number of ☞machine code instructions, the processor carries out those instructions very quickly.

RISC microprocessors became commercially available in the late 1980s. They are now widely used in Apple and PC microcomputers and laser printers.

RL (abbreviation of *real life*) the opposite of ☞virtual reality.

rlogin (contraction of *remote login*) ☞UNIX program that enables users to log in on another computer via the Internet. Compare ☞Telnet.

rogue value another name for ☞data terminator.

ROM (acronym for *read-only memory*) a memory device in the form of a collection of integrated circuits (chips), frequently used in microcomputers. ROM chips are loaded with data and programs during manufacture and, unlike ☞RAM (random-access memory) chips, can subsequently only be read, not written to, by computer. However, the contents of the chips are not lost when the power is switched off, as happens in RAM.

ROM is used to form a computer's permanent store of vital information, or of programs that must be readily available but protected from accidental or deliberate change by a user. For example, a microcomputer ☞operating system is often held in ROM memory.

root the account used by system administrators and other superusers in ⮑UNIX systems. Users logged in as root (or in some systems, ⮑avatar) have permission to access and change all the files in the system.

root directory the top directory in a ⮑tree-and-branch filing system. It contains all the other directories.

router a device that pushes traffic through a packet-switched network. On the Internet, traffic travels through a series of routers that relay each *packet* of data to its destination by the best possible route.

RS-232 interface standard type of computer ⮑interface used to connect computers to serial devices. It is used for modems, mice, screens, and serial printers.

RSA name of both an encryption ⮑algorithm and the company (RSA Inc) set up to exploit that algorithm in commercial encryption products. First described 1977 by its inventors, Ronald Rivest, Adi Shamir, and Leonard Adelman, and published in *Scientific American*, the RSA algorithm is used in the free program ⮑Pretty Good Privacy (PGP) and in commercial products released by RSA Laboratories. As of mid-1996, it had not been cracked.

RSI abbreviation for ⮑*repetitive strain injury*, a condition affecting workers, such as typists, who repeatedly perform certain movements with their hands and wrists.

RSUP (abbreviation for *Reliable SAP Update Protocol*) bandwidth-saving protocol for Novell networks developed by router manufacturer Cisco Systems.

RTF (abbreviation for *Rich Text Format*) file format designed to facilitate the exchange of documents between different word processing programs. RTF text files make it possible to transfer formatting such as font styles or paragraph indents from one program to another.

run-time system programs that must be stored in memory while an application is executed.

run-time version copy of a program that is provided with another application, so that the latter can be run, although it does not provide the full functionality of the program. An example is the provision of run-time versions of Microsoft ⮑Windows with Windows applications for those users who do not have the full version of Windows.

SAA abbreviation for ↪*systems application architecture*.

sampling measurement of an ↪analogue signal (such as an audioor video signal) at regular intervals. The result of the measurement can be converted into a ↪digital signal that can be electronically enhanced, edited or processed.

sans-serif font typeface, such as Helvetica or Gill Sans, the strokes of which terminate in plain ends. Such fonts are very clear – hence their use in posters and signposts – but many designers believe that in running text, ↪serif fonts are easier to read.

scalable font font that can be used at any size and any resolution, on a screen or hard-copy device, such as a laser printer or image setter. Scalable fonts are always ↪outline fonts.

scanner a device that can produce a digital image of a document for input and storage in a computer. It uses technology similar to that of a photocopier. Small scanners can be passed over the document surface by hand; larger versions have a flat bed, like that of a photocopier, on which the input document is placed and scanned.

Scanners are widely used to input graphics for use in ↪desktop publishing. If text is input with a scanner, the image captured is seen by the computer as a single digital picture rather than as separate characters. Consequently, the text cannot be processed by, for example, a word processor unless suitable optical character-recognition software is available to convert the image to its constituent characters. Scanners vary in their resolution, typical hand-held scanners ranging from 75 to 300 dpi. Types include flat-bed, drum, and overhead.

screen another name for monitor.

screen dump the process of making a printed copy of the current VDU screen display. The screen dump is sometimes stored as a data file instead of being printed immediately.

screen grabber software which can take a snapshot of the contents of a computer screen and save it as a picture file. Screen grabbers are useful for creating the screen shots seen in many computer magazines to illustrate software reviews and instructions.

screen saver program designed to prevent a static image from 'burning' itself into the phosphor screen of an idle computer monitor. If the user leaves the computer alone for more than a few minutes, the screen saver automatically displays a moving or changing image – perhaps a sequence of random squiggles, or an animation of flying toasters – on the screen. When the user touches any key, the computer returns to its previous state.

script in communications, a series of instructions for another computer. For example, when users log on to an ISP (Internet Service Provider) or other service, their computers follow a script containing passwords and other information to tell the server who they are.

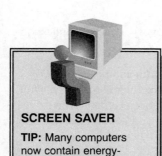

SCREEN SAVER

TIP: Many computers now contain energy-saving circuitry to black out idle screens, rendering screen savers superfluous.

scrollback the automatic scrolling of messages down the screen as they are received in ↪Internet Relay Chat (IRC), ↪bulletin boards or similar forums,.

scrollbar a narrow box along two sides of a ↪window, enabling users to move its contents up, down, left or right. Each end of the scrollbar represents the same end of the document on display, and the ↪mouse is used to move a small 'scrollbox' up and down the bar to scroll the contents or to click on the directional arrows.

scrolling the action by which data displayed on a VDU screen are automatically moved upwards and out of sight as new lines of data are added at the bottom.

SCSI (abbreviation for *small computer system interface*) standard method for connecting ↪peripheral devices (such as printers, scanners and CD-ROM drives) to a computer. A group of peripherals linked in series to a single SCSI ↪port is called a *daisy-chain*.

SDK (abbreviation for *software development kit*) suite of programs supplied to software developers to help them develop applications for environments such as Microsoft Windows and Microsoft Office.

search engine remotely accessible program to help users find information on the Internet. Commercial search engines such as ↪AltaVista and ↪Lycos comprise databases of documents, ↪URLs, ↪USENET articles and more, which can be searched by keying-in a key word or phrase. The databases are compiled by a mixture of automated agents (↪spiders) and ↪webmasters registering their sites. Some search engines, such as Yahoo, also work as catalogues, with items carefully indexed by category and cross-referenced.

Search engine	Web address	Description
AltaVista	www.altavista.digital.com	funded by DEC; select word search
Infoseek	guide-p.infoseek.com	powerful engine searches whole Web or focuses on 9 major topic sections; provides related sites
Lycos	www.lycos.com	extensive index of documents, including by words in title, headings, subheadings and hyperlinks
UK Index	www.ukindex.co.uk	database of almost exclusively UK sites with vetted selection
WebCrawler	webcrawler.com	database created using ↪spider (automated search routine)
Yahoo	www.yahoo.com	search-tree offering constant refinement of choice

ɔme major search engines

searching extracting a specific item from a large body of data, such as a file or table. The method used depends on how the data are organized. For example, a

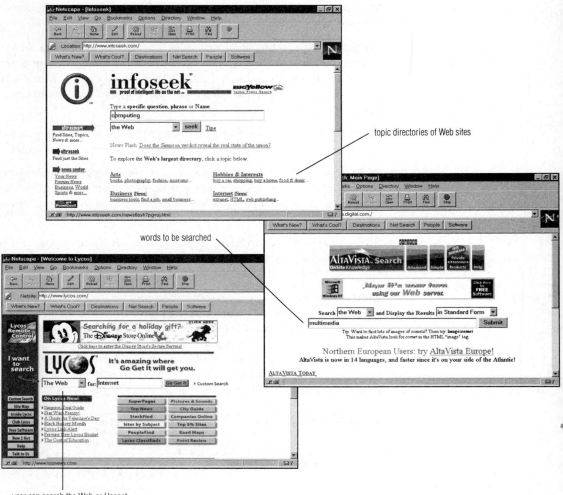

topic directories of Web sites

words to be searched

user can search the Web or Usenet

search engine
User interfaces of some typical Internet search engines. The user may search by a selection of keywords in particular subject areas.

binary search, which requires the data to be in sequence, involves first deciding which half of the data contains the required item, then which quarter, then which eighth, and so on until the item is found.

search request a structured request by a user for information from a ⌐database. This may be a simple request for all the entries that have a single field meeting a certain condition. For example, a user searching a file of car-registration details might request a list of all the records that have 'VOLKSWAGEN' in the ⌐field recording the make of car. In more complex examples, the user may construct a search request using operators like AND, OR, NOT, CONTAINING, and BETWEEN.

An example of a search request using all these operators is:

CAR SEARCH

registration number *containing* XTW *and* make Volkswagen *and* model Polo *and* body hatchback *and* colour white *or* black *and* registered *between* 1989 *and* 1991.

This search request would produce a list of all the white or black Volkswagen Polo hatchbacks registered between 1990 and 1996 that contained the letters XTW in their registration number.

SECAM (acronym for *Système Electronique Couleur Avec Mémoire*) television and video standard used in France, some states in Eastern Europe, and a few other countries. It is broadly similar to the ⌐PAL system used in most of Europe.

sector part of the magnetic structure created on a disc surface during ⌐disc formatting so that data can be stored on it. The disc is first divided into circular tracks and then each circular track is divided into a number of sectors.

secure HTTP communications protocol that provides the basis for privacy-enhanced or encrypted communications between a web ⌐browser and a ⌐server. Secure HTTP enables users to send private information such as credit card numbers and addresses over the Internet.

secure socket layer (SSL) in computing, standard protocol built into Web ⌐browsers such as Netscape and Internet Explorer, which provides an encrypted channel for private information such as credit card numbers and passwords

Considered a key technology to allow commerce across the World Wide Web, SSL began appearing on the Net 1995.

security protection against loss or misuse of data; see ⌐data security.

seek time time taken for a read-write head to reach a particular item of data on a ⌐disc track.

Sega Japanese ⌐games console and software manufacturer. Sega's most successful game is *Sonic the Hedgehog*.

sendmail ⌐UNIX program for sending ⌐e-mail via ⌐TCP/IP (Transport Control Protocol/Internet Protocol) using ⌐SMTP (simple mail transfer protocol).

sensor a device designed to detect a physical state or measure a physical quantity, and produce an input signal for a computer.

For example, a sensor may detect the fact that a printer has run out of paper or may measure the temperature in a kiln.

The signal from a sensor is usually in the form of an analogue voltage, and must therefore be converted to a digital signal, by means of an ⌐analogue-to-digital converter, before it can be input.

sequence-control register or *program counter* a special memory location used to hold the address of the next instruction to be fetched from the immediate

SECURE HTTP

TIP: Most web browsers will warn you if data you are about to disclose over the network will not be covered by secure HTTP.

access memory for execution by the computer (see ↩fetch-execute cycle). It is located in the control unit of the ↩central processing unit.

sequential file a file in which the records are arranged in order of a ↩key field and the computer can use a searching technique, like a ↩binary search, to access a specific record. See ↩file access.

serial device a device that communicates binary data by sending the bits that represent each character one by one along a single data line, unlike a parallel device.

serial file a file in which the records are not stored in any particular order and therefore a specific record can be accessed only by reading through all the previous records. See ↩file access.

serial interface an ↩interface through which data is transmitted one bit at a time. Compare with parallel interface.

Serial Line Internet Protocol in computing, method of connecting a computer to the Internet; usually abbreviated to ↩SLIP.

serif font typeface, such as Times or Palatino, the strokes of which terminate in ornamental curves or cross-strokes. These are said to aid legibility.

server computer used as a store of software and data for use by other computers on a ↩network. See ↩file server.

SGML

An example of an SGML source file. No on-screen formatting is used; headings and paragraphs are tagged as such and only appear in a different typeface in the final display.

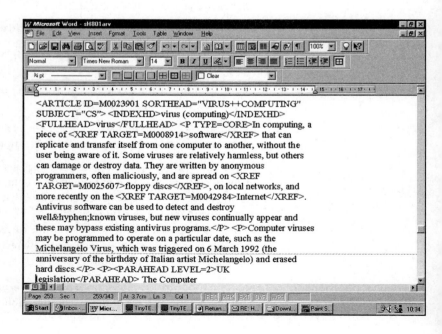

set-top box box containing decoding equipment for satellite or cable television broadcasts. Such boxes represent a means of linking television sets to a network such as the ⮞Internet, enabling people to browse the ⮞World Wide Web using their televisions as the monitor, or to view ⮞video-on-demand.

SGML (Abbreviation for *standard gneralized markup language*) ⮞International Standards Organization standard describing how the structure (features such as headers, columns, margins, and tables) of a text can be identified so that it can be used, probably via ⮞filters, in applications such as ⮞desktop publishing and ⮞electronic publishing. HTML and VRML are both types of SGML.

shared memory bus architecture (SMBA) system of ⮞buses that allows parallel computers to share ⮞RAM for greater processing power.

shareware software distributed free via the Internet or on discs given away with magazines. Users have the opportunity to test its functionality and ability to meet their requirements before paying a small registration fee (of the order of £25–50) directly to the author. This may bring additional functionality, documentation, and occasional upgrades. Shareware is not copyright-free. Compare with ⮞public-domain software.

Shareware

try before you buy Shareware is computer software that is distributed on the principle that users can try it before they buy it. Shareware is not *free* software, and it is still protected by copyright laws. The essential difference between shareware and ordinary commercial software is that users are permitted to run a shareware program to test it for a reasonable time – perhaps for 30 days – before registering and paying for it. Users who do not pay for it are on their honour, if any, to stop using it.

Because shareware is freely distributed, it avoids many of the costs of commercial distribution. Shareware programs are usually circulated without boxes and manuals, and there are no dealers to take a cut of the profits. Shareware libraries are allowed to make a small charge to cover the cost of any discs, and on-line services may charge for connection time while a program is downloaded to a user's personal computer, but these sums are small. As a result, shareware is usually much cheaper than commercial software, and it can be very good value.

The best shareware authors are often members of an American organization, the ASP (Association of Shareware Professionals), which acts as a sort of trade body.

heyday The shareware market was most successful in the early days of the IBM Personal Computer, launched in the USA in 1981. At the time, there was relatively little commercial software around, there were not many shops selling programs, and commercial standards were relatively low. Good shareware programs such as PC-Write and PC-File generated millions of dollars' worth of sales. Today, sophisticated software suites such as Microsoft Works and ClarisWorks are widely available and cheap, so most shareware programs are simpler utilities that often could not be distributed on a commercial basis. However, there are still exceptions, such as PaintShop Pro, and id Software's games, such as *Doom*.

don't pay, don't use Software writers have made a variety of attempts to encourage users to pay for programs when the test period runs out. Payment may, for example, be rewarded with an upgraded version of the program, a printed manual, and support if there are problems. Some programmers include warnings or advertising messages that nag the user into paying (often called 'nagware'). Some programrs limit their software ('crippleware'), or stop it from working after 30 days. This is no longer shareware by the standards of the ASP.

Many programmers take advantage of the distribution system that has grown up around shareware, including shareware libraries (which distribute programs by post), on-line bulletin boards (from which programs may be downloaded), CD-ROMs, and computer magazine cover discs. Some authors are giving their programs away (*freeware*) while others ask for a postcard, a bottle of an alcoholic beverage, a donation to a named charity, or just a smile.

Today, shareware is not as popular as it has been, and there are fewer shareware libraries in operation. However, the future is not necessarily bleak. Many computer users have now become used to downloading programs over the Internet, and this means many more users have easy access to shareware. Also we may be moving away from large, complex programs towards an age of software components that 'plug in' to 'container' programs like World Wide Web browsers. These components – written in for example, Sun's Java language or Microsoft's Visual Basic – can easily be written by individuals and small companies and could well be distributed as shareware.

Jack Schofield

shell program that mediates access to a particular system or server. Windows 95 is a shell that interposes a ↝graphical user interface and other utilities between the operator and ↝MS-DOS. In DOS itself, the file COMMAND.COM is a shell that makes the operating system display a ↝prompt and enables it to interpret user instructions. Shells can also be used to improve computer security.

shell account cheap method of accessing the ↝Internet via another computer, usually a ↝UNIX machine. Users with a shell account are given text-only access (via the telephone) to another computer connected to the Net.

shell script the ↝UNIX equivalent of batch files created for a program shell. Essentially, shell scripts allow users to create their own commands by creating a file that contains the sequence of commands they want to run and then designating the file as executable. Thereafter, typing the name of the file executes the sequence of commands.

Shockwave ↝application that enables interactive and multimedia features, such as movies, sounds, and animations, to be embedded in web pages. Unlike ↝Java, which achieves these effects by using a special programming language, Shockwave allows developers to add items created with conventional ↝authoring tools such as ↝Director or Freehand.

shortcut keyboard combination or icon which activates a procedure otherwise available only through pull-down menus and ↝dialog boxes. Most commercial software comes with built-in keyboard shortcuts and ↝pushbuttons, and many allow users to create their own custom shortcuts. In Windows 95, a shortcut is an icon that launches a program direct from the desktop.

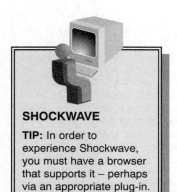

SHOCKWAVE

TIP: In order to experience Shockwave, you must have a browser that supports it – perhaps via an appropriate plug-in.

shovelware material used to fill (usually) a large-capacity disc, such as a ⌐CD-ROM, by 'shovelling it in' without changing or updating it to suit the new format. The term is also used for a disc that is full of old or low-cost material, such as shareware programs or the texts of out-of-copyright books.

signal processing the digitizing of an ⌐analogue signal such as a voice stream.

signature (or *.sig*) in computing, personal information appended to a message by the sender of an ⌐e-mail message or ⌐USENET posting in order to add a human touch. Signatures, which are optional, usually carry the sender's real name and e-mail address, and may also include the writer's occupation, telephone number, and the ⌐URL of his or her ⌐home page. Many have a short quote, motto or slogan, and a few incorporate ⌐ASCII art. .Sig is the name of the file in which signature information is stored on a ⌐UNIX system.

SIGNATURE

TIP: It is considered bad netiquette to post a signature of more than four lines or so.

silicon chip ⌐integrated circuit with microscopically small electrical components on a piece of silicon crystal only a few millimetres square.

One may contain more than a million components. A chip is mounted in a rectangular plastic package and linked via gold wires to metal pins, so that it can be connected to a printed circuit board for use in electronic devices, such as computers, calculators, television sets, car dashboards, and domestic appliances.

Silicon Graphics, Inc (SGI) manufacturer of high-performance workstations and software designed primarily for graphics and image processing.

Simple Mail Transfer Protocol in computing, protocol for transferring electronic mail between computers, commonly abbreviated to ⌐SMTP.

Simple Network Management Protocol agreed method of managing a computer network, commonly abbreviated to ⌐SNMP.

simulation short for ⌐computer simulation.

Sinclair Clive Marles 1940– . British electronics engineer. He produced the first widely available pocket calculator, pocket and wristwatch televisions, a series of home computers, and the innovative but commercially disastrous C5 personal transport (a low cyclelike three-wheeled vehicle powered by a washing-machine motor).

SIPC (abbreviation for *simply interactive PC*) easy-to-use and cheaply-priced computer planned by ⌐Microsoft, ⌐Intel and Toshiba for release 1997. The SIPC will be a sealed unit that can be connected to the telephone, television, hi-fi and other domestic electronic apparatus.

site location at which computers are used. If a company uses only ⌐IBM computers, for example, it is known as an IBM site. The term is also used for a computer which acts as a ⌐server for files that can be accessed via the ⌐World Wide Web, also called a *web site*.

site licence licence issued with commercial software entitling the purchaser to install the program on a fixed number of computers.

16-bit term describing the ability to process 16 ⮑bits at a time. The Intel 286 series of microprocessors are examples of 16-bit processors.

The term is used slightly differently to specify the quality of the sound produced by ⮑soundcards, where it refers to digital audio resolution; the quality of sound produced by a 16-bit soundcard is roughly equivalent to that produced by a compact disc.

64-bit term describing the ability to process 64 ⮑bits simultaneously. In 1996 the most powerful widely available processors on the mass market were 64-bit processors such as the ⮑Pentium, developed by Intel and released 1995. Other commonly used 64-bit processors included the Alpha ⮑RISC chip made by ⮑DEC and some of the chips used in Sparcstations made by ⮑Sun.

slide show in computing ⮑presentation graphics programs, facility to display a presentation electronically instead of outputting it onto film or paper. The program displays the images ('slides') using the computer's full screen or an overhead projector. Slide shows are a versatile display method: presenters can customize timings to suit what they have to say and incorporate sound and movies into their presentations.

SLIP (abbreviation for *serial line Internet protocol*) the older of two standard methods for connecting a computer to the Internet via a modem and telephone line. Unlike ⮑PPP (Point-to-Point Protocol), a SLIP connection needs to have its ⮑IP address reset every time it is used, and offers no ⮑error detection.

Smalltalk the first high-level programming language used in ⮑object-oriented applications.

smart term for any piece of equipment that works with the help of a microprocessor: a 'smart' carburetter, for example, maintains the correct proportion of air-to-petrol vapour in a car engine by electronically monitoring engine temperature, acceleration, and other variables. Designers are incorporating smart technology into an increasing range of products, such as smart toasters, which can prevent toast from burning. Smart furniture, such as chairs with cushions that adjust themselves according the size and weight of the person sitting in them, is a typical area of current research.

Architects are already making smart buildings, especially large office blocks and hospitals. Such buildings are wired with sensors to monitor heating, lighting and air quality. A central computer automatically performs simple tasks such as turning lights out when there is nobody in a room, adjusting air conditioning and even darkening photo-electric windows to counteract bright sunlight.

smart card plastic card with an embedded microprocessor and memory. It can store, for example, personal data, identification, and bank-account details, to enable it to be used as a credit or debit card. The card can be loaded with credits, which are then spent electronically, and reloaded as needed. Possible other uses range from hotel door 'keys' to passports.

The smart card was invented by French journalist Juan Moreno in 1974. By the year 2000 it will be possible to make cards with as much computing power as the leading personal computers of 1990.

smiley alternative term for ↝emoticon, named after the original smiling face :-).

SMPTE (abbreviation for the *Society of Motion Picture and Television Engineers*) US organization founded 1916 to advance the theory and application of motion-imaging technology including film, television, video, computer imaging, and telecommunications.

The SMPTE has 8,500 members in 72 countries, including engineers, executives, technical directors, camerapeople, editors, and consultants. It is based in White Plains, New York.

SMTP (abbreviation for *simple mail transfer protocol*) the basic protocol for transferring electronic mail between computers. SMTP is an agreed procedure for identifying the host, sending and receiving data and checking e-mail addresses.

SNA abbreviation for ↝*system network architecture*.

snail mail in the computing community, nickname for the conventional postal service. E-mail can deliver messages within minutes while conventional postal services take at least a day. One's postal address is therefore a 'snail mail address'.

sniffer software tool that analyses the transport data attached to ↝packets sent across a network, used to monitor the network's efficiency and level of usage. Hackers (see ↝hacking) also use sniffers to collect people's passwords for ↝Telnet connections.

SNMP (abbreviation for *Simple Network Management Protocol*) agreed method of managing a computer network. SNMP governs the overall structure of the Internet, in particular its arrangement around ↝hubs and ↝nodes.

socket mechanism for creating a connection to an application on another computer. A socket combines an ↝IP address (denoting the host computer on a network) with a port number describing the application (perhaps ↝FTP or ↝SMTP) the user requires.

Socks the First Cat on the Internet. Socks is the real-life cat belonging to President Bill Clinton's family and a resident of the White House when the White House Web site was set up in 1995.

soft-sectored disc another name for an unformatted blank disc; see ↝disc formatting.

software a collection of programs and procedures for making a computer perform a specific task, as opposed to ↝hardware, the physical components of a

SOCKS

TIP: Visitors to the Web site http://www. whitehouse.gov may click on an icon to hear Socks meow.

Software applications

start simple The Internet and multimedia may enjoy all the hype, but the most useful software programs you can buy for a personal computer are the old faithfuls of word processor, database, and spreadsheet, with maybe a drawing package and another for creating presentation slides.

Full-strength business programs are extremely powerful, but also rather complicated, and many people find they do not use a quarter of the available features. For the novice, the best approach, and the best value, are offered by integrated packages, such as ClarisWorks or Microsoft Works. These generally combine word processing, spreadsheet, database and drawing, and are good value for money.

The best way to buy full-strength software, such as Microsoft's Word word processor, or Lotus's 1–2–3 spreadsheet, is in a suite, such as Microsoft Office or Lotus SmartSuite. These are more expensive and usually include word processor, spreadsheet, database, and presentation graphics software, and maybe extras like a diary/organizer.

In practice, most computer buyers do not need to purchase their basic software, because it is included with the computer. These software **bundles** typically include an integrated package or suite, home finance software, reference works like encyclopedias, and some educational and entertainment titles.

Computer manufacturers and retailers buy the software cheaply in bulk, so it often represents excellent value. Beginners should not worry which particular package they are getting, since most of the big-name products are of similar quality.

However, it pays to examine the software bundle carefully. Some vendors cut corners by supplying inferior software, outdated versions, or editions with American spellings and voices. Sometimes they do not supply instruction manuals or the original discs, and occasionally they have copied the software illegally, leaving the buyer technically in breach of copyright.

Whether software is bundled or purchased separately, it is worth registering with the publisher. You may then be notified when 'bugs' (errors) are found and when new versions are published, and you may receive discounts on other products.

You will also get free telephone support, though usually only for 3–6 months. Most support calls relate to installation and learning, so it pays to start using the software straightaway.

do you need to upgrade? Most major software packages are upgraded every 12–18 months. For many users this is a source of irritation rather than jubilation, and although publishers offer discounts, many people prefer to stick with the version they are familiar with rather than suffer the upheaval of upgrading – especially since the new version often requires a more powerful computer.

Businesses seldom skip more than one generation of software, since support is harder to find on old versions, and it may confuse new recruits used to working on the latest releases. But home users can continue for years with older software which still suits them and their computer.

other software sources An alternative source of cheap software is **shareware** programs published by independent authors, who distribute them for free and rely on people's honesty to pay a small fee if they use them. Shareware and free software are often available on magazine cover discs, and via the Internet, though anyone downloading software from the Internet should beware of viruses.

In future, the Internet may become the major medium for software distribution, and could revolutionize the way software is produced and sold. Cheap **network computers** may have no internal applications software, but call up small programs (applets) over the network as and when they are required, perhaps on a pay-as-you-use basis.

Alternatively, conventional packaged software may still be sold, but made up of self-contained components, produced by a mix of large publishers and small independents. This componentware will be tailored to the individual user. Computer enthusiasts may do this themselves, but most people will buy assemblages of components specially related to their profession, hobbies, or age-group.

Paul Bray

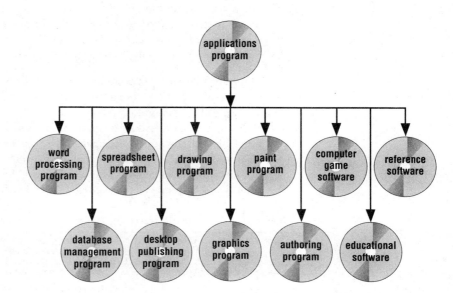

computer system. Software is created by programmers and is either distributed on a suitable medium, such as the ⌐floppy disc, or built into the computer in the form of ⌐firmware. Examples of software include ⌐operating systems, ⌐compilers, and applications programs, such as payrolls. No computer can function without some form of software.

software agent see ⌐intelligent agent.

software piracy unauthorized duplication of computer software. Although some software piracy is done by companies for financial gain, most piracy is done by private individuals who lend discs to friends or copy programs from the workplace to their computers at home.

Software manufacturers' attempts to protect their property – for example, by using special codes to prevent programs from being installed more than once from each set of discs – have proved unpopular with users and bypassable by determined copiers. Because computer data is so easy to duplicate, and the use of unauthorized software is so hard to detect, it appears nigh impossible to enforce anti-piracy law. The only sure way to prevent it appears to be for manufacturers to sell each copy of their software with a ⌐dongle – a coded plug that must actually be fitted to the computer for the software to function.

In the UK, unauthorized copying of software is covered by the Copyright, Designs and Patents Act 1988, which makes it a criminal offence to copy or distribute programs or to run them on more than one computer without the manufacturer's express permission in the software licence. It is also illegal to loan software to anyone else for copying, or for companies to encourage employees to make or use illegal copies of software at work. The maximum penalty is two years in prison and an unlimited fine, and offenders may also face civil prosecution for damages by the makers of the pirated software.

SOFTWARE PIRACY

TIP: It is also illegal to loan software to anyone else for copying, or for companies to encourage employees to make or use illegal copies of software at work.

software project life cycle various stages of development in the writing of a major program (software), from the identification of a requirement to the installation, maintenance, and support of the finished program. The process includes ⮑systems analysis and ⮑systems design.

software suite a set of complementary programs which can be bought separately, or (at a considerable saving) as a ⮑bundled package. ⮑office suites are an especially common form of software suite.

Examples include: Adobe's graphics software which includes Photoshop (for processing photographs), Pagemaker (for page layout) and Illustrator (for creating illustrations); and Macromedia's multimedia software, which comprises Director (for creating presentations), xRes2 (for editing images), SoundEdit (for editing sound) and Extreme 3D (for 3-D modelling and animation).

Package	Manufacturer	Description
ClarisWorks	Claris	with word processor, spreadsheet, database and paint and draw programs; flexible and creative document design
Microsoft Works	Microsoft	with ⮑Wizards to help create the required document; pre-installed on many new PCs
Perfect Works	Corel	includes paint and draw packages

Some major software suites

Sony Japanese electronics hardware company that produced the Walkman, the first easily portable cassette player with headphones, 1980. It diversified into entertainment by the purchase of CBS Records 1988 and Columbia Pictures 1989. They also manufacture computing ⮑games consoles.

During the 1970s Sony developed the Betamax video-cassette format, which technicians rated as more advanced than the rival VHS system developed by the Matsushita Corporation, but the latter eventually triumphed in the marketplace. Sony's chair, Akio Morita, is co-author of *A Japan That Can Say No* 1989 and sequels. Consolidated operating profits for the first quarter of 1992 were 151 million, after more than a year of decline.

In Sept 1996 Sony delayed the launch of its digital versatile disc (DVD) players until spring 1997.

sorting arranging data in sequence. When sorting a collection, or file, of data made up of several different ⮑fields, one must be chosen as the *key field* used to establish the correct sequence. For example, the data in a company's mailing list might include fields for each customer's first names, surname, address, and telephone number. For most purposes the company would wish the records to be sorted alphabetically by surname; therefore, the surname field would be chosen as the key field.

The choice of sorting method involves a compromise between running time, memory usage, and complexity. Those used include *selection sorting*, in which the smallest item is found and exchanged with the first item, the second smallest exchanged with the second item, and so on; *bubble sorting*, in which adjacent items are continually exchanged until the data are in sequence; and *insertion sorting*, in which each item is placed in the correct position and subsequent items moved down to make a place for it.

SoundBlaster the most popular type of ⌒soundcard for IBM-compatible PCs.

soundcard printed circuit board that, coupled with a set of speakers, enables a computer to reproduce music and sound effects.

source code the original instructions written by computer programmers. Before these instructions can be understood, they must be processed by a ⌒compiler and turned into ⌒machine code.

source language the language in which a program is written, as opposed to ⌒machine code, which is the form in which the program's instructions are carried out by the computer. Source languages are classified as either ⌒high-level languages or ⌒low-level languages, according to whether each notation in the source language stands for many or only one instruction in machine code.

Programs in high-level languages are translated into machine code by either a ⌒compiler or an ⌒interpreter program. Low-level programs are translated into machine code by means of an ⌒assembler program. The program, before translation, is called the *source program*; after translation into machine code it is called the *object program*.

source program a program written in a ⌒source language.

spamming advertising on the ⌒Internet by broadcasting to many or all ⌒newsgroups regardless of relevance. Spamming is contrary to ⌒netiquette, the Net's conduct code, and is likely to result in the advertiser being bombarded by ⌒flames (angry messages), and ⌒'dumping' (the downloading of large, useless files).

speech chip see ⌒DSP.

speech recognition or *voice input* any technique by which a computer can understand ordinary speech. Spoken words are divided into 'frames', each lasting about one-thirtieth of a second, which are converted to a wave form. These are then compared with a series of stored frames to determine the most likely word. Research into speech recognition started in 1938, but the technology did not become sufficiently developed for commercial applications until the late 1980s.

There are three types: *separate word recognition* for distinguishing up to several hundred separately spoken words; *connected speech recognition* for speech in which there is a short pause between words; and *continuous speech recognition* for normal but carefully articulated speech.

speech synthesis or *voice output* computer-based technology for generating speech. A speech synthesizer is controlled by a computer, which supplies strings of codes representing basic speech sounds (phonemes); together these make up words. Speech-synthesis applications include children's toys, car and aircraft warning systems, and talking books for the blind.

speech writing system computing system that enables data to be input by voice. It includes a microphone, and ⮜soundcard that plugs into the computer and converts the analogue signals of the voice to digital signals. Examples include DragonDictate, and IBM's Personal Dictation System released 1994.

The user must read sample sentences to the computer on first use to familiarize it with individual pronunciation. Early speech writers were very inaccurate and slow but by the mid-1990s speeds of 80 words per minute with 95–99% accuracy were achievable.

spider program that combs the ⮜Internet for new documents such as web pages and ⮜FTP files. Spiders start their work by retrieving a document such as a Web page and then following all the links and references contained in it. They repeat the process with the followed links, supplying all the references they find to a database that can be searched via a ⮜search engine.

spooling the process in which information to be printed is stored temporarily in a file, the printing being carried out later. It is used to prevent a relatively slow printer from holding up the system at critical times, and to enable several computers or programs to share one printer.

spreadsheet a program that mimics a sheet of ruled paper, divided into columns and rows. The user enters values in the sheet, then instructs the program to perform some operation on them, such as totalling a column or finding the average of a series of numbers.

Highly complex numerical analyses may be built up from these simple steps.

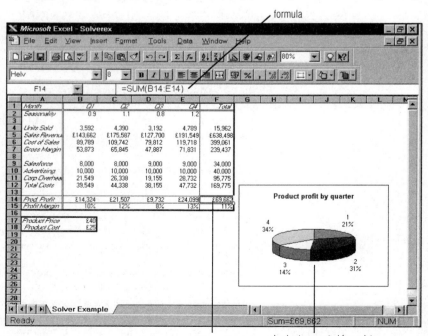

spreadsheet
A typical spreadsheet software package. The data it contains may be output in a graphical form, enabling the production of charts and diagrams.

Software	Manufacturer	Description
1-2-3	Lotus	Long-established and full-featured; able to work with e-mail programs, strong on complex analyses
Excel	Microsoft	Powerful and user-friendly; with built-in functions and ⮌Wizards
Quattro Pro	Corel	Extensive built-in functions; good value; provides visual representation of formulas

Some major spreadsheet programs

Spreadsheets are widely used in business for forecasting and financial control. The first spreadsheet program, Software Arts' VisiCalc, appeared 1979. The best known include ⮌Lotus 1–2–3 and Microsoft ⮌Excel.

Sprint US telecommunications company supplying data and long-distance voice connections. It was founded in 1899 as the Brown Telephone Company.

Sprint began offering long-distance service under the Sprint brand name in 1986. The company was the first to connect coast-to-coast fibre-optic transmissions.

sprite a graphics object made up of a pattern of ⮌pixels (picture elements) defined by a computer programmer. Some ⮌high-level languages and ⮌applications programs contain routines that allow a user to define the shape, colours, and other characteristics of individual graphics objects. These objects can then be manipulated and combined to produce animated games or graphic screen displays.

SQL (abbreviation for *structured query language*) high-level computer language designed for use with ⮌relational databases. Although it can be used by programmers in the same way as other languages, it is often used as a means for programs to communicate with each other. Typically, one program (called the 'client') uses SQL to request data from a database 'server'.
Although originally developed by IBM, SQL is now widely used on many types of computer.

SRAM (acronym for *static random-access memory*) computer memory device in the form of a silicon chip used to provide ⮌immediate access memory. SRAM is faster but more expensive than ⮌DRAM (dynamic random-access memory).

DRAM loses its contents unless they are read and rewritten every 2 milliseconds or so. This process is called *refreshing* the memory. SRAM does not require such frequent refreshing.

stack a method of storing data in which the most recent item stored will be the first to be retrieved. The technique is commonly called 'last in, first out'.

Stacks are used to solve problems involving nested structures; for example, to analyse an arithmetical expression containing subexpressions in parentheses, or to work out a route between two points when there are many different paths.

stand-alone computer self-contained computer, usually a microcomputer, that is not connected to a network of computers and can be used in isolation from any other device.

standards any agreed system or protocol that helps different pieces of software or different computers to work together.

In the fast-moving area of computer technology, standards have sometimes developed haphazardly: market forces brought about de facto standards such as the ⌐MS-DOS operating system for PCs, or the 3.5 in floppy disc. If computers are to communicate over a network, however, standards must be co-ordinated: the ⌐World Wide Web, for example, works because everybody who uses it agrees to follow the same conventions, such as using ⌐HTML to build web documents. Other standards, like ⌐SMTP – the procedure for sending e-mail – exist to make cross-platform communication (for example between a ⌐UNIX machine and a ⌐Macintosh) possible. Bodies involved with this process include: the ⌐Internet Architecture Board, which lays down basic procedures by promulgating ⌐RFCs; the International Standards Organization, which produces the Yellow Book of standards for CD-ROMs; and the ⌐Open Software Foundation.

Industry standards

why standards are needed In computing, standards are vital in two areas: compatibility and interoperability. Compatibility affects both hardware and software, but if two machines are 'software compatible' then they will run the same programs. Interoperability refers to the ability of two computers to work together, usually by exchanging data. For example, two incompatible computers can interoperate if they both support the same networking protocol, such as the Internet's TCP/IP. Compatibility is the basis of the computer industry, while interoperability is the basis of the World Wide Web.

The computer industry recognizes two sorts of standard, known as de jure and de facto standards. The **de jure standards** have been discussed and ratified by recognized standards bodies such as America's IEEE (Institution of Electrical and Electronics Engineers) and the ISO (International Standards Organization). The **de facto standards** are the ones that have been accepted by a compelling proportion of the marketplace. Personal computers based on Intel processors running Microsoft's MS-DOS and Windows operating systems are a de facto standard, even though the elements that make up a PC are proprietary (owned by their manufacturers) and not 'open' or based on agreed standards.

Standards are an important way of avoiding 'lock in'. A proprietary product that cannot be obtained from alternative sources 'locks' users to a particular supplier. Also, the availability of written standards means that products can be designed and tested to see whether they meet a known specification, and given a certificate or brand label if they do. Such products should then be compatible or able to interoperate with each other, though this is not always the case. (Products designed to the same specification sometimes fail to interoperate because the specification has been written too loosely, or because vendors have interpreted it differently.)

With de facto standards there are rarely any 'test suites' to ensure compatibility, and buyers have to rely on manufacturers' claims, press reports, and their own experience. An early 'test' for IBM PC-compatibility, for example, was the ability to run a game, Microsoft's *Flight Simulator*.

drawbacks The drawback with standards is that the computer industry develops very rapidly while standards bodies are notoriously slow-moving. Also, standards bodies often include too many options and compromises to satisfy the competing manufacturers represented on their various committees. The resulting standard may be too late, too unwieldy, or too expensive to achieve success in the marketplace, as happened with the ISO's highly-touted OSI (Open Systems Interconnection) standards for networking. Real customers will often buy a cheaper, faster, proprietary solution if it is readily available and meets their needs.

However, because manufacturers of key products can demand large sums for proprietary systems (thanks to 'lock in'), and because they sometimes go bust, the industry recognizes the value of standards. These provide a choice of products and this tends to drive down prices, which almost everyone likes. Also, developing an industry standard product can still be extremely profitable, and suppliers sometimes put their proprietary designs under a standards umbrella to encourage their adoption – as Microsoft has done with its object-oriented software architecture, ActiveX.

Jack Schofield

start bit ↪bit used in ↪asynchronous communications to indicate the beginning of a piece of data.

startup screen screen displayed by a PC while it loads its ↪operating system and other resident software. Well-known startup screens include the Windows 95 'flying window' motif and the Macintosh 'smiling face'. It is also possible to create a custom start-up screen, perhaps incorporating a favourite image or corporate logo.

static IP address (abbreviation for *static Internet Protocol address* an ↪IP address which is permanently assigned to a particular user. Most Internet Service Providers (ISPs) use ↪dynamic IP addressing for their customers. Static IP addressing is, however, generally used by businesses or any organization running its own site and is also available for individuals from some ISPs, such as Demon Internet, allowing them to set up ↪FTP or Web sites on their home computers. Static IP addressing also allows a higher degree of tracking an individual user's actions on the Internet.

steganography camouflaging messages in large computer files, especially those carrying audio, video or graphics, by appropriating a small percentage of their constituent data. For example, a graphics file measuring 500×500 ↪pixels, using 32 ↪bits to represent each pixel, contains 8 million bits. A single bit of each pixel (perhaps the 1st, the 15th or the 32nd) could be used to insert some 5,000 words of text, chopped into individual bits, without making any perceptible difference to the image. The text message itself can be encrypted using ↪Pretty Good Privacy (PGP) for added security.

stepper motor electric motor that can be precisely controlled by signals from a computer. The motor turns through a precise angle each time it receives a signal pulse from the computer. By varying the rate at which signal pulses are produced, the motor can be run at different speeds or turned through an exact angle and then stopped. Switching circuits can be constructed to allow the computer to reverse the direction of the motor.

By combining two or more motors, complex movement control becomes possible. For example, if stepper motors are used to power the wheels of a small vehicle, a computer can manoeuvre the vehicle in any direction.

Stepper motors are commonly used in small-scale applications where computer-controlled movement is required. In larger applications, where greater power is necessary, pneumatic or hydraulic systems are usually preferred.

Sterling Bruce 1954–   . US science fiction writer generally credited as being one of the inventors of the ⮑cyberpunk genre.

Stoll Clifford. US astronomer whose books *The Cuckoo's Egg* 1994 and *Silicon Snake Oil* 1995, express an oblique, and at times sceptical, view of the benefits and consequences of computerization.

stop bit ⮑bit used in ⮑asynchronous communications to indicate the end of a piece of data.

store-and-forward technology in computing, general term for systems like ⮑UUCP and e-mail, which work by storing data that has been received and then forwarding it on demand to the authorized recipient. Most of the Internet is based on store-and-forward technology.

story board in film and television, technique for reviewing a particular story or scene before it is expensively filmed, animated, or scripted.

The scene is broken down into key frames or moments, and sketched in varying detail onto boards with accompanying text outlining the plot's progress.

streaming sending data, for example video frames or radio broadcasts, in a steady flow over the Internet. Streaming requires data to pass through a special channel or dedicated connection; conventional ⮑packets, which travel by a multiplicity of routes, may arrive in the wrong order or be duplicated on the way. ⮑RealAudio and ⮑CU-SeeMe make use of streaming.

string a group of characters manipulated as a single object by the computer. In its simplest form a string may consist of a single letter or word – for example, the single word SMITH might be established as a string for processing by a computer. A string can also consist of a combination of words, spaces, and numbers – for example, 33 HIGH STREET ANYTOWN ALLSHIRE could be established as a single string.

Most high-level languages have a variety of string-handling ⮑functions. For example, functions may be provided to read a character from any given position in a string or to count automatically the number of characters in a string.

structured programming in computing, the process of writing a program in small, independent parts. This makes it easier to control a program's development and to design and test its individual component parts. Structured programs are built up from units called *modules*, which normally correspond to single ⮑procedures or ⮑functions. Some programming languages, such as PASCAL and Modula-2, are better suited to structured programming than others.

style sheet pre-set group of formats used in word processing, presentation graphics and page layout programs. Style sheets impose margins, fonts, point sizes, alignments, and other criteria to give text a uniform appearance. In a page layout program, designers might use different style sheets for headings, picture captions, and main text.

subject drift tendency for postings in ⌐UseNet, and sometimes entire newsgroups, to wander away from their original subject matter. As threads accumulate in response to a posting, the subject heading is retained, but the discussions can rapidly go off at a tangent. Thus a thread headed 'Re: Ice cream – favourite flavours' might actually be a long-running discussion about Napoleon.

subroutine a small section of a program that is executed ('called') from another part of the program. Subroutines provide a method of performing the same task at more than one point in the program, and also of separating the details of a program from its main logic. In some computer languages, subroutines are similar to ⌐functions or ⌐procedures.

substring a portion of a ⌐string. In searching a text database, for example, specifying that a sequence of letters is a substring will widen the search from just matching words to other words in which that sequence of letters appears. For example, searching a database on the string 'computer' will not retrieve entries which use 'computing' or 'compute'. Searching on the substring 'comput' however, will retrieve all three. The technique adds flexibility when the exact syntax of the search term is unknown.

subsystem hardware and/or software which performs a specific function within a larger system. ⌐Silicon Graphics, for example, uses subsystems to perform the many calculations needed for computer animation.

Sun Microsystems US-based computer manufacturer founded 1982 with the motto 'the network is the computer'. Sun specializes in office networks, workstations, servers, and the operating systems to run them. Sun pioneered the concept of open systems – technology which is available free to other manufacturers – and in 1995 released Java, the platform-independent programming language which now drives much of the ⌐World Wide Web.

supercomputer the fastest, most powerful type of computer, capable of performing its basic operations in picoseconds (thousand-billionths of a second), rather than nanoseconds (billionths of a second), like most other computers.

To achieve these extraordinary speeds, supercomputers use several processors working together and techniques such as cooling processors down to nearly absolute zero temperature, so that their components conduct electricity many times faster than normal. Supercomputers are used in weather forecasting, fluid dynamics and aerodynamics. Manufacturers include Cray, Fujitsu, and NEC.

Of the world's 500 most powerful supercomputers 232 are in the USA, 109 in Japan, and 140 in Europe, with 23 in the UK. In 1992 Fujitsu announced the launch of the first computer capable of performing 300 billion calculations a second. In 1996 University of Tokyo researchers completed a computer able to perform 1.08 trillion floating-point operations per second.

support a particular type of hardware or software that is compatible with a relevant standard or another type of hardware or software. A given printer might, for example, support 600 dpi (dots per inch) resolution, or a particular computer system might support ⇔SVGA graphics.

support environment a collection of programs (⇔software) used to help people design and write other programs. At its simplest, this includes a ⇔text editor (word-processing software) and a ⇔compiler for translating programs into executable form; but it can also include interactive debuggers for helping to locate faults, data dictionaries for keeping track of the data used, and rapid prototyping tools for producing quick, experimental mock-ups of programs.

surfing exploring the ⇔Internet. The term is rather misleading: the glitches, delays, and complexities of the system mean the experience is more like wading through mud.

SVGA (abbreviation for *super video graphics array*) a graphic display standard providing higher resolution than ⇔VGA. SVGA screens have resolutions of either 800 x 600 or 1,024 x 768.

swap to move segments of data in and out of memory. For fast operation as much data as possible is required in main memory, but it is generally not possible to include all data at the same time. Swapping is the operation of writing and reading from the backup store, often a special space on the disc.

symbolic address a symbol used in ⇔assembly language programming to represent the binary ⇔address of a memory location.

symbolic processor computer purpose-built to run so-called symbol-manipulation programs rather than programs involving a great deal of numerical computation. They exist principally for the ⇔artificial intelligence language ⇔LISP, although some have also been built to run ⇔PROLOG.

synchronous regular. Most communication within a computer system is synchronous, controlled by the computer's own internal clock, while communication between computers is usually ⇔asynchronous. Synchronous telecommunications are, however, becoming more widely used.

Syquest manufacturer of removal ⇔hard disc drives. Syquest drives are most commonly associated with the Apple ⇔Macintosh, and are used to transport large files from one location to another.

sysop (contraction of *system operator*) the operator of a ⇔bulletin board system (BBS).

System 7 operating system used by Apple ⇔Macintosh computers, introduced in 1991. System 7 is designed to be an intuitive, easy-to-use interface, with icons, windows and a mouse. A series of control panels and system extensions customize and enhance the capabilities of the program. Apple plan to introduce System 8, an improved and Internet-friendly operating system in 1997.

system administrator (or *sysadmin*) person who runs and maintains a computer system, especially a ⌐local area network (LAN). The responsibilities of a systems administrator typically include installing hardware and software, supervising system security, fixing faults, and organizing training.

system flow chart type of ⌐flow chart used to describe the flow of data through a particular computer system.

system implementation in computing, the process of installing a new computer system.

To ensure that a system's implementation takes place as efficiently and with as little disruption as possible, a number of tasks are necessary. These include ordering and installing new equipment, ordering new stationery and storage media, training personnel, converting data files into new formats, drawing up an overall implementation plan, and preparing for a period of either ⌐parallel running or ⌐pilot running.

SYSTEM.INI (abbreviation for *System Initialization*) file used by Microsoft Windows to store information about which parts of Windows to load and how to set itself up on the PC on which it is running, for example SYSTEM.INI specifies drivers for the keyboard, graphics card, and sound card, if any.

System Network Architecture (SNA) a set of communication protocols developed by IBM and incorporated in hardware and software implementations. See also ⌐TCP/IP and ⌐Open Systems Interconnection (OSI).

system requirements minimum specification necessary in order to use a particular piece of hardware or software.

systems analysis the investigation of a business activity or clerical procedure, with a view to deciding if and how it can be computerized. The analyst discusses the existing procedures with the people involved, observes the flow of data through the business, and draws up an outline specification of the required computer system. The next step is ⌐systems design.

Systems in use in the 1990s include Yourdon, SSADM (Structured Systems Analysis and Design Methodology), and Soft Systems Methodology.

systems application architecture (SAA) an IBM model for client-server computing. SAA makes use of ⌐CUA (common user access) to ensure that commands and keystrokes are used consistently in different applications.

systems design the detailed design of an ⌐applications package. The designer breaks the system down into component programs, and designs the required input forms, screen layouts, and printouts. Systems design forms a link between systems analysis and ⌐programming.

systems program a program that performs a task related to the operation and performance of the computer system itself. For example, a systems program might control the operation of the display screen, or control and organize backing storage. In contrast, an ⌐applications program is designed to carry out tasks for the benefit of the computer user.

SYSTEM REQUIREMENTS

TIP: some system requirements err on the low side. In general, assume that performance will be slow if your system matches the minimum.

T1 link digital telephone line which can transfer data at 1.544 megabits per second. T-1 lines are a type of ⌐Integrated Services Digital Network (ISDN) communication.

T3 digital telephone standard that transmits data at 44.736 megabits per second, widely used for ⌐Integrated Services Digital Network (ISDN) lines.

tape streamer a backing storage device consisting of a continuous loop of magnetic tape. Tape streamers are largely used to store dumps (rapid backup copies) of important data files (see ⌐data security).

TAPI (abbreviation for *Telephony Application Programming Interface*) program included in ⌐Windows 95 to enable applications to use the telephone. A ⌐CD-ROM reference work might use TAPI to access updated information over the Internet, and a word processing program might use it to send an ⌐e-mail or fax.

TAR UNIX-based compression routine in common use on the Internet.

taskbar strip at the bottom of a ⌐Windows 95 screen containing icons ('task buttons') of all programs launched in the current session. The taskbar makes it possible to switch between applications simply by clicking the mouse on a task button.

TCP/IP (abbreviation for *transport control protocol/Internet protocol*) set o network protocols, developed principally by the US Department of Defense. TCP/IP is widely used, particularly in ⌐Unix and on the ⌐Internet and it is now incorporated into operating systems, such as Windows 95.

telco hacker's contraction of *telecommunications company*.

TeleAdapt US company that specializes in supplying worldwide telephone and power adaptor plugs for mobile laptop users.
TeleAdapt is based in Campbell, California, and has offices in London and Sydney.

telecommuting working from home using a telephone, fax, and ⌐modem to keep in touch with the office of the employing company. In the mid 1990s, it was estimated that 5% of US workers and 2.3% (600,000) of the British workforce were telecommuters.
Most telecommuters are self-employed, or sales people spending much of their time on the road. However, the number of part-time telecommuters, for example working one day per week at home, is growing.

telemedicine the use of computer communications to improve medical practice and training.

Telephony Application Programming Interface Windows 95 program, commonly abbreviated to ⌐TAPI.

teletext broadcast system of displaying information on a television screen. The information – typically about news items, entertainment, sport, and finance – is constantly updated. Teletext is a form of ⟿videotext, pioneered in Britain by the British Broadcasting Corporation (BBC) with Ceefax and by Independent Television with Teletext.

teletype (TTY) ⟿UNIX computer used as a remote terminal to communicate with another computer.

Telnet Internet utility that enables a user to work on a remote computer as if directly connected. Telnet connections to a remote computer system are typically much cheaper than long-distance telephone calls; the user makes a local call to an Internet access provider and the rest of the connection is handled via the Internet at no additional cost. ⟿Bulletin board systems usually work via Telnet.

template file that lays down a document's format. Templates are used in word processing, spreadsheet, and other programs to specify all the styles used in a document, such as fonts, margins, macros, formulas and so on. They are widely used to automate the production of documents such as memos, mailings and reports, making sure that they have a uniform appearance.

terabyte 1,024 ⟿gigabytes, or 1,099,511,627,776 ⟿bytes.

terminal a device consisting of a keyboard and display screen (⟿VDU) to enable the operator to communicate with the computer. The terminal may be physically attached to the computer or linked to it by a telephone line (remote terminal). A 'dumb' terminal has no processor of its own, whereas an 'intelligent' terminal has its own processor and takes some of the processing load away from the main computer.

terminal emulation communications program such as ⟿Telnet that allows a computer to emulate a terminal or workstation of a remote host. The host accepts instructions from the remote computer as if it were one of its own workstations.

terminate and stay resident (TSR) term given to a program that remains in the memory – for example, a clock, calculator, or thesaurus. The program is run by the use of a ⟿hot key.

test data data designed to test whether a new computer program is functioning correctly. The test data are carefully chosen to ensure that all possible branches of the program are tested. The expected results of running the data are written down and are then compared with the actual results obtained using the program.

test message a message in ⟿USENET that is posted simply to make sure that one's software or network connections are working properly.

T_EX (pronounced 'tek') ⟿public domain text formatting and typesetting system, developed by Donald Knuth and widely used for producing mathematical and technical documents. Unlike ⟿desktop publishing applications, T_EX is not ⟿WYSIWYG, although in some implementations screen preview of pages is possible.

text editor a program that allows the user to edit text on the screen and to store it in a file. Text editors are similar to ⌐word processors, except that they lack the ability to format text into paragraphs and pages and to apply different typefaces and styles.

TFT display another name for ⌐active matrix LCD.

32-bit term describing the ability to process 32 ⌐bits at a time. The Intel 386 and 486 series of microprocessors are examples of 32-bit processors.

The term is also used to specify the quality of sound produced by ⌐soundcards, where increased speed indicates the ability to produce more fully detailed (and therefore more realistic) sound. Windows NT, OS/2, and Windows 95 are all examples of 32-bit operating systems.

thread subject line of electronic messages within an on-line topic or conference. Most on-line conferencing systems use some kind of threading; one advantage is that it makes it easy for readers of a particular conference or forum to skip over sections that do not interest them. Threading is an important feature of off-line readers, as otherwise it is difficult to tell how individual messages relate to one another.

3-D graphics graphics defined by width, height, and depth (in mathematical terms, x, y, and z axes). In ***business applications*** such as spreadsheets, 3-D graphics allow users to display complex relationships between several different types of data. In ***computer animation***, 3-D graphics allow animators to create characters that look rounded and real enough to interact with humans, such as the cartoon characters in the film *Who Framed Roger Rabbit?* 1988 or the liquid-metal man in *Terminator 2* 1991.

thumbnail a small version of a larger image used for reference. A ⌐PhotoCD or ⌐clip art collection might initially present images as thumbnails, while publishing programs include the facility for designers to produce thumbnail page layouts.

TIFF (acronym for ***tagged image file format***) a ⌐graphics file format.

tiling arrangement of ⌐windows in a ⌐graphical user interface system so that they do not overlap.

time out pre-set period of time during which a computer waits for a response from a device or another computer. For example, when sending a fax, a computer will time out the telephone call if the receiving fax machine fails to answer.

time-sharing a way of enabling several users to access the same computer at the same time. The computer rapidly switches between user ⌐terminals and programs, allowing each user to work as if he or she had sole use of the system.

Time-sharing was common in the 1960s and 1970s before the spread of cheaper computers, and looks set to make a comeback in the late 1990s, with the advent of ***network computing***.

timestamp ⌐digital signature that 'fixes' a document in time, so that any later alterations can be readily detected.

TinyMUD one of the oldest and most popular ⤸MUDs, named for the the efficiency of its program code.

TinySex cybersex on ⤸TinyMUD.

TLA (abbreviation for *three letter acronym*) hackers' self-fulfilling reference to the apparent ubiquity of three-letter abbreviations (all popularly and wrongly referred to as acronyms) in the computing world. Anyone who has used a DOS-based CPU and a ⤸VGA or ⤸LCD ⤸VDU (or, indeed, an ⤸IBM ⤸MPC) to create ⤸GIFs, ⤸WAVs or ⤸PDF files, or who has hooked up to an ISP (⤸Internet Service Provider) to access IRC, WWW, a BBS or a ⤸MUD, or to get an ⤸FAQ by ⤸FTP, will be familiar with this syndrome. Some hackers are so addicted to using TLAs that a four-letter acronym is known mockingly as an 'ETLA' – *Extended Three-Letter Acronym.*

TN3270 variation of ⤸Telnet used to connect to IBM mainframes.

toggle to switch between two settings. In software a toggle is usually triggered by the same code, so it is important that this code only has two meanings. An example is the use of the same character in a text file to indicate both opening and closing quotation marks; if the same character is also used to mean an apostrophe, then conversion, via a toggle switch, for a ⤸desktop publishing system that uses different opening and closing quotation marks, will not be carried out correctly.

Token Ring protocol for ⤸local area networks, developed by IBM.

toolbar area at the top or side of a screen with ⤸pushbuttons and other features to perform frequently used tasks. For example, the toolbar of a ⤸paint program might offer quick access to different brushes, spraycans, erasers, and other useful tools. Many commercial programs enable users to create their own custom toolbars to suit their specific purposes.

Toolbook multimedia authoring tool created by the US company Asymetrix. Versions are available for @Windows NT@ to enable the management of course material distributed across the Internet.

topology the arrangement of devices in a ⤸network. Common topologies include *star networks*, where a central computer manages network access, and *ring networks*, where users can establish direct connections with other work stations.

touch screen an input device allowing the user to communicate with the computer by touching a display screen with a finger. In this way, the user can point to a required ⤸menu option or item of data. Touch screens are used less widely than other pointing devices such as the ⤸mouse or ⤸joystick.

Typically, the screen is able to detect the touch either because the finger presses against a sensitive membrane or because it interrupts a grid of light beams crossing the screen surface.

touch sensor in a computer-controlled robot, a device used to give the robot a sense of touch, allowing it to manipulate delicate objects or move automatically about a room. Touch sensors provide the feedback necessary for the robot to adjust the force of its movements and the pressure of its grip. The main types include the strain gauge and the microswitch.

trace a method of checking that a computer program is functioning correctly by causing the changing values of all the ⌐variables involved to be displayed while the program is running. In this way it becomes possible to narrow down the search for a bug, or error, in the program to the exact instruction that causes the variables to take unexpected values.

traceroute network ⌐utility program that allows the user to find out the ⌐bang path taken by ⌐packets of data sent across the ⌐Internet. Traceroute can help to debug a network, or check how it works.

track part of the magnetic structure created on a disc surface during ⌐disc formatting so that data can be stored on it. The disc is first divided into circular tracks and then each circular track is divided into a number of sectors.

trackball ⌐input device that carries out the same function as a ⌐mouse, but remains stationary. In a trackball the ball controlling the cursor position is operated directly with the fingers.

tracking amount of space between text characters. Many word processing and page layout programs allow users to adjust tracking for a wide-spaced or slightly condensed appearance.

traffic messages sent over a network such as the Internet.

transaction file a file that contains all the additions, deletions, and amendments required during ⌐file updating to produce a new version of a master file.

transistor–transistor logic (TTL) the type of integrated circuit most commonly used in building electronic products. In TTL chips the bipolar transistors are directly connected (usually collector to base). In mass-produced items, large numbers of TTL chips are commonly replaced by a small number of ⌐uncommitted logic arrays (ULAs), or logic gate arrays.

transition way in which one image changes to another in a ⌐slide show, animation or multimedia presentation.

Different transitions have a different effect on the viewer: slow mixes (fades) are gentler on the eye than sudden blackouts, and wipes – in which one scene replaces the next like a blind being pulled across the screen – are an especially dynamic type of transition.

translation program a program that translates another program written in a high-level language or assembly language into the machine-code instructions that a computer can obey. See ⌐assembler, ⌐compiler, and ⌐interpreter.

transputer a member of a family of microprocessors designed for parallel processing, developed in the UK by Inmos. In the circuits of a standard computer the processing of data takes place in sequence; in a transputer's circuits processing takes place in parallel, greatly reducing computing time for those programs that have been specifically written for it. The transputer implements a special programming language called OCCAM.

tree-and-branch filing system in computing, a filing system where all files are stored within directories, like folders in a filing cabinet. These directories may in turn be stored within further directories. The root directory contains all the other directories and may be thought of as equivalent to the filing cabinet. Another way of picturing the system is as a tree with branches from which grow smaller branches, ending in leaves (individual files).

tree-and-branch filing system
The directory filing structure used by computers. The structure can be likened to an upside-down tree, with the root at the top and branching downwards and outwards into sub-directories.

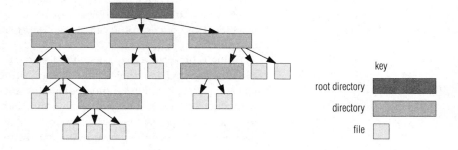

key

root directory

directory

file

Trinitron ↩monitor based on a cathode-ray tube developed by ↩Sony, designed to give a sharper image and more uniform brightness than conventional monitors.

Trojan horse a ↩virus program that appears to function normally but, while undetected by the normal user, causes damage to other files or circumvents security procedures.
    The earliest appeared in the UK in about 1988.

trolling mischievously posting a deliberately erroneous or obtuse message to a ↩newsgroup in order to tempt others to reply – usually in a way that makes them appear gullible, intemperate or foolish.

TrueType scalable font system, jointly developed by Apple and Microsoft. It allows scalable fonts to be used by non-PostScript printers. Such printers are usually cheaper.

Trumpet popular shareware ↩TCP/IP program for Windows or ↩MS-DOS.

truncation error an ↩error that occurs when a decimal result is cut off (truncated) after the maximum number of places allowed by the computer's level of accuracy.

truth table in electronics, a diagram showing the effect of a particular ↩logic gate on every combination of inputs.

Every possible combination of inputs and outputs for a particular gate or combination of gates is described, thereby defining their action in full. When logic value 1 is written in the table, it indicates a 'high' (or 'yes') input of perhaps 5 volts; logic value 0 indicates a 'low' (or 'no') input of 0 volts.

TSR abbreviation for ↩*terminate and stay resident*.

TTL abbreviation for ↩*transistor–transistor logic*, a family of integrated circuits.

TTY contraction of ↩teletype.

Turing Alan Mathison 1912–1954. English mathematician and logician. In 1936 he described a 'universal computing machine' that could theoretically be programmed to solve any problem capable of solution by a specially designed machine. This concept, now called the *Turing machine*, foreshadowed the digital computer.

Turing is believed to have been the first to suggest (in 1950) the possibility of machine learning and artificial intelligence. His test for distinguishing between real (human) and simulated (computer) thought is known as the *Turing test*: with a person in one room and the machine in another, an interrogator in a third room asks questions of both to try to identify them. When the interrogator cannot distinguish between them by questioning, the machine will have reached a state of humanlike intelligence.

Turing was born in London and studied at Cambridge. During World War II he worked on the Ultra project in the team that cracked the German Enigma cipher code. After the war he worked briefly on the project to design the general computer known as the Automatic Computing Engine, or ACE, and was involved in the pioneering computer developed at Manchester University from 1948.

Turing was concerned with mechanistic interpretations of the natural world and attempted to erect a mathematical theory of the chemical basis of organic growth. He was able to formulate and solve complicated differential equations to express certain examples of symmetry in biology and also certain phenomena such as the shapes of brown and black patches on cows.

He committed suicide following a prosecution for a minor homosexual offence.

Turing machine abstract model of an automatic problem-solving machine, formulated by Alan Turing in 1937. It provides the theoretical basis of modern digital computing.

turnkey system system that the user has only to switch on to have direct access to application software that is usually specific to a particular application area. Turnkey systems often use menus. The user is expected to follow instructions on the screen and to have no knowledge of how the system operates.

turtle small computer-controlled wheeled robot. The turtle's movements are determined by programs written by a computer user, typically using the high-level programming language ⌐LOGO.

TWAIN software standard allowing images to be taken directly from a ⌐scanner or digital camera into any image processing application. Before TWAIN, users were restricted to the scanners explicitly supported by their software; now, the only necessity is that both items follow the TWAIN standard.

24-bit colour term specifying that a ⌐video adapter is able to display more than 16 million colours simultaneously. The human eye processes 16 million colours with every blink, and a computer needs the same number of colours to be able to display pictures of a photographic quality. Powerful microprocessors, large amounts of ⌐RAM, and mass storage media are needed to handle the large computer files involved in holding such complex data.

2-D graphics graphics defined only by width and height (in mathematical terms, x and y axes). Examples of 2-D graphics are the graphics generated by spreadsheets or animated characters with no shading.

256-colour term specifying the numbers of colours that an 8-bit ⌐video adapter or ⌐VGA screen is able to display simultaneously. The earliest VGA screens could handle only 16 colours. By 1996 most new computer systems came equipped with a video adapter and display that could handle 256 colours, allowing the use of more detailed and complex graphics. The extra depth is useful for applications such as games and multimedia encyclopedias.

two's complement number system number system, based on the ⌐binary number system, that allows both positive and negative numbers to be conveniently represented for manipulation by computer.

In the two's complement system the most significant column heading (the furthest to the left) is always taken to represent a negative number.

For example, the four-column two's complement number 1101 stands for –3, since: –8 + 4 + 1 = –3.

UART integrated circuit that converts computer data into ⌒asynchronous signals suitable for transmission via a telephone line, and vice versa. UARTs combine a transmitter (parallel-to-serial converter) and a receiver (serial-to-parallel converter) to provide a 'bridge' between the parallel signals used by the computer and the serial signals used by communications networks.

ULA abbreviation for ⌒*uncommitted logic array*, a type of integrated circuit.

unbundling marketing or selling products, usually hardware and software, separately rather than as a single package.

uncommitted logic array (ULA) or *gate array* a type of semicustomized integrated circuit in which the logic gates are laid down to a general-purpose design but are not connected to each other. The interconnections can then be set in place according to the requirements of individual manufacturers. Producing ULAs may be cheaper than using a large number of TTL (⌒transistor–transistor logic) chips or commissioning a fully customized chip.

UnCover service comprised of a free searchable database of periodicals known as CARL and a fee-based fax-back facility. Researchers either dial into or access the database via Telnet or the World Wide Web and search for articles from approximately 15,000 periodicals, many not indexed elsewhere. They then select the ones they want, and pay approximately $15 each to have the articles faxed to the location of their choice, usually within 24 hours.

undelete command that allows a user to reinstate deleted text or files. See also ⌒delete.

underflow error an ⌒error that occurs if a number is outside the computer's range and is too small to deal with.

Unicode 16-bit character encoding system, intended to cover all characters in all languages (including Chinese and similar languages) and to be backwards compatible with ⌒ASCII.

Unlike ASCII, which is 8-bit and can therefore represent only 256 characters – insufficient for many diacritics outside the English language – Unicode can represent more than 65,000 characters, big enough to handle almost all written languages, including Japanese, Tibetan, and the International Phonetic Alphabet (IPA). It was created in the 1980s by Apple and Xerox in the US.

uninterruptible power supply (UPS) power supply that includes a battery, so that, in the event of a power failure, it is possible to continue operations. UPSs are normally used to provide time either for a system to be shut down in the usual way (so that files are not corrupted) or for an alternative power supply to be connected. For large systems these operations are usually carried out automatically.

UNIX multiuser ⌒operating system designed for minicomputers but becoming increasingly popular on large microcomputers, workstations, mainframes, and

supercomputers. It was developed by AT&T's Bell Laboratories in the USA during the late 1960s, using the programming language ⌐C. It could therefore run on any machine with a C compiler, so ensuring its wide portability. Its wide range of functions and flexibility, in addition to the fact that it was available free of charge during 1976–83, have made it widely used by universities and in commercial software.

unshielded twisted pair (UTP) form of cabling used for ⌐local area networks, now commonly used as an alternative to coaxial cable.

upgrade improved version of an existing software program. Upgrades are sometimes available free or at low cost to registered owners of previous versions.

UPS abbreviation for *⌐uninterruptible power supply*.

URL (abbreviation for *uniform resource locator*) series of letters and/or numbers specifying the location of a document on the ⌐World Wide Web. Every URL consists of a domain name, a description of the document's location within the host computer and the name of the document itself, separated by full stops and backslashes. Thus *The Times* web site can be found at http://www.The-times.co.uk/news/pages/home.html, and a tribute to Elvis Presley is at http:///www.mit.edu:8001/activities/41West/elvis.html. The complexity of URLs explains why bookmarks and links, which save the user from the chore of typing them in, are so popular.

USENET (acronym for *users' network*) the world's largest ⌐bulletin board system, which brings together people with common interests to exchange views

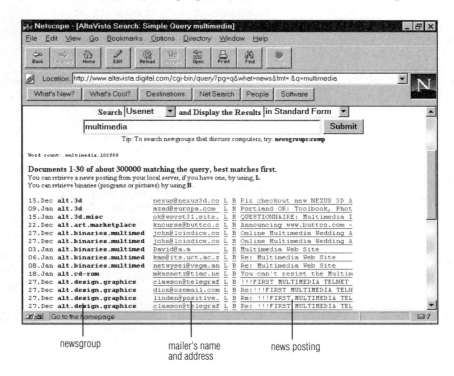

USENET
A typical user interface for the USENET bulletin board service.

newsgroup   mailer's name and address   news posting

Upgrading

why do you need to upgrade? Most personal computers are assembled from commodity components, and frequently have unused spaces and sockets inside, allowing manufacturers to build a variety of specifications from a limited inventory.

It also gives manufacturers an additional marketing tool, because components can be added and swapped with relative ease, making almost every personal computer (PC) upgradable – or, in marketing parlance, 'future-proof'.

Theoretically, this is correct. Almost any part of a PC can be upgraded, from processor and memory to discs and display, and even the entire main circuit board (motherboard). And a host of extra components can be added, internally or externally.

disadvantages Few people actually upgrade their PCs. Some upgrades are beyond the capabilities of the ordinary user. Others are costly, because the original component must be discarded, making the upgraded machine more expensive than one which had the higher specification in the first place.

Moreover, upgrading one component is seldom enough. If you wanted to convert a road car for racing, you might have to replace not only the engine, but the wheels, the brakes, the transmission, the subframe, and the windows.

Similarly with a PC. Once you replace the processor, it may also be necessary to upgrade the memory, discs, disc controller, display and graphics controller. By this time, you might as well have bought a new computer.

The older the PC, the less worthwhile the upgrade. Anything with a 286 or 386 processor is not worth upgrading, whereas a fast 486 or Pentium machine may have a couple of years of useful life left.

upgrading memory The most worthwhile upgrade, which can often be done without affecting the other components, is adding extra memory. Windows 95 requires at least 8Mb of memory to run adequately, and 16Mb can give much improved performance. In many modern PCs, all you have to do is plug in an extra memory module.

Upgrading the processor chip is fairly straightforward, as long as the PC is quite new. But to be worthwhile, the new processor should be considerably faster than the old, such as upgrading from a 486 to a Pentium, and to get full benefit you will almost certainly have to upgrade some other components.

Modern software and data requires undreamed-of amounts of disc space, so upgrading from, say, a 200Mb disc to a 1Gb model can be effective. Most people prefer to install a second hard disc, rather than scrapping the old one. But a cheaper alternative is to double the capacity of the existing disc using compression software.

Rather than upgrading core components, ambitious PC owners would do better to consider adding new ones. Multimedia features (CD-Rom drive, sound card and loudspeakers) can all be added quite cheaply, and without too much trouble. A modem (telephone adaptor) lets you hook up to the Internet, and send and receive faxes. And a tape backup unit lets you take backup copies of files.

final checks Before you upgrade, consider all the components you may have to change and any knock-on effects, and calculate the cost (including your time); you may find it will be almost as much as buying a new PC.

Then check that the PC has physical space for the new chips, drive or card, and make sure that you can return or exchange the new components if they turn out to be incompatible. Ask the PC manufacturer's advice, and check that you are not invalidating any warranty.

Finally, however minor the upgrade, always take backup copies of all programs and data first. You never know!

Paul Bray

and information. It consists of ⌐e-mail messages and articles organized into
⌐newsgroups. USENET is uncensored and governed by the rules of ⌐netiquette.

user-friendly term used to describe the ease of use of a computer system,
particularly for those with little understanding or familiarity with computers. Even
for experienced users, user-friendly programs are quicker to learn.

user ID (contraction of *user identification*) name or nickname that identifies
the user of a computer system or network. See also ⌐password.

user interface the procedures and methods through which the user operates a
program. These might include ⌐menus, input forms, error messages, and keyboard
procedures. A ⌐graphical user interface (GUI or WIMP) is one that makes use of
icons (small pictures) and allows the user to make menu selections with a mouse.
The study of the ways in which people interact with computers is a subbranch of
ergonomics. It aims to make it easier for people to use computers effectively and
comfortably, and has become a focus of research for many national and
international programmes.

utility program a systems program designed to perform a specific task related to
the operation of the computer when requested to do so by the computer user.
For example, a utility program might be used to complete a screen dump, format
a disc, or convert the format of a data file so that it can be accessed by a different
applications program.

UTP abbreviation for *⌐unshielded twisted pair*.

UUCP (acronym for *UNIX to UNIX Copy Program*) protocol which allows
⌐UNIX users to share files, read ⌐USENET articles and exchange ⌐e-mail. The
system is based on computers regularly 'polling' (connecting to) each other to
swap data. Polling can take place via an ordinary telephone connection or over
the Internet.

UUENCODE ⌐utility program that converts a ⌐binary file (typically, a program
or graphics file) into ⌐ASCII text suitable for inclusion in e-mail or ⌐USENET
messages. The recipient then *UUdecodes* the text file, reconverting it from ASCII
to the original binary file.

UUNET Technologies, Inc US-based provider of Internet access. UUNET was
the first commercial Internet Service Provider, founded in 1987; the company now
has an international network of ⌐PoPs and is a major ⌐backbone provider. It
acquired ⌐PIPEX from Unipalm 1996.

Vactor (contraction of *virtual actor*) animated character moved and voiced by an actor behind the scenes using a ⌐Waldo and dataglove to control the character.

validation the process of checking input data to ensure that it is complete, accurate, and reasonable. Although it would be impossible to guarantee that only valid data are entered into a computer, a suitable combination of validation checks should ensure that most errors are detected.

Common validation checks include:

character-type check Each input data item is checked to ensure that it does not contain invalid characters.

For example, an input name might be checked to ensure that it contains only letters of the alphabet, or an input six-figure date might be checked to ensure it contains only numbers.

field-length check The number of characters in an input field is checked to ensure that the correct number of characters has been entered. For example, a six-figure date field might be checked to ensure that it does contain exactly six digits.

control-total check The arithmetic total of a specific field from a group of records is calculated – for example, the hours worked by a group of employees might be added together – and then input with the data to which it refers. The program recalculates the control total and compares it with the one entered to ensure that entry errors have not been made.

hash-total check An otherwise meaningless control total is calculated – for example, by adding together account numbers. Even though the total has no arithmetic meaning, it can still be used to check the validity of the input account numbers.

parity check Parity bits are added to binary number codes to ensure that each number in a set of data has the same ⌐parity (that each binary number has an even number of 1s, for example). The binary numbers can then be checked to ensure that their parity remains the same. This check is often applied to data after it has been transferred from one part of the computer to another; for example, from a disc drive into the immediate-access memory.

check digit A digit is calculated from the digits of a code number and then added to that number as an extra digit. For example, in the ISBN (International Standard Book Number) 0 631 90057 8, the 8 is a check digit calculated from the book code number 063190057 and then added to it to make the full ISBN. When the full code number is input, the computer recalculates the check digit and compares it with the one entered. If the entered and calculated check digits do not match, the computer reports that an entry error of some kind has been made.

range check An input numerical data item is checked to ensure that its value falls in a sensible range. For example, an input two-digit day of the month might be checked to ensure that it is in the range 01 to 31.

variable a quantity that can take different values. Variables can be used to represent different items of data in the course of a program.

A computer programmer will choose a symbol to represent each variable used in a program. The computer will then automatically assign a memory location to store the current value of each variable, and use the chosen symbol to identify this location.

For example, the letter *P* might be chosen by a programmer to represent the price of an article. The computer would automatically reserve a memory location with the symbolic address *P* to store the price being currently processed.

Different programming languages place different restrictions on the choice of symbols used to represent variables. Some languages only allow a single letter followed, where required, by a single number. Other languages allow a much freer choice, allowing, for example, the use of the full word 'price' to represent the price of an article.

A *global variable* is one that can be accessed by any program instruction; a *local variable* is one that can only be accessed by the instructions within a particular subroutine.

VDU abbreviation for ⌐*visual display unit*.

vector graphics computer graphics that are stored in the computer memory by using geometric formulas. Vector graphics can be transformed (enlarged, rotated, stretched, and so on) without loss of picture resolution. It is also possible to select and transform any of the components of a vector-graphics display because each is separately defined in the computer memory. In these respects vector graphics are superior to ⌐raster graphics. Vector graphics are typically used for drawing applications, allowing the user to create and modify technical diagrams such as designs for houses or cars.

verification the process of checking that data being input to a computer have been accurately copied from a source document.

This may be done visually, by checking the original copy of the data against the copy shown on the VDU screen. A more thorough method is to enter the data twice, using two different keyboard operators, and then to check the two sets of input copies against each other. The checking is normally carried out by the computer itself, any differences between the two copies being reported for correction by one of the the keyboard operators.

Where large quantities of data have to be input, a separate machine called a *verifier* may be used to prepare fully verified tapes or discs for direct input to the main computer.

Veronica software tool for searching for files on the ⌐Internet. Veronica is broadly similar to ⌐Archie, but whereas the latter searches anonymous ⌐FTP sites, Veronica searches ⌐Gopher servers.

Veronica is sometimes said to stand for 'very easy rodent-oriented net-wide index to computerized archives' and is sometimes also known as ⌐*Archie's girlfriend*.

vertical spam on ⌐USENET, spam which consists of many, often repetitive, messages per day posted to the same newsgroup or small set of newsgroups. The effect is to drown out other, more useful, conversation in the newsgroup.

VESA local bus hardware configuration laid down by the Video Electronics Standards Association for computers based on the ⌐Intel 486 chip. A VESA local bus speeds up operations by providing a dedicated link between microprocessor to monitor.

VGA (abbreviation for *video graphics array*) a colour display system that provides either 16 colours on screen and a resolution of 640 x 480, or 256 colours with a resolution of 320 x 200. ⌐SVGA (Super VGA) provides even higher resolution and more colours.

video accelerator card in computing, circuit board that contains a special microchip to process display data, freeing the ⌐central processing unit (CPU) for other tasks. A video accelerator card speeds up the performance of computers running ⌐Windows and other ⌐graphical user interfaces (GUIs) which place a heavy demand on processors.

video adapter an ⌐expansion board that allows display of graphics and colour. Commonly used video adapters for IBM PC-based systems are Hercules, CGA, EGA, VGA, XGA, and SVGA.

video adapter card circuit board that provides the data needed to create a display on a ⌐monitor. Common adapter cards include ⌐VGA and ⌐SVGA.

video capture board ⌐expansion board for a personal computer which digitizes an incoming stream of analogue video. Video capture boards vary widely in the amount of data they can handle; the cheapest can handle only single frames, while the most expensive and full-featured can handle full-motion video. Once the video stream has been digitized, it can be stored, copied, digitally edited or retouched on the computer.

Video CD ⌐CD-ROM that conforms to Philips' White Book standard for displaying full-motion digital video using ⌐MPEG data compression. Video CD is used to store films such as *Top Gun* on CD-ROM for playback on Philips ⌐CD-i players and personal computers or consoles equipped with an MPEG decoder in hardware and/or software.

videoconferencing system which allows people in different locations to interact via video and audio. It is essentially multiparty telephone conferencing with pictures. Older videoconferencing systems required expensive equipment set up in a special-purpose room. By the mid 1990s, newer systems became available for desktop videoconferencing using much cheaper equipment so that videoconferencing facilities could be deployed to individual users' desks.

video dialtone US legislation passed in Oct 1995, to allow telephone companies to sell information and video services as well as straight telephone connections. The result is expected to be increased competition in both telephone and television services.

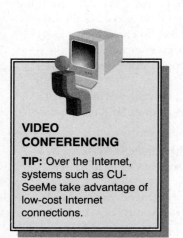

VIDEO CONFERENCING

TIP: Over the Internet, systems such as CU-SeeMe take advantage of low-cost Internet connections.

video file file, such as an ⮑MPEG or ⮑AVI file, that contains compressed video information.

video graphics card ⮑expansion board that gives personal computers their display capability. The video graphics card must match the display monitor in functionality.

video-on-demand (VOD) system for transmission of video by cable where specific videos can be selected from a choice button on the remote control that brings up a menu on screen. Once a choice has been selected, a set-top box sends a query to the video server where the video is stored in compressed format. The server sends the video back through the system where it is decompressed by the set-top box. Trials were underway in Europe and the USA 1996.

videophone telephone allowing the sending and receiving of pictures as well as voice.

videotext system in which information (text and simple pictures) is displayed on a television (video) screen. There are two basic systems, known as ⮑teletext and ⮑viewdata. In the teletext system information is broadcast with the ordinary television signals, whereas in the viewdata system information is relayed to the screen from a central data bank via the telephone network. Both systems require the use of a television receiver (or a connected VTR) with special decoder.

viewdata system of displaying information on a television screen in which the information is extracted from a computer data bank and transmitted via the telephone lines. It is one form of ⮑videotext. The British Post Office (now British Telecom) developed the first viewdata system, Prestel, 1975. Similar systems are now in widespread use in other countries. Users have access to a large store of information, presented on the screen in the form of 'pages'.

Prestel has hundreds of thousands of pages, presenting all kinds of information, from local weather and restaurant menus to share prices and airport timetables. Since viewdata uses telephone lines, it can become a two-way interactive information system, making possible, for example, home banking and shopping. In contrast, the only user input allowed by the ⮑teletext system is to select the information to be displayed.

virtual without physical existence. Some computers have virtual memory, making their immediate-access memory seem larger than it is. ⮑Virtual reality is a computer simulation of a whole physical environment.

virtual community group of people joined by using the same electronic conferencing system. The sense of virtual community can be extremely strong, going beyond simply exchanging mutually useful information to helping with real-life events such as family illnesses and financial crises.

virtual corporation company with no real-life headquarters but whose employees and/or individual contractors are linked via telecommunications.

VIRTUAL COMMUNITY

TIP: The most detailed examination of virtual communities is Howard Rheingold's book *The Virtual Community* 1992.

Virtuality British computing company founded in a garage in 1987 by Dr Jonathan Waldern and three friends. Originally called W Industries, Virtuality pioneered 'virtual reality' games machines, where players wear head-mounted displays, launching its first commercial products in 1991. Virtuality machines found in arcades across the world have provided most people's first, and often their only, experience of virtual reality.

virtual memory a technique whereby a portion of the computer backing storage, or external, ↩memory is used as an extension of its immediate-access, or internal, memory. The contents of an area of the immediate-access memory are stored on, say, a hard disc while they are not needed, and brought back into main memory when required.

The process, called paging or segmentation, is controlled by the computer ↩operating system and is hidden from the programmer, to whom the computer's internal memory appears larger than it really is. The technique can be successfully implemented only if very fast backing store is available, so that 'pages' of memory can be rapidly switched into and out of the immediate-access memory.

virtual reality advanced form of computer simulation, in which a participant has the illusion of being part of an artificial environment. The participant views the environment through two tiny television screens (one for each eye) built into a visor. Sensors detect movements of the participant's head or body, causing the apparent viewing position to change. Gloves (datagloves) fitted with sensors may be worn, which allow the participant seemingly to pick up and move objects in the environment.

The technology is still under development but is expected to have widespread applications; for example, in military and surgical training, architecture, and home entertainment.

Virtual Reality Modelling Language method of displaying three-dimensional images on a web page, usually abbreviated to ↩VRML.

virus a piece of ↩software that can replicate and transfer itself from one computer to another, without the user being aware of it. Some viruses are relatively harmless, but others can damage or destroy data. They are written by anonymous programmers, often maliciously, and are spread on ↩floppy discs, on local networks, and more recently on the ↩Internet. Antivirus software can be used to detect and destroy well-known viruses, but new viruses continually appear and these may bypass existing antivirus programs.

Computer viruses may be programmed to operate on a particular date, such as the Michelangelo Virus, which was triggered on 6 March 1992 (the anniversary of the birthday of Italian artist Michelangelo) and erased hard discs.

UK legislation The Computer Misuse Act of 1990 made the release of computer viruses an offence. In Nov 1995 Christopher Pile (known as the Black Baron) was sentenced to 18 months in prison for writing a virus, becoming the first person to be imprisoned for this offence.

Internet virus A virus which is spread via Microsoft ↩Word documents was discovered on the Internet in 1995. The virus comes in the form of a Word ⮑macro program. The first virus of this kind was harmless, but a malicious version appeared soon after, capable of causing serious damage to the infected system.

vision system computer-based device for interpreting visual signals from a video camera. Computer vision is important in robotics where sensory abilities would considerably increase the flexibility and usefulness of a robot.

Although some vision systems exist for recognizing simple shapes, the technology is still in its infancy.

Visual Basic computer language based on ⮑BASIC.

visual display unit (VDU) computer terminal consisting of a keyboard for input data and a screen for displaying output. The oldest and the most popular type of VDU screen is the cathode-ray tube (CRT), which uses essentially the same technology as a television screen. Other types use plasma display technology and ⮑liquid-crystal displays.

visualization turning numerical data into graphics. A simple example is to create a bar chart from a set of sales figures; more complex types of visualization include fractals and other forms of computer-generated art.

visual programming programming method that uses a system of graphics, instead of text, to build software.

VLSI (abbreviation for *very large-scale integration*) in electronics, the early-1990s' level of advanced technology in the microminiaturization of ⮑integrated circuits, and an order of magnitude smaller than ⮑LSI (large-scale integration).

VMS operating system created in 1978 by ⮑DEC for its VAX minicomputers. VMS was for many years a popular operating system for hackers (see ⮑hacking), although it has now been largely eclipsed by ⮑UNIX.

V numbers series of ⮑protocols issued by the International Telecommunication Union defining the rate at which modems transfer data. The numbers have come to designate a modem's speed: V.32 modems transmit at up to 9,600 ⮑bits per second (bps); V.32b is at up to 14,400 bps and V.34 at up to 28,800 bps.

voice input in computing and electronics, an alternative name for ⮑speech recognition.

voice mail ⮑electronic mail including spoken messages and audio. Messages can also be generated electronically using ⮑speech synthesis. In offices, voice mail systems are often included in computerized telephone switchboards.

voice modem ⮑modem which handles voice as well as data communications, so that it can be used to add the capabilities of a ⮑voice mail system to a personal computer.

Primarily aimed at small and home-based businesses, voice modems use a built-in ⮑DSP and typically also include fax facilities.

voice output in computing and electronics, an alternative name for ⌐speech synthesis.

voice-to-MIDI converter microphone which sends human vocal input to a synthesizer.

This system of singing to run a synthesizer does not work well unless the singer has perfect pitch, so it is not commonly used.

volatile memory ⌐memory that loses its contents when the power supply to the computer is disconnected.

Von Neumann John, (originally Johann) 1903–1957. Hungarian-born US scientist and mathematician, a pioneer of computer design. He invented his 'rings of operators' (called Von Neumann algebras) in the late 1930s, and also contributed to set theory, game theory, quantum mechanics, cybernetics (with his theory of self-reproducing automata, called *Von Neumann machines*), and the development of the atomic and hydrogen bombs.

He designed and supervised the construction of the first computer able to use a flexible stored program (named MANIAC-1) at the Institute for Advanced Study at Princeton from 1940–52. This work laid the foundations for the design of all subsequent programmable computers.

Von Neumann was born in Budapest and studied in Germany and Switzerland. In 1930 he emigrated to the USA, where he became professor at Princeton 1931, and from 1933 he was a member of the Institute for Advanced Study there. He also held a number of advisory posts with the US government 1940–54.

Von Neumann's book *The Mathematical Foundations of Quantum Mechanics* 1932 defended mathematically the uncertainty principle of German physicist Werner Heisenberg. In 1944, Von Neumann showed that matrix mechanics and wave mechanics were equivalent.

The monumental *Theory of Games and Economic Behavior* 1944, written with Oskar Morgenstern (1902–1977), laid the foundations for modern game theory.

vPoP (acronym for *virtual point of presence*) telephone link which enables users to connect to a distant point of presence (⌐PoP) for the price of a local call.

VRAM (acronym for *video random-access memory*) form of ⌐RAM that allows simultaneous access by two different devices, so that graphics can be handled at the same time as data is updated. VRAM improves graphic display performance.

VR browser application that enables PC users to 'walk through' a ⌐virtual reality scene on their monitors.

VRML (acronym for *Virtual Reality Modelling Language*) method of displaying three-dimensional images on a ⌐web page. VRML, which functions as a counterpart to ⌐HTML, is a platform-independent language that creates a ⌐virtual reality scene which users can 'walk' through and follow links much like a conventional web page.

In some contexts, VRML can replace conventional computer interfaces with their icons, menus, files, and folders. It is possible to use VRML to create, for example, a virtual museum with all the elements of a real museum, including corridors, display cases and multimedia demonstrations. Other possibilities include a web market containing stalls with goods that can be 'handled' using a mouse, or a virtual library of 'books' which can be taken off 'shelves'.

VT-100 type number of a simple character-based computer terminal originally supplied by ⤴DEC (Digital Equipment Corporation). VT-100 terminal emulation is commonly provided in personal computer communications software and may be useful for logging on to minicomputers and networks via the Internet.

W3 Consortium computing industry group which seeks to promote standards and coordinate developments in the World Wide Web. Founded in 1994 and based at the Massachusetts Institute of Technology (MIT), the Consortium is directed by Tim ↝Berners-Lee, inventor of the Web. The W3 Consortium is behind many initiatives, including the ↝HTML standard for building web pages and the ↝PICS content rating system.

WAIS (abbreviation for Wide Area Information Server) software tool for searching for and retrieving information from a range of archives on the ↝Internet.

wait state situation when the ↝central processing unit or a ↝bus is idle. Wait states are necessary because system components run at different speeds.

Waldo a mechanical device, such as a gripper arm, that follows the movements of a human limb. Waldos were developed by the nuclear industry in the 1940s for handling hazardous substances at a safe distance, and were named after a 1942 story by science-fiction writer Robert Heinlein.

walkthrough another name for ↝flythrough.

wallpaper design used as a background 'desktop pattern' on ↝graphical user interfaces (GUIs) such as ↝Windows or ↝System 7, and visible when no windows are open. Users can choose from a range of different wallpapers, including plain colours, textures and repeating patterns, or a design their own.

WAN abbreviation for *wide area ↝network*.

wand in ↝virtual reality, simple input device to allow users to interact with onscreen objects in three dimensions.

Wang An 1920–1990. Chinese-born US engineer, founder of Wang Laboratories 1951, one of the world's largest computer companies in the 1970s. In 1948 he invented the computer memory core, the most common device used for storing computer data before the invention of the integrated circuit (chip).

Wang emigrated to the USA 1945. He developed his own company with the $500,000 he received from IBM from the sale of his patent. One of his early contracts was the first electronic scoreboard, installed at New York's Shea Stadium. His company took off in 1964 with the introduction of a desktop calculator. Later, Wang switched with great success to the newly emerging market for word-processing systems based on cheap silicon chips, turning Wang Laboratories into a multibillion-dollar company. But with the advent of the personal computer, the company fell behind. Wang Laboratories made a loss of $400 million 1989.

wAreZ slang for pirated games or other applications that can be downloaded using ↝FTP.

WAV (abbreviation of *Windows WAVeform*) audio file format for ↝IBM-compatible PCs, widely used to distribute sounds over the Internet. WAV files, which contain a digitized recording of a sound, bear the suffix .wav.

wavetable synthesizer ⌐MIDI synthesizer that uses sampling – recordings of actual musical instruments – to create sounds. The authenticity of the sound source means that wavetable synthesizers can achieve very realistic results.

web authoring tool software for creating ⌐web pages. The basic web authoring tool is ⌐HTML, the source code that determines how a web page is constructed and how it looks. Other programs, such as ⌐Java and ⌐VRML, can also be incorporated to enhance web pages with animations and interactive features. Commercial authoring tools include HoTMetaL PRO, HTML Assistant, and WebAuthor.

Web browser client software that allows to access the World Wide Web. See ⌐browser.

Webmaster ⌐system administrator for a server on the ⌐World Wide Web.

web page a ⌐hypertext document on the ⌐World Wide Web.

WWW address (URL)

icons link to required audio
and video plug-ins

hot spots

user clicks on 'Enter' - a hypertext   . . . a menu page of graphic   . . . and selects an interactive
link to . . .   hotspots . . .   game

web page
An example of how pages
on the World Wide Web
may be linked to take the
user to additional pages of
information.

webzine magazine published on the Web, instead of on paper. Notable examples include *HotWired* (a digital version of ⌐*Wired* magazine), *Slate* (a serious periodical funded by ⌐Microsoft), and *Suck* (satire). Electronic versions of printed magazines (such as *Elle* or *Vogue*) do not, in the strict sense of the word, qualify as webzines, for they rarely offer any substantial content which is not available on the news stand.

WELL, the (acronym for *Whole Earth 'Lectronic Link*) San Francisco-based electronic conferencing system. It was founded in 1984 by Stewart ↝Brand, with Larry Brilliant, Matthew McClure, and Kevin Kelly (later founding editor of ↝*Wired* magazine). The WELL includes among its 11,000 members a mix of leading journalists and writers, Grateful Dead fans, and technological inventors. The WELL featured in the 1995 arrest of hacker Kevin ↝Mitnick, and was the site where the first few Computers, Freedom, and Privacy conferences (annual gatherings to discuss the future impact of technology) were planned. The WELL was bought 1994 by Reebok founder Bruce Katz.

whois searchable database of every registered ↝domain and the names of their users. A special application, also called Whois, is needed to search the database.

wide area network a ↝network that connects computers distributed over a wide geographical area.

Wiener Norbert 1894–1964. US mathematician, credited with the establishment of the science of cybernetics in his book *Cybernetics* 1948. In mathematics, he laid the foundation of the study of stochastic processes (those dependent on random events), particularly Brownian motion.

Wiener was born in Columbia, Missouri, and received his PhD from Harvard at the age of 19. He then went to Europe to study under leading mathematicians (Bertrand Russell at Cambridge, England, and David Hilbert at Göttingen, Germany). From 1919 he taught at the Massachusetts Institute of Technology, becoming professor 1932.

Wiener devoted much of his efforts to methodology, developing mathematical approaches that could usefully be applied to continuously changing processes.

During World War II, Wiener worked on the control of anti-aircraft guns (which required him to consider factors such as the machinery itself, the gunner, and the unpredictable evasive action on the part of the target's pilot), on filtering 'noise' from useful information for radar, and on coding and decoding. His investigations stimulated his interest in information transfer and processes such as information feedback.

wild card character which represents 'any character' in a search or command. When comparing ↝strings, the computer does not seek a precise match for a wild card character. The most useful wildcards are ?, which matches any single character, and *, which matches any number of characters, including zero. Hence the ↝DOS commands DEL *.* – delete all files – and COPY *.DOC – copy all files with the filename extension 'DOC'.

Wilkes Maurice Vincent 1913–   . English mathematician who led the team at Cambridge University that built the EDSAC (electronic delay storage automatic calculator) 1949, one of the earliest of the British electronic computers.

Wilkes was born in Dudley and studied at Cambridge. During World War II he became involved with the development of radar.

He was director of the Cambridge Mathematical Laboratory 1946–80.

In the late 1940s Wilkes and his team began to build the EDSAC. At the time, electronic computers were in their infancy. Wilkes chose the serial mode, in which the information in the computer is processed in sequence (and not several parts at once, as in the parallel type). This design incorporated mercury delay lines (developed at the Massachusetts Institute of Technology, USA) as the elements of the memory.

In May 1949 the EDSAC ran its first program and became the first delay-line computer in the world. From early 1950 it offered a regular computing facility to the members of Cambridge University, the first general-purpose computer service. Much time was spent by the research group on programming and on the compilation of a library of programs. The EDSAC was in operation until 1958.

EDSAC II came into service 1957. This was a parallel-processing machine and the delay line was abandoned in favour of magnetic storage methods.

WIMP (acronym for *windows, icons, menus, pointing device*) another name for ⌐graphical user interface (GUI).

Winchester drive an old-fashioned term for ⌐hard disc.

WinCode program developed by US company Snappy Inc, that uses a process known as bit-shifting to ⌐uuencode and uudecode binary programs and files in 7-bit ASCII text so that they can be transmitted via on-line systems and over the Internet. Several other coding systems are also used, and recent versions of WinCode can handle most of the common formats. WinCode is a copyright program distributed as freeware.

window a rectangular area on the screen of a ⌐graphical user interface. A window is used to display data and can be manipulated in various ways by the computer user.

Windows ⌐graphical user interface (GUI) from Microsoft that has become the standard for IBM PCs and clones. There are two versions of Windows: *Windows 95*, designed for homes and offices uses the ⌐MS-DOS operating system; Windows NT is a 32-bit ⌐multi-user and ⌐multitasking operating system, used by engineers, scientists, and other professions that require a high-processing capacity. Windows NT is seen as a rival to ⌐UNIX.

Windows WAVeform audio file format commonly abbreviated to ⌐WAV.

WIN.INI (acronym for *Windows initialization*) file used by Microsoft Windows to store a range of settings that in general govern the appearance of Windows and some Windows applications. Changes made via Windows 3's Control Panel program are often stored in WIN.INI, though there is an increasing tendency for programs to use their own .INI files.

Winsock (contraction of *Windows socket*) program that supplies an interface between Windows software and a ⌐TCP/IP application.

Wired US computing magazine founded 1993 by Jane Metcalfe and Louis Rossetto to serve as the voice of the 'digital revolution'. It is based in San Francisco. In addition to its flagship US magazine, *Wired's* parent company, Wired Ventures, publishes editions in Japan and the UK.

WIRED

TIP: Wired Ventures manages a number of advertising-supported sites on the World Wide Web, including The Netizen http://www. netizen.com, Muckraker http://www.muckraker.com, and HotWired http://www.hotwired.com. It also owns the satirical site Suck http://www. suck.com and the search engine HotBot http://www.hotbot.com. By 1996, Wired had become such a strongly recognized magazine that there were a number of parodies, including ReWired and, on the Web, HowTired http://www. howtired.com.

wired gloves interface worn on the hands for ⌐virtual reality applications. The gloves detect the movement of the hands, enabling the user to 'touch' and 'move' objects in a virtual environment.

wire frame method of creating three-dimensional computerized animations by drawing a series of frames showing the moving image in outline, like a moving skeleton. When the designer is satisfied with the action of the wire-frame figure, he or she adds the 'skin', superimposing textures to give the final effect.

wizard interactive tool developed by ⌐Microsoft that 'talks' users of a program through a complex operation, such as creating a ⌐template or a presentation. The wizard presents the user with a series of ⌐dialog boxes asking simple questions in ordinary language, which the user answers by choosing ⌐radio buttons, check boxes and entering information by keyboard.

The term wizard stems from programmers' slang, where it means an expert in a particular piece of software or hardware, capable of answering all manner of queries, fixing faults and dealing with emergencies.

word a group of bits (binary digits) that a computer's central processing unit treats as a single working unit. The size of a word varies from one computer to another and, in general, increasing the word length leads to a faster and more powerful computer. In the late 1970s and early 1980s, most microcomputers were 8-bit machines. During the 1980s 16-bit microcomputers were introduced and 32-bit microcomputers are now available. Mainframe computers may be 32-bit or 64-bit machines.

Word word processing program for the IBM PC and Apple ⌐Macintosh produced by ⌐Microsoft. Word began 1983 as an ⌐MS-DOS program, but was much less successful than its rival, ⌐WordPerfect and development ceased 1993. However, with the arrival of ⌐Windows 3.0, Word for Windows established itself as the leading Windows word processor 1991.

WordPerfect word processing program for various computers produced by WordPerfect Corp. It was first released 1982 and by 1987 was the dominant ⌐MS-DOS word processor, rapidly eclipsing the previous leader, WordStar, by offering many more features, despite having the reputation of being difficult to learn.

WordPerfect Corp was slow to release a version of WordPerfect for ⌐Windows, and when it did appear 1992 it suffered in comparison with Microsoft ⌐Word. Word has retained its market lead during 1996, but recent versions of WordPerfect have been rated highly.

word processor a program that allows the input, amendment, manipulation, storage, and retrieval of text; or a computer system that runs such software. Since word-processing programs became available to microcomputers, the method has largely replaced the typewriter for producing letters or other text. Typical facilities include insert, delete, cut and paste, reformat, search and replace, copy, print, mail merge, and spelling check.

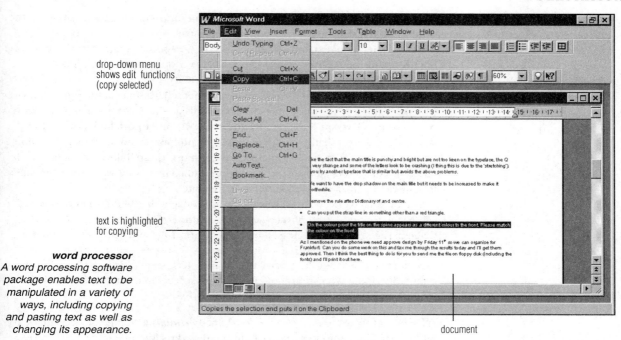

drop-down menu
shows edit functions
(copy selected)

text is highlighted
for copying

word processor
*A word processing software
package enables text to be
manipulated in a variety of
ways, including copying
and pasting text as well as
changing its appearance.*

document

*Some major word
processing programs*

Software	Manufacturer	Description
TopCopy	Top Level	professional program provides integration with database and accounts
Word	Microsoft	market leader; powerful and easy to use with sophisticated spell checking
Word Pro	Lotus	formerly Ami Pro; good value program strong on tabling and charting
WordPerfect	Corel	full-featured, including format and spell checking; customizable interface

The leading word processing programs include Lotus Word Pro, Microsoft Word, and WordPerfect.

workgroup small group of computer users who need to share data and computer facilities.

workstation high-performance desktop computer with strong graphics capabilities, traditionally used for engineering (↪CAD and ↪CAM), scientific research, and desktop publishing. Frequently based on fast RISC (reduced instruction-set computer) chips, workstations generally offer more processing power than microcomputers (although the distinction between workstations and the more powerful microcomputer models is becoming increasingly blurred). Most workstations use ↪UNIX as their operating system, and have good networking facilities.

World Wide Web (WWW) ⌐hypertext system for publishing information on the ⌐Internet. World Wide Web documents ('web pages') are text files coded using ⌐HTML to include text and graphics, stored on a special computer (a web server) connected to the Internet. Web pages may also contain ⌐Java ⌐applets for enhanced animation, video, sound, and interactivity.

Every web page has a ⌐URL (Uniform Resource Locator) – a unique address (usually starting with `http://www`) which tells a ⌐browser program (such as Netscape or Microsoft Explorer) where to find it. An important feature of the World Wide Web is that most documents contain links enabling readers to follow whichever aspects of a subject interest them most. These links may connect to different computers all over the world. Interlinked or nested web pages belonging to a single organization are known as a 'web site'.

The original World Wide Web program was created in 1990 for internal use at CERN, the Geneva-based physics research centre, by Tim Berners-Lee and Robert Cailliau. The system was released on the Internet 1991, but only caught on in 1993, following the release of ⌐Mosaic, an easy-to-use PC-compatible browser. The exponential growth of the Internet since then has been widely attributed to the popularity of the Web: from the 600-odd web servers in existence in December 1993, the total had exceeded 80,000 by July 1996.

WORM (acronym for *write once read many times*) a storage device, similar to ⌐CD-ROM. The computer can write to the disc directly, but cannot later erase or overwrite the same area. WORMs are mainly used for archiving and backup copies.

worm ⌐virus designed to spread from computer to computer across a network. Worms replicate themselves while 'hiding' in a computer's memory, causing systems to 'crash' or slow down, but do not infect other programs or destroy data directly.

The most celebrated worm was the 'Internet worm' of November 1988. Released onto the Internet by Robert Morris, Jr., a graduate student at Cornell University, it infected some 6,000 systems via a loophole in §UNIX e-mail and finger procedures. Morris claimed that a programming bug had caused the worm to replicate far more virulently than he had intended, and took swift measures to publish an 'antidote' on the network – but by then, many machines had already been disconnected from it. Morris was later convicted, fined, and sentenced to 400 hours community service.

write-once technology technology that allows a user to write data onto an optical disc once. After that, the data is permanent and can be read any number of times.

write protection device on discs and tapes that provides ⌐data security by allowing data to be read but not deleted, altered, or overwritten.

WYSIWYG (acronym for *what you see is what you get*) a program that attempts to display on the screen a faithful representation of the final printed output. For example, a WYSIWYG ⌐word processor would show actual page layout – line widths, page breaks, and the sizes and styles of type.

x ⌒wild card character often used to describe versions of hardware or software. One might, therefore, refer to Windows 3.x (any version of Windows, from 3.0 to 3.31), System 7.x (any version of System 7) or a x86 chip (any of the chips manufactured by ⌒Intel with serial numbers ending in 86).

X.25 communications protocol for sending ⌒packets of data over a network.

X.400 standard maintained by the ITU (International Telecommunications Union, formerly the CCITT) which forms the basis for a Message Handling System. X.400 is used as a shorthand term for a number of recommendations and standards involved in running some electronic mail systems over telecommunications lines.

X.500 directory standards for network addresses, issued by the ⌒Comité Consultatif International Téléphonique et Télégraphique (CCITT).

Xerox PARC Xerox Corporation's Palo Alto Research Center. During the 1970s and 1980s, Xerox PARC spawned a series of major computing innovations, including ⌒Ethernet networks, the ⌒mouse and the ⌒graphical user interface (GUI). Laser printing, ⌒Smalltalk and the LAN (⌒local area network) and the first (never-manufactured) personal computer were also developed there.

Xerox never capitalized on these inventions, leaving entreprenuers such as Steve ⌒Jobs and Bill ⌒Gates to bring them into the marketplace, but Xerox PARC remains at the cutting edge of computer innovations.

XGA (abbreviation for ***extended graphics array***) colour display system which provides either 256 colours on screen and a resolution of 1,024 x 768 ⌒pixels or 25,536 colours with a resolution of 640 x 480. This gives a much sharper image than, for example, ⌒VGA, which can only display 480 lines of 640 pixels.

Xmodem an ⌒FTP ⌒protocol designed to make transmitting files via telephone speedy and error-free.

XON/XOFF control commands used when two devices ⌒handshake using a modem connection. XON starts or resumes transmission of data and XOFF pauses it. XON and XOFF can be manually activated by control-Q and control-S respectively.

XOR (contraction of ***exclusive or***) search filter meaning 'A or B, but not both'. Thus a search for 'chocolate xor biscuit' might yield 'chocolate', 'biscuit', 'chocolate cake' and 'shortbread biscuit' but never 'chocolate biscuit'. See also ⌒Boolean algebra.

X-Windows ⌒graphical user interface for UNIX. X-Windows was developed at the Massachusetts Institute of Technology, and is ultimately intended to be a standard for windowing systems. X-Windows is now controlled by X-OPEN as part of the drive towards open systems in the UNIX world.

Yahoo ⌒search engine for the ⌒World Wide Web, based on a catalogue of indexed resources. Yahoo, for several years the only search engine on the Web, was created at Stanford University by David Filo and Jerry Yang.

year 2000 problem faced by computer professionals, the industry, and users towards the close of the 20th century because most computers use only 6 digits to record the date. Thus, 10 August 1962 is recorded as 10/08/62, 081062 , or a similar format. Because the year is represented by only two characters, computers all over the world need reprogramming to prevent them assuming that the figures 00 stand for 1900. The consequences could be devastating, including pension funds and payrolls being unable to make payments, accounting systems refusing to issue cheques, landlords crediting lessees with 99 years rent and many companies going out of business. Action to minimize these problems started in the mid-1990s.

user can key in indexed word to be searched . . .

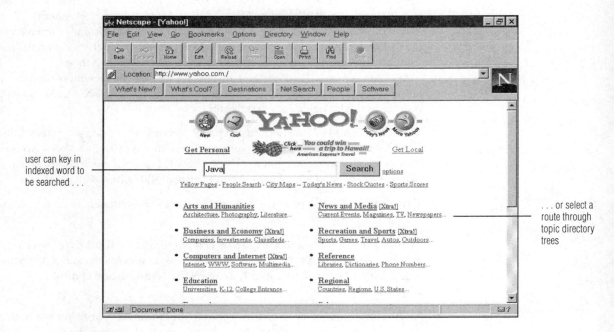

. . . or select a route through topic directory trees

Yahoo
The Yahoo World Wide Web user interface, which enables the user to search for occurrences of a particular word, or to browse through particular subject areas.

z-buffer ⌐buffer for storing depth information for displaying three-dimensional graphics. (Two dimensional images may be displayed using x,y coordinates but the third dimension implies x, y, and z.) In a graphics card, z-buffer memory keeps track of which onscreen elements are visible and which are hidden behind other objects.

zero wait state term applied to ⌐central processing units that run without wait states – that is, without waiting for slower chips.

ZIF socket (acronym for *zero insertion force socket*) socket on a computer's ⌐motherboard that enables a chip to be easily removed or inserted by use of a lever. ZIF sockets are usually used only for expensive ⌐microprocessors that are designed to be upgraded.

Zimmermann Phil(ip) R 1955– . US security consultant and author of the encryption program ⌐Pretty Good Privacy (PGP). He was an obscure security consultant in Colorado, with an interest in cryptography until the ready availability of PGP caught the eye of the US Justice Department, which in 1993 began investigating whether Zimmermann had violated US export restrictions on strong encryption products. He consistently denied having released PGP to the Net, and in 1996 the Justice Department dropped the investigation without indicting him.

Zip drive portable disc drive manufactured by ⌐Iomega. Zip drives can store 100 ⌐megabytes on each 3.5-in disc.

zipped file a file that has been compressed using the ⌐PKZIP program.

Zmodem ⌐FTP ⌐protocol for transferring files across the ⌐Internet. It offers the facility to use ⌐wild cards to search files and to resume interrupted transfers where they left off.

Appendix: thematic lists of computing, multimedia, and Internet terms

audio
biographies
bulletin boards and USENET
communications
companies
computer architecture
computer control
computer types
data processing
data representation
data storage
electronic mail
graphics
input devices
Internet and on-line services
multimedia and interactivity
networks
organizations
output devices
programming
programming languages
security and freedom of information
software and applications
software programs and operating systems
standards and protocols
systems analysis
user interface
video
virtual reality

AUDIO
audio file
AVI
CD-quality sound
digital audio tape
digital signal processor
FM synthesizer
line input
MIDI
mixer
Moog, Robert
polyphony
RealAudio
SoundBlaster
speech chip
speech synthesis
speech writing system
voice modem
voice-to-MIDI converter
WAV

BIOGRAPHIES
Andreessen, Marc
Barlow, John Perry
Barnsley, Michael
Berners-Lee, Tim
Brand, Stewart
Cerf, Vinton
Clark, James
Cray, Seymour Roger
Gates, Bill
Gibson, William
Gore, Al
Herzog, Bertram
Jobs, Steve
Kahle, Brewster
Kapor, Mitch
Kay, Alan
Lanier, Jaron
Mandelbrot, Benoit
Mitnick, Kevin
Moog, Robert
Moore, Gordon
Negroponte, Nicholas
Nelson, Ted
Sterling, Bruce
Stoll, Clifford
Zimmermann, Phil

BULLETIN BOARDS AND USENET
alt heirarchy
anonymous remailer
article
Big Seven

binary newsgroup
bozofilter
bulletin board
bulletin board system
call for votes
cancelbot
CancelMoose
Computer Underground Digest
cross-posting
dot
electronic conferencing
expire
Fidonet
flame
flame war
follow-up post
freenet
frequently asked questions
hierarchy
killfile
lurk
moderator
netiquette
newbie
news server
newsgroup
newsreader
NNTP
off-line reader
pseudonym
public news server
quoting
scrollback
.sig
signature
subject drift
sysop
test message
trolling
USENET
vertical spam

COMMUNICATIONS
acoustic coupler
ADSL
asynchronous
asynchronous transfer mode
authentication
auto-responder
backbone
bandwidth
baseband
baud
bits per second

blink
bridge
broadband
brouter
cable modem
cellular modem
cellular phone
clickstream
client
client/server
codec
communications
Communications Decency Act
communications program
Compulink Information Exchange
computer-mediated communication
computer-supported collaborative
  work
dial-up connection
digital data transmission
direct broadcast system
duplex
Electronic Communications Privacy
  Act
electronic data interchange
fax
fax modem
flow control
frame relay
full duplex
half duplex
handle
handshake
Hayes Computer Products
hub
internal modem
inverse multiplexing
ITU
KA9Q
kermit
kilostream link
leased line
MCI
microbilling
mobile phone
modem
modem tax
NO CARRIER
null-modem
Open Systems Interconnection
packet radio
phreaking
PSTN
RSUP

script
secure HTTP
Sprint
T1 link
T3
telco
telecommuting
telemedicine
time out
UART
V numbers
video dialtone
videoconferencing
videophone
virtual community
virtual corporation
voice modem
voice-to-MIDI converter
X.25
X.400
X.500

COMPANIES
Acorn
Adobe
America Online
Amiga
Big Blue
CompuServe
Corel
Creative Labs
DEC
Demon Internet
Hayes Computer Products
Hewlett-Packard
IBM
id Software
Industrial Light & Magic
Intel
Iomega
MCI
Microsoft Corp.
Netcom
NeXT Technologies Inc
Nintendo
Novell
Philips
Pipex
Pixar
RSA
Sega
Silicon Graphics Inc.
Sony
Sprint

Sun Microsystems
Syquest
TeleAdapt
UUNET Technologies Inc.
Virtuality
Xerox PARC

COMPUTER ARCHITECTURE
accelerator board
access
access time
accumulator
active matrix LCD
adder
address
address bus
alligator clips
alpha channel
alpha disc
analog computer
architecture
arithmetic and logic unit
ARM
ASIC board
backup
BIOS
boot disc
bridge
brouter
buffer
bus
cache memory
central processing unit
Centronics interface
CGA
chip
chip-set
CISC
client/server architecture
Clipper chip
clock interrupt
clock speed
clone
co-processor
coaxial cable
COM ports
complementary metal-oxide
  semiconductor
configuration
console
control unit
coprocessor
copy protection
Cray, Seymour Roger

Creative Labs
cylinder
data bus
daughterboard
DCE
DEC
decoder
digital data transmission
digital monitor
digital signal processor
direct connection
display
distributed processing
DRAM
drive bay
DX
edge connector
EEPROM
EGA
EISA
EPROM
Ethernet
executable file
expansion board
external modem
fetch-execute cycle
file server
firmware
flash memory
flat screen
floating point unit
font-end processor
footprint
function key
games console
generation
geographical information system
gigabyte
graphics card
hardware
hertz
Hewlett-Packard
high memory
HPGL
HyperCard
IBM
immediate access memory
information technology
integrated circuit
Intel
interrupt
IRQ
ISA bus
jack

Jobs, Steve
jumper
light-emitting diode
liquid crystal display
local area network
local bus
LSI
memory resident
microchip
microcomputer
microprocessor
Microsoft Corp.
MIDI
minicomputer
mips
MMX
monitor
Moore, Gordon
motherboard
multi-user system
multitasking
nanotechnology
NetWare
network interface card
neural network
NeXT Technologies Inc
optical fibre
original equipment manufacturer
overdrive chip
parallel device
passive matrix display
PCI
PCI bus
PCMCIA
Pentium
peripheral device
platform
port
POSIX
printed circuit board
processing cycle
processor
ROM
protected mode
quad-speed
real-time system
register
reverse engineering
RISC
RS-232 interface
run-time system
screen
sequence-control register
serial device
serial interface/port

set-top box
shared memory bus architecture
silicon chip
SIPC
smart card
socket
soft-sectored disc
SoundBlaster
speech chip
SRAM
stand-alone computer
SVGA
SX
synchronous
TeleAdapt
256-colour
time-sharing
transistor-transistor logic
Trinitron
2D graphics
3D graphics
TTY
uncommitted logic array
uninterruptible power supply
unshielded twisted pair
VESA local bus
VGA
video accelerator card
video adapter
video adapter card
video graphics card
visual display unit
VRAM
VT100
wavetable synthesizer
wide area network
Windows
workstation
XGA
zero wait state

COMPUTER CONTROL
Advanced Technology Attachment
  Packet Interface
analog-to-digital converter
audit trail
authorization
auto-responder
AUTOEXEC.BAT
automatic fallback
backup
balloon help
bang
bang path

batch file
BIOS
blind carbon copy
blind signature
blink
bookmark
Boolean algebra
bozo filter
browse
Capstone
carbon copy
channel
client/server architecture
codec
CONFIG.SYS
console
context-sensitive help
copy protection
CTS/RTS
current directory
daemon
data logging
default
delete
desktop
device driver
digital-to-analog converter
digitize
DIP switch
direct memory access
disc optimizer
distributed processing
DMA channel
downtime
dynamic data exchange
Elm
Energy Star
error detection
escape sequence
expanded memory
extended memory
F1
feedback
file allocation table
file server
flag
flash upgrade
FLOP
FM synthesizer
formatting
full duplex
gain
GPF
grep
groupware

hit
hot-swapping
hotlist
HPGL
human-computer interaction
I/O
incremental backup
ISA bus
launch
liquid crystal display
local area network
local bus
memory address
memory resident
monitor
Motorola
MTBF
multi-threading
NetWare
neural network
Newton
object linking and embedding
off line
on line
on-line help
on-site warranty
PCMCIA
peer-to-peer networking
pen-based computer
PING
plug and play
print
print spooler
prompt
protected mode
Raid
refresh
response time
return-to-base warranty
root
router
sampling
security
sensor
signal processing
small computer systems interface
smart
soft-sectored disc
start bit
startup screen
stepper motor
stop bit
subsystem
support
SVGA

system administrator
system requirements
taskbar
Telnet
terminal emulation
time out
TN3270
topology
touch sensor
undelete
uninterruptible power supply
unshielded twisted pair
VGA
video adapter
vision system
VRAM
wait state
wide area network
Windows
XON/XOFF

COMPUTER TYPES
Acorn
Amiga
Apple
Archimedes
computer
dedicated computer
digital computer
fifth-generation computer
IBM-compatible
IF socket
laptop computer
Macintosh
mainframe
network computer
Newton
notebook computer
pen-based computer
personal computer
personal digital assistant
portable computer
PowerPC
supercomputer

DATA PROCESSING
anamorphic projection
annotate
augmented reality
authoring
batch processing
binary search
character type check
check digit
compound document

content provider
control total
crop
data capture
data flow chart
data preparation
data processing
data protection
digital composition
digital retouching
direct access
document
documentation
drag and drop
dump
editing
EDP
electronic mail
error correction
extruded shape
field
field-length check
file
file access
file generation
file merging
file sorting
file transfer
file updating
floating point unit
forms
frame
GIGO
hash total
header
indexed sequential file
interpolation
justification
key-to-disc system
logical error
master file
media
off-line editing
overlay
random access
range check
record
searching
serial file
16-bit
64-bit
sorting
style sheet
32-bit
24-bit colour

ansaction file
ree-and-branch filing system
urnaround document
alidation
erification
vord processing

DATA REPRESENTATION
lphanumeric data
nalogue
nchor
>
g>
SCII
SCII art

inary file
inary number code
inary number system
it
it map
it-mapped font
lock
yte
apture
ase-sensitive
haracter
haracter set
leartext
lip art
ontrol character
orruption of data
lata
ligit
ligital
ligital photography
lingbat
louble precision
lumb terminal
EBCDIC
EIS
extended character set
ilter
ixed font
greeking
greyscale
hexadecimal number system
hinting
hyperlink
information technology
instruction set
interlacing
jaggies
kilobyte
lathe shape

machine-readable
magnetic-ink character recognition
mask
megabyte
model
null character
object linking and embedding
outline font
Pantone
parity
parse
PCX
PostScript
proportional font
?
QWERTY
redundancy
sans-serif font
scalable font
.sig
smiley
Standard Generalized Markup
    Language
thumbnail
tiling
tracking
TrueType
typeface
typography
Unicode
wild card

DATA STORAGE
access
access time
archive
backing storage
binary large object
cache memory
bubble memory
CD-R
CD-ROM
clipboard
compact disc
compression
data compression
data recovery
defragmentation program
digital audio tape
directory
directory tree
disc
disc compression
disc drive
disc formatting

Discman
document image processing
download
DSP
EDO RAM
EEPROM
encapsulate
EPROM
export file
field
file
file allocation table
file extension
file format
flash memory
floppy disc
floptical disc
folder
formatting
fragmentation
frame buffer
gigabyte
grandfather-father-son system
graphic file format
hard disc
hard-sectored disc
hashing
hidden file
IDEA
image compression
immediate access memory
instruction register
inverted file
Iomega
JPEG
key field
kilobyte
log file
lossless compression
lossy compression
magnetic tape
mass storage system
media
megabyte
memory
mirror site
multisession
nonvolatile memory
optical disc
page
paging
PKZip
proxy server
queue
Raid

RAM
RAM disc
read-only storage
ROM
root directory
search request
sector
sequential file
swap
Syquest
SYSTEM.INI
tape streamer
TAR
terabyte
track
UART
upload
video file
volatile memory
WIN.INI
Winchester drive
Write Once Read Many
write-protection
z-buffer
zipped file

ELECTRONIC MAIL
acronyms
address book
advertising
alias
attachment
BinHex
blind carbon copy
bounce
bozo filter
carbon copy
daemon
electronic mail
Elm
emoticon
Eudora
finger
firewall
forgery
FTPmail
header
Internet mail
LISTSERV
mail reflector
mail server software
mail-bombing
mail-enabled
mailbox
mailbox name

mailing list
Majordomo
message ID
MIME
net abuse
net police
Netfind
NNTP
Pine
PING
post
postmaster
privacy enhanced mail
RiPEM
sendmail
signature
smiley
SMTP
snail mail
store-and-forwarded technology
thread
voice mail
WinCode

GRAPHICS
aliasing
anti-aliasing
Barnsley, Michael
Bezier curve
computer art
contouring
digital photography
digital retouching
dithering
document image processing
fractal
Gouraud shading
graphic file format
graphics card
halftone
Herzog, Bertram
hologram
holography
image compression
image processing
Industrial Light & Magic
inline graphics
interpolation
Kay, Alan
key frame
lathe shape
Mandelbrot, Benoit
morphing
paint program
PaintShop Pro

Pantone
phong shading
PICT
Pixar
QuickDraw
raster image processor
ray-tracing
remote imaging
rendering
Silicon Graphics Inc.
TIFF
transition
virtual art
visualization
wire frame

INPUT DEVICES
bar code
digital camera
digitizer
document reader
Dvorak keyboard
echo
graphics tablet
handwriting recognition
I/O
input device
intercast
joystick
keyboard
light pen
line input
look-and-feel
machine-readable
magnetic strip
magnetic-ink character
point-of-sale terminal
recognition
mark sensing
menu
mouse
optical character recognition
optical mark recognition
QWERTY
scanner
speech recognition
speech writing system
touch screen
trackball
voice input
write-once technology
X-Windows

MULTIMEDIA AND
INTERACTIVITY
audio file
authoring
authoring tools
AutoCAD
avatar
AVI
Brand, Stewart
CD-I
CD-ROM
CD-ROM drive
CD-ROM XA
CDTV
CinePak
compact disc
Deep Blue
destination page
digital versatile disc
digital video interactive
Director
distance learning
Doom
edutainment
electronic publishing
FlashPix
flythrough
FM synthesizer
fractal
frame
full-motion video
Furry MUCK
gain
games console
General MIDI
gesture recognition
href
HTML
hyperlink
hypermedia
hyperreality
hypertext
infotainment
interactive
interactive computing
interactive media
Interactive Multimedia Association
interactive video
JPEG
kiosk
Kodak
MIME
MIT Media Lab
mixer

MMX
MOO
MPC
MPEG
MUD
multimedia
MUSE
MUSH
new media
Nintendo
Philips
PhotoCD
playstation
QuickTime
Sega
Shockwave
Sony
sound card
TinyMUD
tinysex
Toolbook
video capture board
virtual reality

NETWORKS
access privileges
account
ARPAnet
BITNET
browse
chain letter
chat
ClariNet
CoSy
CWIS
DARPAnet
desktop video
DIANE
EcoNet
encapsulate
Ethernet
gateway
Global Information Infrastructure
GreenNet
host
infobahn
information superhighway
Integrated Services Digital Network
intranet
JANET
knowbot
LINX, the
Minitel
mirror site

Modem
multicasting
multiplexer
National Information Infrastructure
navigate
network
network interface card
network operating system
node
NREN
NSFnet
off-line reader
packet
packet switching
PeaceNet
PING
.plan
polling
PoP
RARE
remote terminal
router
server
set-top box
sniffer
SNMP
SuperJANET
System Network Architecture
TAPI
Telnet
Token Ring
topology
traceroute
traffic
Trumpet
Veronica
vPoP
WELL, The
whois
Wide Area Information Server
worm

ORGANIZATIONS
British Computer Society
CERN
Commercial Internet Exchange
Computer Professionals for Social
   Responsibility
Electronic Frontier Foundation
ESPRIT
Free Software Foundation
GCHQ
Institute of Electrical and Electronic
   Engineers

Interactive Multimedia Association
International Standards Organization
Internet Architecture Board
Internet Engineering Task Force
Internet Society
InterNIC
ITU
MIT Media Lab
National Computing Centre
National Institute of Standards and
   Technology
National Security Agency
Open Software Foundation
RARE
SMPTE
W3 Consortium

OUTPUT DEVICES
bit map
bit-mapped font
bubble-jet printer
CD-R
CMYK
colour depth
daisywheel
desktop publishing
digital monitor
Discman
display
dot matrix printer
dot pitch
dpi
dumb terminal
electronic publishing
encapsulated PostScript
fax
font
greeking
greyscale
hard copy
hinting
impact printer
ink-jet printer
interlacing
inverse video
laser printer
light-emitting diode
line printer
microfiche
microform
outline font
output device
page description language
page printer

PCL
PICT
pixel
plasma display
plotter
polyphony
PostScript
printer
QuickDraw
raster graphics
resolution
RGB
scalable font
screen dump
scrolling
serial interface/port
serif font
slide show
speech synthesis
TIFF
TrueType
typeface
vector graphics
visual display unit
voice output

PROGRAMMING
absolute
algorithm
application program interface
argument
array
artificial intelligence
benchmark
beta version
binary search
Boolean algebra
bubble sort
bug
checksum
data terminator
debugging
decimal number system
declarative programming
developer
driver
dry running
error
error message
execution error
filter
flow chart
functional programming
fuzzy logic

global variable
heuristics
interrupt
iteration
jump
library program
local variable
logic gate
macro
null character
null string
object-oriented programming
octal number system
overflow error
parameter
patch
pop-up menu
program
program documentation
program files
program flow chart
program loop
programming
public-domain software
RAMdisc
random number
recursion
relative
reserved word
rogue value
rounding error
run-time error
SDK
shareware
source code
sprite
stack
string
structured programming
subroutine
symbolic processor
syntax error
systems program
test data
toggle
trace
truncation error
truth table
underflow error
user documentation
variable
virtual
virtual memory

PROGRAMMING LANGUAGES

Ada
ALGOL
assembler
assembly language
BASIC
C
C++
COBOL
code
command language
compiler
FORTRAN
high-level language
interpreter
Java
LISP
LOGO
low-level language
machine code
mnemonic
Nelson, Ted
object program
PASCAL
portability
procedural programming
procedure
programming language
PROLOG
shell script
SmallTalk
source program
SQL
substring
translation program
virtual reality markup language
Visual Basic
visual programming

SECURITY AND FREEDOM OF INFORMATION

access priveleges
anonymous FTP
authentication
biometrics
blue-ribbon campaign
censorship
Clipper chip
computer crime
Computer Misuse Act
Computer Underground Digest
copyright
cracker
cryptography
cyberlaw
cypherpunk
Data Encryption Standard
Data Protection Act
data recovery
data security
Diffie-Hellman key exchange system
digital signature
Electronic Communications Privacy Act
Electronic Frontier Foundation
encryption
firewall
First Amendment
forgery
GCHQ
Good Times virus
IDEA
intellectual property
intellectual property rights
International Traffic in Arms Regulations
Kerberos
key
key escrow
log off
log on
Mitnick, Kevin
National Security Agency
nondisclosure agreement
password
PIN
Pretty Good Privacy
privacy
privacy enhanced mail
public key
public-key cryptography
registration
RiPEM
RSA
secure HTTP
secure socket layer
steganography
user ID
write-protection
year 2000
Zimmermann, Phil

SOFTWARE AND APPLICATIONS

active window
add-on
Adobe
agent
anti-virus software
applet
application
application program interface
applications package
artificial intelligence
audit trail
authoring tools
backup
beta
BinHex
bit map
bit-mapped font
blocking software
BMP
boot
bot
bug
bulletin board
bundling
CAL
cancelbot
Capstone
checksum
CinePak
client
clone
collision detection
communications program
computer game
computer graphics
computer numerical control
computer program
computer simulation
computer-aided design
computer-aided manufacturing
Corba
Corel
crawler
critical path analysis
CUA
data dictionary
database
delete
demo
desktop publishing
device driver
dialler
dingbat
disc optimizer
distributed processing
document image processing
drawing program
dynamic data exchange
dynamic link library

electronic book
electronic mail
electronic publishing
emulator
engine
expert system
file extension
file format
flash upgrade
flight simulator
Free Software Foundation
freeware
fuzzy logic
Gates, Bill
geographical information system
GIF
GNU
Good Times virus
greeking
greyscale
groupware
guiltware
hash function
helper application
hinting
hypertext
id Software
import file
Kapor, Mitch
killer application
knowbot
knowledge-based system
Laplink
legacy
Lynx
mail merge
mail server software
mail-enabled
Majordomo
microbilling
Microsoft Corp.
morphing
MSCDEX.EXE
multimedia
network operating system
newsreader
Novell
off-line browser
off-line reader
office suite
open systems
operating system
outline font
paint program
PCI

PCX
PDF
personal productivity software
PICT
Pine
playstation
plug-in
presentation graphics
print spooler
process control
Program Manager
program trading
public-domain software
RAMdisc
relational database
RiPEM
rlogin
robot
RTF
run-time version
sampling
screen grabber
scrollbar
SDK
search engine
search request
sendmail
shell
shovelware
site licence
slide show
sniffer
software
software piracy
software project lifecycle
software suite
spider
spreadsheet
Standard Generalized Markup
    Language
subsystem
system application architecture
SYSTEM.INI
TAPI
template
terminate and stay resident
text editor
TIFF
traceroute
tree-and-branch filing system
Trojan horse
TrueType
TWAIN
unbundling
undelete

upgrade
utility program
UUCP
UUencode
videotext
virtual reality
virus
VMS
wAreZ
WAV
whois
WIN.INI
WinCode
wire frame
word processor
worm
x

**SOFTWARE PROGRAMS AND
OPERATING SYSTEMS**
Acrobat
ActiveX
Adobe Type Manager
AltaVista
AutoCAD
ChromaKey
CoSy
CP/M
CU-SeeMe
Director
DOS
EMACS
Eudora
Excel
GZip
Hytelnet
Internet Explorer
Linux
LISTSERV
Lotus 1-2-3
Lotus Notes
Lynx
Microsoft Word
MS-DOS
NeXTStep
OS/2
PaintShop Pro
PKZip
PowerPoint
Pretty Good Privacy
RealAudio
Shockwave
System 7
Toolbook
Trumpet

UNIX
Windows
Windows NT
Winsock
WordPerfect
Yahoo

STANDARDS AND PROTOCOLS
ADSL
Advanced Technology Attachment
    Packet Interface
American National Standards Institute
anonymous FTP
asynchronous transfer mode
AT command set
Cerf, Vinton
CGI
Comité Consultatif International
    Téléphonique et Télégraphique
Corba
CSLIP
CUA
Data Encryption Standard
display control interface
EISA
ESPRIT
FlashPix
frame relay
General MIDI
High Sierra format
high-definition television
IBM
International Standards Organization
Internet Architecture Board
Internet Engineering Task Force
ISO 9660
ITU
KA9Q
LDAP
Microsoft Corp.
MIDI
MIME
MPR-II
National Institute of Standards and
    Technology
NNTP
NTSC
Open Software Foundation
Open Systems Interconnection
PAL
POP3
POSIX
PPP
protocol

RFC
RSUP
screen saver
SECAM
secure HTTP
secure socket layer
SMTP
SNMP
standards
T3
TWAIN
V numbers
W3 Consortium
X.25
X.400
Xmodem

SYSTEMS ANALYSIS
parallel running
pilot running
software project lifecycle
system flow chart
system implementation
systems analysis
systems design
turnkey system

USER INTERFACE
carriage return
check box
click
combo box
command line interface
computer personnel
cursor
desktop
dialog box
dongle
double click
drop-down list
end user
ergonomics
graphical user interface
hot key
human-computer interaction
icon
interface
point and click
pointing device
pop-up menu
pull-down menu
push-button
radio button
repetitive strain injury

right-click
shortcut
tiling
toggle
toolbar
user interface
user-friendly
window
Wizard
workstation
WYSIWYG
zero wait state

VIDEO
CinePak
digital composition
full-motion video
inline video
nonlinear video editing
NTSC
PAL
QuickTime
SECAM
SMPTE
story board
video accelerator card
video adapter
video adapter card
video CD
video file
video graphics card
video-on-demand
visual display unit

VIRTUAL REALITY
anamorphic projection
collision detection
DataGlove
flight simulator
flythrough
force feedback
gesture recognition
immersive
Lanier, Jaron
parallax
RL
Vactor
virtual reality
virtual reality markup language
Virtuality
VR browser
Waldo
wand
wired gloves